CANADIAN CASES IN THE PHILOSOPHY OF LAW

THIRD EDITION

CANADIAN CASES IN THE PHILOSOPHY OF LAW

THIRD EDITION

EDITED BY J.E. BICKENBACH

broadview press

Canadian Cataloguing in Publication Data

Main entry under title:
Canadian cases in the philosophy of law

3rd ed.
ISBN 1-55111-160-8

1. Law — Canada — Philosophy. 2. Law — Canada — Cases.
I. Bickenbach, Jerome Edmund.

KE427.C35 1997   340'.1   C97-932122-0
KF379.C35 1997

Broadview Press
Post Office Box 1243, Peterborough, Ontario, Canada K9J 7H5

in the United States of America:
3576 California Road, Orchard Park, NY 14127

in the United Kingdom:
B.R.A.D. Book Representation & Distribution Ltd., 244A,
London Road, Hadleigh, Essex SS7 2DE

Broadview Press gratefully acknowledges the support of the Canada Council, the Ontario Arts Council, and the Ministry of Canadian Heritage.

Typesetting and assembly: True to Type Inc., Mississauga, Canada.

PRINTED IN CANADA

TABLE OF CONTENTS

PREFACE TO THE FIRST EDITION

Editors should neither be seen nor heard. Though I strongly approve of this maxim, there are exceptions. This book is intended as a supplementary teaching tool for courses in the philosophy of law, as well as the sociology and politics of Canadian law. My job as editor has been to select the cases and to trim them down to size, sometimes drastically. It seems to me the reader deserves to know the guidelines I used for both tasks.

First, why Canadian cases? It has been my experience that students have a fairly good grasp of what a district attorney does, why a barrister is different from a solicitor, the difference between misdemeanours and felonies, what it means to "take the fifth" or "turn state's evidence," and what the due process of law entails. But beyond these tidbits of American and English law, most Canadian students are woefully unfamiliar with their own law. Worse yet, they tend to assume there are no differences when, indeed, there are some important ones.

So, one of my principles of selection was to highlight some of the issues and approaches in Canadian legal culture. I include cases that reflect Canadian history and values, as well as ones involving language and culture, the treatment of aboriginals, the role of the state and its institutions, and the character of the Canadian constitution. I also include cases that display some, often very subtle, features of the Canadian approach to the interpretation of basic human rights.

Secondly, why these Canadian cases? My second principle of selection was that every case must exemplify at least one issue of interest to philosophers and other social theorists. Of course, there are many issues to choose from so I opted for a representative sample of basic issues – protection of rights and autonomy, the nature of justice and responsibility – and, under these headings, tried to get as much variety as possible, subject to the first principle already mentioned. I looked for cases that took contrasting positions on similar legal issues, as well as cases that exemplified different techniques of legal reasoning. And I also looked for cases that were inherently interesting.

I should quickly add that although many of these cases are very recent judgments of the highest court of the land, it has not been my intention to represent the current state of the law on any issue. Some of the cases included in this collection are not only out of date, they have been expressly overruled by other cases or by legislation.

Finally, why these excerpts from the cases? Generally, I trusted my pedagogical intuitions about what would be useful as a supplementary teaching tool. I asked myself: is there enough to make the facts and other circumstances intelligible and the legal questions clear? Is the court's basic argument – good, bad or indifferent – set out in enough detail to do it justice? Is there enough text to raise questions and problems, but not so much as to bury them under irrelevant detail and legal dross? Is the excerpt coherent but economical, fair but lean?

The editing was, to be sure, severe. As anyone who has read a court of appeal or Supreme Court of Canada judicial judgment will know, every case contains a sizable chunk of preliminary material that can safely be excised. There is usually a review of the history of the litigation and the decisions of the courts below, a presentation of the relevant statutory materials, a review of previous decisions in the area, and so on. Often too, the judgment contains majority, concurring, and dissenting opinions and it is only necessary to look at one or two. And, truth to be told, sometimes judges grind many irrelevant axes along the way.

But it was not always easy to see what could or could not be cut out. Happily, I was able to rely on the editorial skill, good sense, and perspicaciousness of Ms. Pam Cross who assisted me in preparing this book. Her contribution was immense and I thank her for it.

Jerome E. Bickenbach
Kingston, March 1991

PREFACE TO THE SECOND EDITION

There have been many changes in this, the second edition of *Canadian Cases in the Philosophy of Law*. Although only two years have passed since the first edition, many interesting and philosophically significant decisions by Canadian courts in that brief time have earned a place in this collection. But, since I wanted to keep the size and cost down my eagerness to add new cases was tempered by the need to delete old ones. I have taken out nine cases; for all except three, they have been replaced by others that raise the same philosophical issues, only more clearly or in a more interesting manner. I regret having to remove the entire "Language and Cultural Rights" section of Part II, but my experience has been that these cases do not raise the issue of French language rights in a manner that generates interest or discussion.

This Second Edition is improved in several ways. Ten new cases have been added: the *Oakes* case, a highly influential section 1 analysis; a case on the scope of rights protection (*Dolphin Delivery*) and one on the range of remedies available once an infringement has been found (*Schachter*) in the section on Charter adjudications; the Supreme Court of Canada's controversial pornography decision (*Butler*) in the freedom of expression section; and two cases on the vexing problem of suicide and assisted suicide (*Astaforoff and Rodriguez*) in Part IV. In Part VI, Responsibility, there are three important changes. I have added a recent case on "objective *mens rea*" (*Hundel*) and a case involving a defence based on the battered wife syndrome (*Lavallee*). In the area of civil liability, I include an interesting case that tries to recast the duties physicians owe to their patients in terms of a fiduciary relationship (*Norberg v. Wynrib*). Finally, I have replaced the Federal Court of Appeal decision on the constitutionality of capital punishment by the Supreme Court's subsequent decision (*Kindler*).

I have also gone back through all of the cases and expanded the edited selection by as much as 30 percent. I discovered as I used the collection that, more than once, the excerpt was too heavily edited to fully comprehend the argument being made. As I went back over the cases, whenever I found an ellipsis I asked myself whether what was left out could, possibly, find its way back in, for the sake of readability and clarity. I have continued the practice of eliminating citations to legal authorities, although I include the date of the case referred to.

I wish to thank Broadview Press, and especially editor Don LePan, for encouraging me to go back to the law library and try again. I still conceive of this collection as a teaching tool, and hope now it may be a more effective one.

Jerome E. Bickenbach
Kingston, April 1993

PREFACE TO THE THIRD EDITION

It has been four years since the last edition of *Canadian Cases in the Philosophy of Law* and there has been considerable judicial activity in that time. There were many new and philosophically interesting cases for me to choose from. My eagerness to add a new case was tempered by the realization that, for considerations of space and utility, including it might mean deleting another case. In the end, I added twelve new cases and removed eleven cases. I have tried to maintain the balance between the sections, both in terms of number of cases and their overall length. The most changes occurred in the Parts where their has been the most judicial activity – Fundamental Freedoms and Equality Rights.

In particular, I have added into Part I the *Bertrand* about the constitutionality of the proposed Quebec referendum which identifies issues of the limits of judicial review, in the face of a political act of succession. In Part II, I added three new cases: the *Attis* case about the limits in what can be done to prevent a anti-Semitic activist from poisoning the teaching environment; the *RJR-MacDonald* case which looks at freedom of expression as it applies to tobacco advertising; and the *Native Women's Association* case that explores a side of freedom of expression that is rarely discussed, namely whether the state has an obligation to facilitate expression. In Equality Rights, Part III I added the *Egan* decision because it captures many of the on-going jurisprudential issues on discrimination and equality that the Supreme Court of Canada has been struggling with, and the *Eaton* case which debates the issue of whether a child's special educational needs justify the sacrifice in equality that seems to require integration into the mainstream. I decided to add another dimension to Part IV (and changed its name to Autonomy and Self-determination) and add two cases that involve the rights of parents to make decisions for the children. The *B.(R.)* case looks at the issue of "parental liberty" in the instance of parents who refuse to consent to medical treatment for their child on religious grounds. The *Latimer* case considers the more extreme example of a parent who kills his child to save her from a live of pain and disability. In Part V (which I also renamed Procedural Justice), I have included two cases that explore different facets of the "principles of fundamental justice". The *Carosella* case asks whether an accused person's right to defend himself against a criminal charge of indecent assault can demand as evidence the confidential notes of a meeting between his alleged victim and a sexual assault counselor. In *Heywood* the issue is whether the language of a criminal code provision is procedurally unfair because it is overly

11

broad in its scope. Finally, in Part VI, two cases were added to expand on the criminal side of responsibility. The first is the *Jacob* case that asks why should going topless on a hot and humid day constitute criminal indecency. The second, the *Belczowski* case, looks more closely at the nature of criminal punishment and considers whether the long-standing disqualification of prisoners from the right to vote is justifiable.

Jerome E. Bickenbach
Kingston, June 1997

FOR MORGAN BICKENBACH-DAVIES, WHO HELPED WHEN-
EVER SHE COULD . . . AND STILL TRIES.

I CONSTITUTIONAL LAW

The cases in this Part deal with various aspects of the constitution of Canada, broadly understood. Constitutional law has long been of interest to philosophers and political theorists because it is the area of law concerned with the legal foundations of the state – the distribution of legislative powers and sources of political authority, the relationship between the individual and the state, and the ground rules of political institutions and processes. But with the arrival of the *Charter of Rights and Freedoms* on April 17, 1982, this interest greatly increased. It was predicted that since the *Charter* set out the fundamental rights and freedoms of classical liberalism in relatively clear and unqualified language, judicial attempts at applying these rights and freedoms to particular situations were bound to raise important questions in moral and political theory. The *Charter* cases throughout this collection show that this prediction has come to pass.

It is important not to forget, though, that constitutional law is far more than a list of rights and freedoms. The constitution of a state, be it written or unwritten, captures both a political arrangement – the nuts and bolts of the processes of government – and a consensus about the political character of the society. This is evident in the cases included in this Part that debate the scope and application of the *Charter*. But at an even deeper level, constitutional law illuminates the nature of law itself. It is important, therefore, to try to look beyond the surface issues debated in each case to the deeper theoretical questions that are raised.

A: THE CONSTITUTION

REFERENCE RE RESOLUTION TO AMEND THE CONSTITUTION OF CANADA

Supreme Court of Canada

[1981] 1 S.C.R. 753

This is not a typical constitutional case; indeed it is studied by comparative constitutional law scholars because it is unique, involves circumstances that may never arise again and involves basic issues of constitutional law.

Procedurally speaking, it is a *reference* case. Canadian constitutional law makes it possible for either the federal government or, as here, one or more provincial governments, to "refer" for opinion to the Supreme Court of Canada "important questions of law or fact." This procedure for bringing a case before the highest court of the land is usually saved for difficult questions of constitutional law, in particular those concerning the division of legislative powers. The procedure enables either level of government to test the constitutionality of legislation before it is a fait accompli. Unlike other cases, in which the legal issue has to be raised by a plaintiff and then argued before the lower courts – which can take years – in a reference case the issue goes directly to the final legal adjudicator, the Supreme Court of Canada.

At issue in this reference case was the procedure being followed to patriate the constitution: was it proper for the federal government to break the constitutional links between the United Kingdom and Canada and add the *Canadian Charter of Rights and Freedoms* to the constitution of Canada without the consent of all the provinces? Along the way to solving this extremely complex question, the court paused to consider the nature of the Canadian constitution and the difference between law and convention.

* * * *

Mr. Justice Martland and Justices Ritchie, Dickson, Beetz, Chouinard and Lamer:

A substantial part of the rules of the Canadian Constitution are written. They are contained not in a single document called a Constitution but in a great variety of statutes some of which have been enacted by the Parliament of Westminster, such as the *British North American Act 1867...*, or by the Parliament of Canada, such as the *Alberta Act, 1905...*, or by the provincial legislatures, such as the provincial electoral acts. They are also to be found in orders in council like the Imperial Order in Council of May 16, 1871, admitting British Columbia into the Union, and the Imperial Order in Council of June 26, 1873, admitting Prince Edward Island into the Union.

Another part of the Constitution of Canada consists of the rules of the common law. These are rules which the courts have developed over the centuries in the discharge of their judicial duties. An important portion of these rules concerns the prerogative of the Crown. Sections 9 and 15 of the *B.N.A. Act* provide:

9. The Executive Government and authority of and over Canada is hereby declared to continue and be vested in the Queen.

15. The Commander-in-Chief of the Land and Naval Militia, and all Naval and Military Forces, of and in Canada, is hereby declared to continue and be vested in the Queen.

But the Act does not otherwise say very much with respect to the elements of "Executive Government and authority" and one must look at the common law to find out what they are, apart from authority delegated to the Executive by statute.

The common law provides that the authority of the Crown includes for instance the prerogative of mercy or clemency..., and the power to incorporate by charter so as to confer a general capacity analogous to that of a natural person....The royal prerogative puts the Crown in a preferred position as a creditor..., or with respect to the inheritance of lands for defect of heirs..., or in relation to the ownership of precious metals....It is also under the prerogative and the common law that the Crown appoints and receives ambassadors, declares war, concludes treaties and it is in the name of the Queen that passports are issued.

Those parts of the Constitution of Canada which are composed of statutory rules and common law rules are generically referred to as the law of the Constitution. In cases of doubt or dispute, it is the function of the courts to declare what the law is and since the law is sometimes breached, it is generally the function of the courts to ascertain whether it has in fact been breached in specific instances and, if so, to apply such sanctions as are contemplated by the law, whether they be punitive sanctions or civil sanctions such as a declaration of nullity. Thus, when a federal or provincial statute is found by the courts to be in excess of the legislative competence of the legislature which has enacted it, it is declared null and void and the courts refuse to give effect to it. In this sense it can be said that the law of the Constitution is administered or enforced by the courts.

But many Canadians would perhaps be surprised to learn that important parts of the Constitution of Canada, with which they are the most familiar because they are directly involved when they exercise their right to vote at federal and provincial elections, are nowhere to be found in the law of the Constitution. For instance it is a fundamental requirement of the Constitution that if the Opposition obtains the majority at the polls, the government must tender its resignation forthwith. But fundamental as it is, this requirement of the Constitution does not form part of the law of the Constitution.

It is also a constitutional requirement that the person who is appointed Prime Minister or Premier by the Crown and who is the effective head of the government should have the support of the elected branch of the legislature; in practice this means in most cases the leader of the political party which has won a majority of seats at a general election. Other ministers are appointed by the Crown on the advice of the Prime Minister or Premier when he forms or reshuffles his cabinet. Ministers must continuously have the confidence of the elected branch of the legislature, individually and collectively. Should they lose it, they must either resign or ask the Crown for a dissolution of the legislature and the holding of a general election. Most of the powers of the Crown under the prerogative are exercised only upon the advice of the Prime Minister or the Cabinet which means that they are effectively exercised by the latter, together with the innumerable statutory powers delegated to the Crown in council.

Yet none of these essential rules of the Constitution can be said to be a law of the Constitution. It was apparently [A. V.] Dicey who, in the first edition of his *Law of the Constitution*, in 1885, called them "the conventions of the constitution"...an expression which quickly became current. What Dicey described under these terms are the principles and rules of responsible government, several of which are stated above and which regulate the relations between the Crown, the Prime Minister, the Cabinet, and the two Houses of Parliament. These rules developed in Great Britain by way of custom and precedent during the nineteenth century and were exported to such British colonies as were granted self-government.

Dicey first gave the impression that constitutional conventions are a peculiarly British and modern phenomenon. But he recognized in later editions that different conventions are found in other constitutions. As Sir William Holdsworth wrote...:

> In fact conventions must grow up at all times and in all places where the powers of government are vested in different persons or bodies – where in other words there is a mixed constitution. "The constituent parts of a state," said Burke, "are we obliged to hold their public faith with each other, and with all those who derive any serious interest under their engagements, as much as the whole state is bound to keep its faith with separate communities." Necessarily conventional rules spring up to regulate the working of the various parts of the constitution, their relations to one another, and to the subject."

Within the British Empire, powers of government were vested in different bodies which provided a fertile ground for the growth of new constitutional conventions unknown to Dicey whereby self-governing colonies acquired equal and independent status within the Commonwealth. Many of these culminated in the *Statute of Westminster*, 1931....

A federal constitution provides for the distribution of powers between various legislatures and governments and may also constitute a fertile ground for the growth of constitutional conventions between those legislatures and governments. It is conceivable for instance that usage and practice might give birth to conventions in Canada relating to the holding of federal- provincial conferences, the appointment of Lieutenant-Governors, the reservation and disallowance of provincial legislation....

The main purpose of constitutional conventions is to ensure that the legal framework of the Constitution will be operated in accordance with the prevailing constitutional values or principles of the period. For example, the constitutional value which is the pivot of the conventions stated above and relating to responsible government is the democratic principle: the powers of the state must be exercised in accordance with the wishes of the electorate; and the constitutional value or principle which anchors the conventions regulating the relationship between the members of the Commonwealth is the independence of the former British colonies.

Being based on custom and precedent, constitutional conventions are usually unwritten rules. Some of them however may be reduced to writing and expressed in the proceedings and documents of imperial conferences, or in the preamble of statutes such as the *Statute of Westminster*, 1931, or in the proceedings and documents of federal-provincial conferences. They are often referred to and recognized in statements made by members of governments.

The conventional rules of the Constitution present one striking peculiarity. In contradistinction to the laws of the Constitution, they are not enforced by the courts. One reason for this situation is that, unlike common law rules, conventions are not judge-made rules. They are not based on judicial precedents but on precedents established by the institutions of government themselves. Nor are they in the nature of statutory commands which it is the function and duty of the courts to obey and enforce. Furthermore, to enforce them would mean to administer some formal sanction when they are breached. But the legal system from which they are distinct does not contemplate formal sanctions for their breach.

Perhaps the main reason why conventional rules cannot be enforced by the courts is that they are generally in conflict with the legal rules which they postulate and the courts are bound to enforce the legal rules. The conflict is not of a type which would entail the commission of any illegality. It results from the fact that legal rules create wide powers, discretions and rights which conventions prescribe should be exercised only in a certain limited manner, if at all.

Some examples will illustrate this point.

As a matter of law, the Queen, or the Governor General or the Lieutenant-Governor could refuse assent to every bill passed by both Houses of Parliament or by a Legislative Assembly as the case may be. But by convention they cannot of their own motion refuse to assent to any such bill on any ground, for instance because they disapprove of the policy of the bill. We have here a conflict between a legal rule which creates a complete discretion and a conventional rule which completely neutralizes it. But conventions, like laws, are sometimes violated. And if this particular convention were violated and assent were improperly withheld, the courts would be bound to enforce the law, not the convention. They would refuse to recognize the validity of a vetoed bill. This is what happened in *Gallant v. The King*, (1949)....The Lieutenant-Governor who had withheld assent in *Gallant* apparently did so towards the end of his term of office. Had it been otherwise, it is not inconceivable that his withholding of assent might have produced a political crisis leading to his removal from office which shows that if the remedy for a breach of a convention does not lie with the courts, still the breach is not necessarily without a remedy. The remedy lies with some other institutions of government; furthermore it is not a formal remedy and it may be administered with less certainty or regularity than it would be by a court.

Another example of the conflict between law and convention is provided by a fundamental convention already stated above: if after a general election where the Opposition obtained the majority at the polls the government refused to resign and clung to office, it would thereby commit a fundamental breach of convention, one so serious indeed that it could be regarded as tantamount to a *coup d',tat*. The remedy in this case would lie with the Governor General or the Lieutenant-Governor as the case might be, who would be justified in dismissing the Ministry and in calling on the Opposition to form the government. But should the Crown be slow in taking this course, there is nothing the courts could do about it except at the risk of creating a state of legal discontinuity, that is a form of revolution. An order or a regulation passed by a Minister under statutory authority and otherwise valid could not be invalidated on the ground that, by convention, the Minister ought no longer to be a Minister. A writ of *quo warranto* aimed at Ministers, assuming that *quo warranto* lies against a Minister of the Crown, which is very doubtful, would be of no avail to remove them from office. Required to say by what warrant they occupy their ministerial office, they would answer that they occupy it by the pleasure of the Crown under a commission issued by the Crown and this answer would be a complete one at law; for at law, the government is in office by the pleasure of the Crown although by convention it is there by the will of the people.

This conflict between convention and law which prevents the courts from enforcing conventions also prevents conventions from crystallizing into laws, unless it be by statutory adoption.

It is because the sanctions of conventions rest with institutions of government other than courts, such as the Governor General or the Lieutenant-Governor, or the Houses of Parliament, or with public opinion and ultimately, with the electorate that it is generally said that they are political.

We respectfully adopt the definition of a convention given by the learned Chief Justice of Manitoba, Freedman C.J.M. in the Manitoba Reference...:

> What is a constitutional convention? There is a fairly lengthy literature on the subject. Although there may be shades of difference among the constitutional lawyers, political scientists, and Judges who have contributed to that literature, the essential features of a convention may be set forth with some degree of confidence. Thus there is general agreement that a convention occupies a position somewhere in between a usage or custom on the one hand and a constitutional law on the other. There is general agreement that if one sought to fix that position with greater precision

he would place convention nearer to law than to usage or custom. There is also general agreement that "a convention is a rule which is regarded as obligatory by the officials to whom it applies": Hogg, *Constitutional Law of Canada* (1977)....There is, if not general agreement, at least weighty authority, that the sanction for breach of a convention will be political rather than legal.

It should be borne in mind however that, while they are not laws, some conventions may be more important than some laws. Their importance depends on that of the value or principle which they are meant to safeguard. Also they form an integral part of the Constitution and of the constitutional system. They come within the meaning of the word "Constitution" in the preamble of the *British North America Act, 1867*:

Whereas the Provinces of Canada, Nova Scotia, and New Brunswick have expressed their Desire to be federally united...with a Constitution similar in principle to that of the United Kingdom...

That is why it is perfectly appropriate to say that to violate a convention is to do something which is unconstitutional although it entails no direct legal consequence. But the words "constitutional" and "unconstitutional" may also be used in a strict legal sense, for instance with respect to a statute which is found *ultra vires* or unconstitutional. The foregoing may perhaps be summarized in an equation: constitutional conventions plus constitutional law equal the total Constitution of the country.

EDWARDS V. ATTORNEY-GENERAL OF CANADA

Judicial Committee of the Privy Council

[1930] A.C. 124

This is the famous "persons" case in which five prominent Alberta women – Henrietta Muir Edwards, Emily F. Murphy, Nellie L. McClung, Louise C. McKinney and Irene Parlby – asked the Supreme Court of Canada whether the Governor General's power to appoint "qualified persons" to the Senate meant that women were eligible. The Supreme Court could not find in Canada's constitutional doctrine, *The British North American Act, 1867,* any reason for extending the phrase to include women and unanimously dismissed the appeal. At the time, however, the final court of appeal for Canada was the Judicial Committee of the Privy Council, and this court reversed the judgment. The case is noteworthy for its discussion of early constitutional relationships between Canada and the United Kingdom, soon to be dramatically changed by the *Statute of Westminster, 1931,* as well as its treatment of how the law, even constitutional law, can evolve.

* * * *

Lord Chancellor Sankey:

By s. 24 of the B. N. A. Act, 1867, it is provided that "The Governor General shall from Time to Time, in the Queen's Name, by Instrument under the Great Seal of Canada, summon qualified Persons to the Senate; and, subject to the Provisions of this Act, every Person so summoned shall become and be a Member of the Senate and a Senator."

The question at issue in this appeal is whether the words "qualified Persons" in that section include a woman, and consequently whether women are eligible to be summoned to and become members of the Senate of Canada....

No doubt in any code where women were expressly excluded from public office the problem would present no difficulty, but where instead of such exclusion those entitled to be summoned to or placed in public office are described under the word "person" different considerations arise.

The word is ambiguous and in its original meaning would undoubtedly embrace members of either sex. On the other hand, supposing in an Act of Parliament several centuries ago it had been enacted that any person should be entitled to be elected to a particular office it would have been understood that the word only referred to males, but the cause of this was not because the word "person" could not include females but because at Common Law a woman was incapable of serving a public office. The fact that no woman had served or had claimed to serve such an office is not of great weight when it is remembered that custom would have prevented the claim being made, or the point being contested.

Customs are apt to develop into traditions which are stronger than law and remain unchallenged long after the reason for them has disappeared.

The appeal to history therefore in this particular matter is not conclusive....

Over and above that, their Lordships do not think it right to apply rigidly to Canada of today the decisions and the reasons therefor which commended themselves, probably rightly, to those who had to apply the law in different circumstances, in different centuries to countries in different stages of development. Referring therefore to the judgment of the Chief Justice [of Canada] and those who agreed with him, their Lordships think that the appeal to Roman law and to early English decisions is not of itself a secure foundation on which to build the interpretation of the British North America Act of 1867....

Before discussing the various sections [of the B.N.A. Act] they think it necessary to refer to the circumstances which led up to the passing of the Act.

The communities included within the Britannic system embrace countries and peoples in every stage of social, political and economic development and undergoing a continuous process of evolution. His Majesty the King in Council is the final Court of Appeal from all these communities, and this Board must take great care therefore not to interpret legislation meant to apply to one community by a rigid adherence to the customs and traditions of another. Canada had its difficulties both at home and with the mother country, but soon discovered that union was strength. Delegates from the three maritime Provinces met in Charlottetown on September 1, 1864 to discuss proposals for a maritime union. A delegation from the coalition government of that day proceeded to Charlottetown and placed before the maritime delegates their schemes for a union embracing the Canadian Provinces. As a result the Quebec conference assembled on October 10, continued in session till October 28, and framed a number of resolutions. These resolutions as revised by the delegates from the different Provinces in London in 1866 were based upon a consideration of the rights of others and expressed in a compromise which will remain a lasting monument to the political genius of Canadian statesmen. Upon those resolutions the British North America Act of 1867 was framed and passed by the Imperial legislature. The Quebec resolutions dealing with the Legislative Council – namely, Nos. 6-24 – even if their Lordships are entitled to look at them, do not shed any light on the subject under discussion. They refer generally to the "members" of the Legislative Council.

The British North America Act planted in Canada a living tree capable of growth and expansion within its natural limits. The object of the Act was to grant a Constitution to Canada. "Like all written constitutions it has been subject to development through usage and convention": Canadian Constitutional Studies, Sir Robert Borden (1922), p. 55.

Their Lordships do not conceive it to be the duty of this Board – it is certainly not their desire – to cut down the provisions of the Act by a narrow and technical construction, but rather to give it a large and liberal interpretation so that the Dominion to a great extent, but within certain fixed limits, may be mistress in her own house, as the provinces to a great extent, but within certain fixed limits, are mistresses in theirs. "The Privy council, indeed, has laid down that Courts of law must treat the provisions of the British North America Act by the same methods of construction and exposition which they apply to other statutes. But there are statutes and statutes; and the strict construction deemed proper in the case, for example, of a penal or taxing statute or one passed to regulate the affairs of an English parish, would be often subversive of Parliament's real intent if applied to an Act passed to ensure the peace, order and good government of a British Colony": see Clement's Canadian Constitution, 3rd ed., p. 347.

The learned author of that treatise quotes from the argument of Mr. Mowat and Mr. Edward Blake before the Privy Council in *St. Catherine's Milling and Lumber Co. v. The Queen* (1888): "That Act should be on all occasions interpreted in a large, liberal and comprehensive spirit, considering the magnitude of the subjects with which it purports to deal in very few words." With that their Lordships agree, but as was said by the Lord Chancellor in *Brophy v. Attorney-General of Manitoba* (1895), the question is not what may be supposed to have been intended, but what has been said.

It must be remembered, too, that their Lordships are not here considering the question of the legislative competence either of the Dominion or its Provinces which arises under ss. 91 and 92 of the Act providing for the distribution of legislative powers and assigning to the dominion and its Provinces their respective spheres of Government. Their Lordships are concerned with the interpretation of an Imperial Act, but an Imperial Act which creates a constitution for a new country. Nor are their Lordships deciding any questions as to the rights of women but only a question as to their eligibility for a particular position. No one either male or female has a right to be summoned to the Senate. The real point at issue is whether the Governor-General has a right to summon women to the Senate.

The Act consists of a number of separate heads.

The preamble states that the Provinces of Canada, Nova Scotia and New Brunswick have expressed their desire to be federally united into one Dominion under the Crown of the United Kingdom of Great Britain and Ireland with a constitution similar in principle to that of the United Kingdom.

Head No. 2 refers to the union.

Head no. 3, ss. 9 to 16, to the executive power.

It is in s. 11 that the word "persons," which is used repeatedly in the Act, occurs for the first time.

It provides that the persons who are members of the Privy Council shall be from time to time chosen and summoned by the Governor General.

The word "person" as above mentioned may include members of both sexes, and to those who ask why the word should include females, the obvious answer is why should it not? In these circumstances the burden is upon those who deny that the word includes women to make out their case....

A heavy burden lies on an appellant who seeks to set aside a unanimous judgment of the Supreme Court, and this Board will only set aside such a decision after convincing argument and anxious consideration, but having regard: (1.) To the object of the Act – namely, to provide a constitution for Canada, a responsible and developing State; (2.) That the word "person" is ambiguous and may include members of either sex; (3.) That there are sections in the Act above referred to which show that in some cases the word "person" must include females; (4.) That in some sections the words "male persons" is expressly used when it is desired to confine the matter in issue to males; and (5.) to the provisions of the Interpretation Act; their Lordships have come to the conclusion that the word "persons" in s. 24 includes members both of the male and female sex and that, therefore, the question propounded by the Governor-General must be answered in the affirmative and that women are eligible to be summoned to and become members of the Senate of Canada, and they will humbly advise His Majesty accordingly.

THE QUEEN IN RIGHT OF CANADA V. BEAUREGARD

Supreme Court of Canada

[1986] 2 S.C.R. 56

This case involves complex issues concerning the salaries and pensions of Superior Court Judges. At the heart of the controversy was the question of whether the federal government, which constitutionally must "fix and provide" salaries and pensions for judges, could lower the salaries and reduce the benefits of *incumbent* judges. Mr. Justice Beauregard's argument was that this power would threaten, or at least might be perceived as threatening, the complete freedom that judges must have to render decisions in the cases that come before them. On the way to rejecting this argument, Chief Justice Dickson discussed in general terms the nature of judicial independence, a central, but rarely discussed, constitutional doctrine.

* * * *

Chief Justice Dickson and Justices Estey and Lamer:

1. General considerations

Historically, the generally accepted core of the principle of judicial independence has been the complete liberty of individual judges to hear and decide the cases that come before them: no outsider – be it government, pressure group, individual or even another judge – should interfere in fact, or attempt to interfere, with the way in which a judge conducts his or her case and makes his or her decision. This core continues to be central to the principle of judicial independence. Nevertheless, it is not the entire content of the principle.

Of recent years the general understanding of the principle of judicial independence has grown and been transformed to respond to the modern needs and problems of free and democratic societies. The ability of individual judges to make decisions in discrete cases free from external interference or influence continues, of course, to be an important and necessary component of the principle. Today, however, the principle is far broader. In the words of a leading academic authority on judicial independence, Professor Shimon Shetreet:

The judiciary has developed from a dispute-resolution mechanism, to a significant social institution with an important constitutional role which participates along with other institutions in shaping the life of its community.

There is, therefore, both an individual and a collective or institutional aspect to judicial independence. As stated by Le Dain J. in *Valente v. The Queen* (1985)...:

[Judicial independence] connotes not merely a state of mind or attitude in the actual exercise of judicial functions, but a status or relationship to others, particularly to the Executive Branch of government, that rests on objective conditions or guarantees....

It is generally agreed that judicial independence involves both individual and institutional relationships: the individual independence of a judge, as reflected in such matters as security of tenure, and the institutional independence of the court or tribunal over which he or she presides, as reflected in its institutional or administrative relationships to the executive and legislative branches of government.

The rationale for this two-pronged modern understanding of judicial independence is recognition that the courts are not charged solely with the adjudication of individual cases. That is, of course, one role. It is also the context for a second, different and equally important role, namely, as protector of the Constitution and the fundamental values embodied in it – rule of law, fundamental justice, equality, preservation of the democratic process, to name perhaps the most important. In other words, judicial independence is essential for fair and just dispute-resolution in individual cases. It is also the lifeblood of constitutionalism in democratic societies.

2. Foundations of judicial independence in Canada

It is trite history that the Canadian court system has its primary antecedents in the United Kingdom. (This is not true of our substantive law which has deep roots in both the United Kingdom and France.) In the United Kingdom the cornerstone of the constitutional system has been for centuries, and still is today, the principle of parliamentary supremacy. But it is not the only principle. The rule of law is another. Judicial independence is a third. The history of the Constitution of the United Kingdom reveals continuous growth towards independent judicial authority....Judicial authority in the United Kingdom has matured into a strong and effective means of ensuring that governmental power is exercised in accordance with law. Judicial independence is the essential prerequisite for this judicial authority. In the recent words of Lord Lane: "Few constitutional precepts are more generally accepted there in England, the land which boasts no written constitution, than the necessity for the judiciary to be secure from undue influence and autonomous within its own field."

In Canada, the constitutional foundation for the principle of judicial independence is derived from many sources. Because the sources for the principle are both varied and powerful, the principle itself is probably more integral and important in our constitutional system than it is in the United Kingdom.

Indeed, two of the sources of, or reasons for, judicial independence in Canada do not exist in the United Kingdom. First, Canada is a federal country with a constitutional distribution of powers between federal and provincial governments. As in other federal countries, there is a need for an impartial umpire to resolve disputes between two levels of government as well as between governments and private individuals who rely on the distribution of powers. In most federal countries the courts play this umpiring role. In Canada, since Confederation, it has been assumed and agreed that the courts would play an important constitutional role as umpire of the federal system. Initially, the role of the courts in this regard was not exclusive; in the early years of Confederation the federal government's disallowance power contained in s.55 of the *Constitutional Act, 1867* was also central to federal-provincial dispute-resolution. In time, however, the disallowance power fell into disuse and the courts emerged as the ultimate umpire of the federal system. That role, still fundamental today, requires that the umpire be autonomous and completely independent of the parties involved in federal-provincial disputes.

Secondly, the enactment of the *Canadian Charter of Rights and Freedoms*...conferred on the courts another truly crucial role; the defense of basic individual liberties and human rights against intrusions by all levels and branches of government. Once again, in order to play this deeply constitutional role, judicial independence is essential.

Beyond these two fundamental sources of, or reasons for, judicial independence there is also textual recognition of the principle in the *Constitution Act, 1867*. The preamble to the *Constitution Act, 1867* states that Canada is to have a Constitution "similar in Principle to that of the United Kingdom". Since judicial independence has been for centuries an important principle of the Constitution of the United Kingdom, it is fair to infer that it was transferred to Canada by the constitutional language of the preamble. Furthermore, s. 129 of the *Constitution Act, 1867* continued the courts previously in existence in the federating provinces into the new Dominion. The fundamental traditions of those courts, including judicial independence, were also continued. Additionally, the judicature provisions of the *Constitution Act, 1867*, especially ss. 96, 99 and 100, support judicial authority and independence, at least at the level of superior, district and county courts. As Lord Atkin said in *Corp. of Toronto v. Corp. of York et al.*, [1938]...:

> While legislative power in relation to the constitution, mainte-
> nance and organization of Provincial Courts of Civil Jurisdiction,
> including procedure in civil matters, is confided to the Province,
> the independence of the judges is protected by provisions that the
> judges of the Superior, District, and County Courts shall be
> appointed by the Governor-General (s. 96 of the British North
> America Act, 1867), that the judges of the Superior Courts shall
> hold office during good behaviour (s. 99), and that the salaries of
> the judges of the Superior, District and County Courts shall be
> fixed and provided by the Parliament of Canada (s. 100). These
> are three principal pillars in the temple of justice, and they are not
> to be undermined.

In summary, Canadian constitutional history and current Canadian constitutional law establish clearly the deep roots and contemporary vitality and vibrancy of the principle of judicial independence in Canada. The role of the courts as resolver of disputes, interpreter of the laws and defender of the Constitution requires that they be completely separate in authority and function from *all* other participants in the justice system.

I emphasize the word "all" in the previous sentence because, although judicial independence is usually considered and discussed in terms of the relationship between the judiciary and the executive branch, in this appeal the relevant relationship is between the judiciary and Parliament. Nothing turns on this contextual difference. Although particular care must be taken to preserve the independence of the judiciary from the executive branch (because the executive is so often a litigant before the courts), the principle of judicial independence must also be maintained against all other potential intrusions, including any from the legislative branch....

REFERENCE RE MANITOBA LANGUAGE RIGHTS

Supreme Court of Canada

[1985] 1 S.C.R. 721

This case involves another, once-in-a-lifetime legal puzzle. By section 23 of the *Manitoba Act, 1879,* all Acts of the Manitoba Legislature were to be enacted, printed and published in both English and French. This had not been done, and the government of Manitoba used the device of the reference to bring the issue before the Supreme Court of Canada. Since the law was clear on the point, the Supreme Court had to conclude that all of the unilingual Acts passed since 1879 were invalid and of no force or effect. In effect, this meant that everything that had been done, or not done in the province in accordance with these laws was also invalid. It was a relatively simple matter to translate the legislation into French, but that would take time. In the meantime, what was to be done with the legal vacuum? The court came to the philosophically interesting conclusion that when all specific laws are found to be invalid, there still remains a kind of legal residue that fills the vacuum. What fills the vacuum is the rule of law itself.

* * * *

By the Court:

This Reference combines legal and constitutional questions of the utmost subtlety and complexity with political questions of great sensitivity....

In the present case the unilingual enactments of the Manitoba Legislature are inconsistent with s. 23 of the *Manitoba Act, 1870* since the constitutionally required manner and form for their enactment has not been followed. Thus they are invalid and of no force or effect.

The Rule of Law

1. The Principle

The difficulty with the fact that the unilingual Acts of the Legislature of Manitoba must be declared invalid and of no force or effect is that,

without going further, a legal vacuum will be created with consequent legal chaos in the Province of Manitoba. The Manitoba Legislature has, since 1890, enacted nearly all of its laws in English only.
Thus, to find that the unilingual laws of Manitoba are invalid and of
no force or effect would mean that only laws enacted in both French
and English before 1890 would continue to be valid, and would still
be in force even if the law had purportedly been repealed or amended by a post-1890 unilingual statute; matters that were not regulated
by laws enacted before 1890 would now be unregulated by law, unless
a pre-confederation law or the common law provided a rule.

The situation of the various institutions of provincial government
would be as follows: the courts, administrative tribunals, public officials, municipal corporations, school boards, professional governing
bodies, and all other bodies created by law, to the extent that they
derive their existence from or purport to exercise powers conferred
by Manitoba laws enacted since 1890 in English only, would be acting
without legal authority.

Questions as to the validity of the present composition of the Manitoba Legislature might also be raised. Under the *Manitoba Act, 1870,*
the Legislative Assembly was to be composed of 24 members (s. 14),
and voters were to be male and over 21 (s. 17). By laws enacted after
1890 in English only, the size of the Legislative Assembly was
increased to 57 members, and all persons, both women and men,
over 18 were granted the right to vote.... If these laws are invalid and
of no force or effect, the present composition of the Manitoba Legislature might be invalid. The invalidity of the post-1890 laws would
not touch the existence of the Legislature or its powers since these
are matters of federal constitutional law.

Finally, all legal rights, obligations and other effects which have
purportedly arisen under all Acts of the Manitoba Legislature since
1890 would be open to challenge to the extent that their validity and
enforceability depends upon a regime of unconstitutional unilingual
laws.

In the present case, declaring the Acts of the Legislature of Manitoba invalid and of no force or effect would, without more, undermine the principle of the rule of law. The rule of law, a fundamental
principle of our Constitution, must mean at least two things. First,
that the law is supreme over officials of the government as well as private individuals, and thereby preclusive of the influence of arbitrary
power. Indeed, it is because of the supremacy of law over the government, as established in s. 23 of the *Manitoba Act, 1870* and s. 52 of
the *Constitution Act, 1982,* that this Court must find the unconstitutional laws of Manitoba to be invalid and of no force and effect.

Second, the rule of law requires the creation and maintenance of an actual order of positive laws which preserves and embodies the more general principle of normative order. Law and order are indispensable elements of civilized life. "The rule of law in this sense implies...simply the existence of public order." (W.I. Jennings, *The Law and the Constitution* (5th ed. 1959), at p. 43). As John Locke once said, "A government without laws is, I suppose, a mystery in politics, inconceivable to human capacity and inconsistent with human society"....According to Wade and Phillips, *Constitutional and Administrative Law* (9th ed. 1977), at p. 89: "...the rule of law expresses a preference for law and order within a community rather than anarchy, warfare and constant strife. In this sense, the rule of law is a philosophical view of society which in the Western tradition is linked with basic democratic notions."

It is this second aspect of the rule of law that is of concern in the present situation. The conclusion that the Acts of the Legislature of Manitoba are invalid and of no force or effect means that the positive legal order which has purportedly regulated the affairs of the citizens of Manitoba since 1890 will be destroyed and the rights, obligations and other effects arising under these laws will be invalid and unenforceable. As for the future, since it is reasonable to assume that it will be impossible for the Legislature of Manitoba to rectify *instantaneously* the constitutional defect, the Acts of the Manitoba Legislature will be invalid and of no force or effect until they are translated, re-enacted, printed and published in both languages.

Such results would certainly offend the rule of law. As we stated in the *Patriation Reference*:

> The "rule of law" is a highly textured expression...conveying, for example, a *sense of orderliness, of subjection to known legal rules* and of executive accountability to legal authority.

Dr. Raz has said: "'The rule of law' means literally what it says: the rule of the law....It has two aspects: (1) that people should be ruled by the law and obey it, and (2) that the law should be such that people will be able to be guided by it" (*The Authority of Law* (1979), at pp. 212-13). The rule of law simply cannot be fulfilled in a province that has no positive law.

The constitutional status of the rule of law is beyond question. The preamble to the *Constitution Act, 1982* states:

> Whereas Canada is founded upon principles that recognize the supremacy of God and the rule of law.

This is explicit recognition that "the rule of law [is] a fundamental postulate of our constitutional structure" (*per* Rand J., *Roncarelli v. Duplessis* (1959)). The rule of law has always been understood as the very basis of the English Constitution characterising the political institutions of England from the time of the Norman Conquest. It becomes a postulate of our own constitutional order by way of the preamble to the *Constitution Act, 1982,* and is implicit inclusion in the preamble of the *Constitution Act, 1867* by virtue of the words "with a Constitution similar in principle to that of the United Kingdom".

Additional to the inclusion of the rule of law in the preambles of the *Constitution Acts* of 1867 and 1982, the principle is clearly implicit in the very nature of a constitution. The Constitution, as the supreme law, must be understood as a purposive ordering of social relations providing a basis upon which an actual order of positive laws can be brought into existence. The founders of this nation must have intended, as one of the basic principles of nation building, that Canada be a society of legal order and normative structure: one governed by rule of law. While this is not set out in a specific provision, the principle of the rule of law is clearly a principle of our Constitution.

This court cannot take a narrow and literal approach to constitutional interpretation. The jurisprudence of the court evidences a willingness to supplement textual analysis with historical, contextual and purposive interpretation in order to ascertain the intent of the makers of our Constitution....

2. Application of the Principle of the Rule of Law

It is clear from the above that: (i) the law as stated in s. 23 of the *Manitoba Act, 1870* and s. 52 of the *Constitution Act, 1982* requires that the unilingual Acts of the Manitoba Legislature be declared to be invalid and of no force or effect, and (ii) without more, such a result would violate the rule of law. The task the Court faces is to recognize the unconstitutionality of Manitoba's unilingual laws and the Legislature's duty to comply with the "supreme law" of this country, while avoiding a legal vacuum in Manitoba and ensuring the continuity of the rule of law.

A number of the parties and interveners have suggested that the Court declare the unilingual Acts of the Manitoba Legislature to be invalid and of no force or effect and leave it at that, relying on the legislatures to work out a constitutional amendment. This approach because it would rely on a future and uncertain event, would be inappropriate. A declaration that the laws of Manitoba are invalid and of no legal force or effect would deprive Manitoba of its legal order and cause a transgression of the rule of law. For the Court to allow such a situation to arise and fail to resolve it would be an abdication of its responsibility as protector and preserver of the Constitution....

The only appropriate solution for preserving the rights, obligations and other effects which have arisen under invalid Acts of the Legislature of Manitoba and which are not saved by the *de facto* or other doctrines is to declare that, in order to uphold the rule of law, these rights, obligations and other effects have, and will continue to have, the same force and effect they would have had if they had arisen under valid enactments, for that period of time during which it would be impossible for Manitoba to comply with its constitutional duty under s. 23 of the *Manitoba Act, 1870*. The Province of Manitoba would be faced with chaos and anarchy if the legal rights, obligations and other effects which have been relied upon by the people of Manitoba since 1890 were suddenly open to challenge. The constitutional guarantee of rule of law will not tolerate such chaos and anarchy.

Nor will the constitutional guarantee of rule of law tolerate the Province of Manitoba being without a valid and effectual legal system for the present and future. Thus, it will be necessary to deem temporarily valid and effective the unilingual Acts of the Legislature of Manitoba which would be currently in force, were it not for their constitutional defect, for the period of time during which it would be impossible for the Manitoba Legislature to fulfil its constitutional duty. Since this temporary validation will include the legislation under which the Manitoba Legislature is presently constituted, it will be legally able to re-enact, print and publish its laws in conformity with the dictates of the Constitution once they have been translated....

As concerns the future, the Constitution requires that, from the date of this judgment, all new Acts of the Manitoba Legislature be enacted, printed and published in both French and English. Any Acts of the Legislature that do not meet this requirement will be invalid and of no force or effect.

BERTRAND V. ATTORNEY-GENERAL OF QUEBEC

Quebec Superior Court

[1995] R.J.Q. 2500

On December 6, 1994, Prime Minister Parizeau tabled a draft bill setting out the terms of Quebec's separation for Canada. On June 12, 1995, Quebec's three major parties agreed to the timetable for a referendum on Quebec sovereignty. Since the proposal to separate made no reference to the amending formula in the Constitution Act, 1982, arguably the whole process was unconstitutional. Guy Bertrand asked Quebec's Superior Court to issue an interlocutory injunction to prevent the referendum. The core of Mr Bertrand's argument was simplicity itself: the Government of Quebec was proposing a referendum that would have the effect of disqualifying him, as a citizen of Quebec, from the guarantees of the rights and freedoms found in the *Charter*, and that was an "irreparable harm" which the court, as a guardian of the Constitution, must prevent. Mr. Justice Lesage, clearly supportive of Mr. Bertrand's appeal, explores in this judgement the limits of the law and the power of the courts when it comes to the political question of secession and sovereignty. Courts cannot prevent revolutions or successions. But they declare the law as they see it.

* * * *

Mr. Justice Lesage:

Application for declarations that a draft bill declaring a province sovereign violated the Constitution of Canada and interlocutory injunctions against implementing the bill and holding a referendum on sovereignty.

The plaintiff, whose standing was not challenged, affirms in his statement of claim that "the conduct of the Quebec government, and its deeds and actions in regard to the draft bill respecting sovereignty and the June 12, 1995 agreement, constitute a veritable parliamentary and constitutional *coup d'état*, a fraud on the Canadian Constitution, and a misappropriation of authority the consequence of which will be the violation and denial of the rights and freedoms of the plaintiff and of all Quebec taxpayers".

The draft bill respecting the sovereignty of Quebec is a document tabled by Prime Minister Parizeau in the National Assembly on December 6, 1994, accompanied by a message to all citizens of Quebec, calling on them "to study, criticize or change this draft bill in a great exercise of democratic participation" and to "imagine together" the "declaration of sovereignty of Quebec" that is to serve as a recital to the eventual bill.

The agreement of June 12, 1995, is an agreement between the representatives of three political parties, the Parti québécois, the Bloc québécois and the Action démocratique du Québec, concerning "a common project to be submitted in the referendum" that is contemplated in the draft bill. It refers to this referendum as "the Fall 1995 referendum" and states that: "The elements of this common project will be integrated in the bill that will be tabled in the Fall." The objective is stated as follows:

> To achieve sovereignty for Quebec and a formal proposal for a new economic and political partnership with Canada, aimed among other things at consolidating the existing economic space....

The action brought by the plaintiff is not an action to nullify a government act or an application to invalidate the provisions of some legal rule pursuant to s. 52(1) of the *Constitution Act, 1982*. It is an independent proceeding under s. 24 for the purpose of obtaining such remedy as is "appropriate and just in the circumstances" for the negation of the rights and freedoms guaranteed to the plaintiff by the *Canadian Charter of Rights and Freedoms*.

The plaintiff argues that the government's action and all the expenditures of public funds with a view to achieving Quebec's secession are illegal, as they are made in the context of a project that proposes, in fraudulent violation of the Constitution of Canada, "to separate Quebec from Canada without complying with the amending formula provided in the *Constitution Act, 1982*". He states that the Quebec government is acting anarchically, in violation of public order, placing itself above the supreme law of the land, and that it is preparing to use its majority in the National Assembly to bring about a veritable constitutional *coup d'état*, in which it is involving the population without informing it of its fraud on the Constitution. He pleads bad faith on the part of the defendants and compares their actions to a conspiracy against the state. He characterizes the proceedings undertaken by the Government of Quebec as a constitutional revolution that has no justification under international law.

The plaintiff applies to the court, as the guardian of the Constitution, asking it to protect his rights and freedoms, which are seriously threatened "by the strategy, deeds and actions of the government of Québec as substantiated in the draft bill respecting the sovereignty of Québec and in the text of the agreement between the Parti québécois, the Bloc québécois and the Action démocratique du Québec. He submits that the Quebec government is seriously violating public order instead of governing in accordance with the rule of law."

Some principles

A society's political organization is derived from the sociological and historical wellsprings of the nation. The state is a product of the political organization. Not all states necessarily exercise full sovereignty over their territory and the people that inhabit it. We have the example of the provinces in our federal system, as in any federation. International recognition is a factor in establishing a country's sovereignty.

The constitution of a sovereign country – the set of rules governing the institutions that make up its political organizations – is not always written. The constitution is not a statute, in the sense that it does not emanate from the legislative authority of the country, although it may take the form of a statute. Still less may the constitution be contingent upon a statute. A statute must be consistent with the constitution, and not the converse. That is why the Constitution of Canada is characterized as the "supreme law of Canada."...

The legal system is a manifestation of state sovereignty which must pass muster with the judiciary. In societies that recognize the supremacy of the law, the judiciary exists to enforce the rule of law and, pre-eminently, the laws enacted by the legislature. In a federal system, the legal system includes some rules that govern the distribution of powers between the central state and the federated states. These rules are enforceable by the courts.

The judiciary does not create the law, still less the constitution of which it is an emanation. It interprets them. It is distinguished as well from the executive authority, the government, which alone has the duty and responsibility to act on behalf of the state. The role of the judiciary is circumscribed by the existence of rules of law, which are normally contained in statutes. Now, it is recognized that some constitutional usages, referred to as conventions, are not rules enforceable by the courts: *Reference re Amendment of the Constitution of Canada*....Contrary to a convention, a *coup d'état* or revolution may occur, breaking the continuity of the legal order, and the courts are powerless to intervene.

A country's sovereignty is, in effect, based on the *de facto* exercise of authority over a territory and the people who inhabit it. This exercise is secured through the voluntary or involuntary acceptance of the rules, including the constitution, that govern the relationships between the state and its citizens. These rules may be altered in accordance with the procedure provided by the existing legal system, *i.e.*, by following the path of legality, but they might also be altered by a declaration by some authority that places itself over and above the existing constitution and ensures its physical control of the territory and acceptance by the population.

This latter course is not legal. A new legal order can arise only after the *fait accompli*. This was the experience in Southern Rhodesia. As professor Peter Hogg relates in his *Constitutional Law of Canada*:

In assessing the legality of a regime established by revolution – meaning any break in legal continuity – the issue for the courts is simply whether or not the revolution has been successful. As de Smith says, "legal theorists have no option but to accommodate their concepts to the facts of political life." In *Madzimbamuto v. Lardner-Burke* (1969), the Privy Council had to decide whether validity should be accorded to the acts of the legislature and government of Southern Rhodesia after the "unilateral declaration of independence" (U.D.I.) from Britain. Their lordships held that the post-U.D.I. acts were not valid, because it could not be said "with certainty" that the break-away government was in effective control of the territory which it claimed the right to govern. Their lordships pointed out that Britain was still claiming to be the lawful government and was taking steps to regain control. In a later case, the Appellate Division of the High Court of Rhodesia decided that, having regard to developments since the decision in *Madzimbamuto*, it could "now predict with certainty that sanctions will not succeed in their objective of overthrowing the present government and of restoring the British government to the control of the government of Rhodesia". The Court accordingly held that the existing Rhodesian government was the legal government, and the post-U.D.I. constitution was the only valid constitution.

The matter at issue

Our task is, in the first place, to assess the right claimed by the plaintiff, namely, whether the government's action violates his rights and freedoms under the *Charter*. The *Charter*, introduced by the *Constitution Act, 1982*, is part of the Constitution of Canada. It undeniably applies to Quebec....

The legitimation or forced imposition of a new legal order can in no way be considered a contingency that a court should take into account. The supremacy of law is recognized by the Constitution of Canada...and our superior courts have stated many times that the courts are the guardians of the Constitution. We know of no authority to the contrary.

Section 24(1) is the appropriate remedy for redress of a violation of *Charter* rights and freedoms. The *Charter* applies not only to the Parliament and Government of Canada in respect of all matters with the authority of Parliament, but also to the legislature and government of each province in respect of all matters with the authority of the legislature of each province. It cannot be maintained, as was suggested to us, that governmental acts that create no obligation do not attract the supervision and control of the courts under the *Charter*. This would limit the operation of the *Charter* to rules of law, which can be declared of no force or effect under s. 52. The *Charter* applies to any government action if such action violates the rights and freedoms it guarantees.

It is manifest, if not expressly stated, that the Quebec government has no intention of resorting to the amending formula in the Constitution to accomplish the secession of Quebec. In this regard, the Quebec government is giving itself a mandate that the Constitution of Canada does not confer on it.

The actions taken by the Government of Quebec in view of the secession of Quebec are a repudiation of the Constitution of Canada. If such secession were to occur, the *Charter*, which is part of the Constitution of Canada, would cease to apply to Quebec and the plaintiff would no longer be able to demand compliance therewith....

The court cannot prevent the political forces from operating. On the other hand, it cannot approve a violation of the constitutional order. The events that have been set in motion by the Government of Quebec may lead to such a violation. This is not pure speculation. The government is going to very great lengths to get its way. Using its political authority and public moneys, it is seeking to overthrow the constitutional order. The plaintiff is opposed to this process. The tension that he and other citizens are experiencing can only increase day by day. The threat is a serious one. Similar considerations apply in the case of public order. The harm is irreparable....

Remedy

The plaintiff is asking me to issue a series of injunctions against the defendants and the Government of Quebec, as well as certain injunctions addressed to the chief electoral officer. The court cannot, of course, paralyze the functioning of the National Assembly or prohibit it from debating the issue. That would be an infringement of parliamentary privileges. Moreover, it is preferable that the public discussion be held with full knowledge of the facts.

As to prohibiting the use of public funds for the promotion of the government's constitutional project, no injunction can be issued since no legal provision controlling these types of expenditures, which are made on behalf of the Crown, was drawn to my attention.

However, I take judicial notice that neither the official opposition in Quebec nor the federal government intends to block the holding of the referendum. It must be understood that the people wish to express themselves. To issue an injunction against the holding of the referendum would risk creating a greater wrong than the wrong that it is sought to prevent.

However, a declaratory judgment may be just as if not more effective than an injunction. Moreover, it is the remedy favoured by the courts in constitutional matters, for a variety of reasons. The declaration is not an intrusion into the functioning of the executive or the legislature. It does not open the door to execution proceedings that might appear odious. On the contrary, it allows governments to conceive of ways in which to satisfy the judicial declaration, and thus helps to maintain the balance in our democratic institutions....

To ensure that the plaintiff's remedy is not completely ineffective once judgment becomes final, the only declaration that would, in my opinion, constitute effective relief is to state, as the plaintiff is asking, that the bill that reiterates the terms of the agreement ratified and executed on June 12, 1995...that would grant the National Assembly of Quebec the capacity or power to declare the sovereignty of Quebec without following the amending procedure provided for in the Constitution of Canada, constitutes a serious threat to the rights or freedoms of the plaintiff guaranteed by the *Canadian Charter of Rights and Freedoms*.

B: THE SCOPE OF THE CHARTER

RETAIL, WHOLESALE AND DEPARTMENT STORE UNION,
LOCAL 580 V. DOLPHIN DELIVERY LTD.

Supreme Court of Canada

[1986] 2 S.C.R. 573

What is the scope of judicial review under the *Charter*? And is there a tension between the sweeping words of section 52(1) and the more restrained language of section 32(1)? The concern here is not the purely technical one it might seem on first glance. At stake is the traditional liberal view that there is a fundamental distinction between the "public" and the "private" spheres, and that constitutional guarantees are only required to constrain government action within the public sphere. Does this mean, for example, that powerful private organizations such as corporations can violate our freedoms of speech and association with impunity?

In the *Dolphin Delivery* case precisely this question is at issue. During a labour dispute involving Purolator Courier, the union representing the employees believed that Dolphin Delivery, by continuing to do business with Purolator during the lock-out, was conspiring to defeat the union. The union proposed to engage in "secondary picketing" of Dolphin Delivery. Before they could do so, Dolphin Delivery asked for and was granted an injunction on the grounds that secondary picketing comprises a common law tort of inducing breach of contract. The union appealed arguing that the injunction, and the "private" common law on which it was based, violated their right to freedom of expression and association. The majority based its rejection of the union's appeal on the issue of whether the *Charter* applies to the law concerning "private" matters.

* * * *

Mr. Justice McIntyre, Chief Justice Dickson, and Justices Estey, Chouinard and Le Dain:

Does the Charter apply to the common law?

In my view, there can be no doubt that it does apply....The English text [of s. 52] provides that "any law that is inconsistent with the provisions of the Constitution is, to the extent of the inconsistency, of no force or effect". If this language is not broad enough to include the common law, it should be observed as well that the French text adds strong support to this conclusion in its employment of the words "elle rend inoperantes les dispositions incompatibles *de tout autre regle de droit*". To adopt a construction of s. 52(1) which would exclude from *Charter* application the whole body of the common law which in great part governs the rights and obligations of the individuals in society, would be wholly unrealistic and contrary to the clear language employed in s. 52(1) of the Act.

Does the Charter apply to private litigation?

This question involves consideration of whether or not an individual may found a cause of action or defence against another individual on the basis of a breach of a *Charter* right. In other words, does the *Charter* apply to private litigation divorced completely from any connection with Government? This is a subject of controversy in legal circles and the question has not been dealt with in this Court. One view of the matter rests on the proposition that the *Charter*, like most written constitutions, was set up to regulate the relationship between the individual and the Government. It was intended to restrain government action and to protect the individual. It was not intended in the absence of some governmental action to be applied in private litigation....

I am in agreement with the view that the *Charter* does not apply to private litigation. It is evident from the authorities...that that approach has been adopted by most judges and commentators who have dealt with this question. In my view, s. 32 of the *Charter*, specially dealing with the question of *Charter* application, is conclusive on this issue....Section 32(1) refers to the Parliament and Government of Canada and to the legislatures and governments of the Provinces in respect of all matters within their respective authorities. In this, it may be seen that Parliament and the legislatures are treated as separate or specific branches of government, distinct from the executive branch of government, and therefore where the word "government" is used in s. 32 it refers not to government in its generic sense – meaning the whole of the governmental apparatus of the state – but to a branch of government. The word "government", following as it does the words "Parliament" and "Legislature", must then, it would seem, refer to the executive or administrative branch of government. This is the sense in which one generally speaks of the Government of Canada or of a province. I am of the opinion that the word "government" is used in s. 32 of the *Charter* in the sense of the executive government of Canada and the Provinces....

It is my view that s. 32 of the *Charter* specifies the actors to whom the *Charter* will apply. They are the legislative, executive and administrative branches of government. It will apply to those branches of government whether or not their action is invoked in public or private litigation. It would seem that legislation is the only way in which a legislature may infringe a guaranteed right or freedom. Action by the executive or administrative branches of government will generally depend upon legislation, that is, statutory authority. Such action may also depend, however, on the common law, as in the case of the prerogative. To the extent that it relies on statutory authority which constitutes or results in an infringement of a guaranteed right or freedom, the *Charter* will apply and it will be unconstitutional. The action will also be unconstitutional to the extent that it relies for authority or justification on a rule of the common law which constitutes or creates an infringement of a *Charter* right or freedom. In this way the *Charter* will apply to the common law, whether in public or private litigation. It will apply to the common law, however, only in so far as the common law is the basis of some governmental action which, it is alleged, infringes a guaranteed right or freedom.

The element of governmental intervention necessary to make the *Charter* applicable in an otherwise private action is difficult to define. We have concluded that the *Charter* applies to the common law but not between private parties. The problem here is that this is an action between private parties in which the appellant resists the common law claim of the respondent on the basis of a *Charter* infringement. The argument is made that the common law, which is itself subject to the *Charter*, creates the tort of civil conspiracy and that of inducing a breach of contract. The respondent has sued and has procured the injunction which has enjoined the picketing on the basis of the commission of these torts. The appellants say the injunction infringes their *Charter* right of freedom of expression under s. 2(b). Professor Hogg meets this problem when he suggests, at p. 677 of his text, after concluding that the *Charter* does not apply to private litigation, that:

Private action is, however, a residual category from which it is necessary to subtract those kinds of action to which s. 32 does make the *Charter* applicable....The *Charter* will apply to any rule of the common law that specifically authorizes or directs an abridgement of a guaranteed right....

The fact that a court order is governmental action means that the *Charter* will apply to a purely private arrangement, such as a contract or proprietary interest, but only to the extent that the *Charter* will preclude judicial enforcement of any arrangement in derogation of a guaranteed right.

Professor Hogg, at p. 678, rationalized his position in these words:

In a sense, the common law authorizes any private action that is not prohibited by a positive rule of law. If the *Charter* applied to the common law in that attenuated sense, it would apply to all private activity. But it seems more reasonable to say that the common law offends the *Charter* only when it crystallizes into a rule that can be enforced by the courts. Then, if an enforcement order would infringe a *Charter* right, the *Charter* will apply to preclude the order, and, by necessary implication, to modify the common law rule.

I find the position thus adopted troublesome and, in my view, it should not be accepted as an approach to this problem. While in political science terms it is probably acceptable to treat the courts as one of the three fundamental branches of government, that is, legislative, executive, and judicial, I cannot equate for the purposes of *Charter* application the order of a court with an element of governmental action. This is not to say that the courts are not bound by the *Charter*. The courts are, of course, bound by the *Charter* as they are bound by all law. It is their duty to apply the law, but in doing so they act as neutral arbiters, not as contending parties involved in a dispute. To regard a court order as an element of governmental intervention necessary to invoke the *Charter* would, seems to me, widen the scope of *Charter* application to virtually all private litigation. All cases must end, if carried to completion, with an enforcement order and if the *Charter* precludes the making of the order, where a *Charter* right would be infringed, it would seem that all private litigation would be subject to the *Charter*. In my view, this approach will not provide the answer to the question. A more direct and a more precisely-defined connection between the element of government action and the claim advanced must be present before the *Charter* applies.

An example of such a direct and close connection is to be found in *Re Blainey and Ontario Hockey Ass'n et al.* (1986). In that case, proceedings were brought against the hockey association in the Supreme Court of Ontario on behalf of a 12- year-old girl who had been refused permission to play hockey as a member of a boys' team competing under the auspices of the association. A complaint against the exclusion of the girl on the basis of her sex alone had been made under the provisions of the *Human Rights Code, 1981* (Ont.)...to the Ontario Human Rights Commission. It was argued that the hockey association provided a service ordinarily available to members of the public without discrimination because of sex, and therefore that the discrimination against the girl contravened this legislation. The commission considered that it could not act in the matter because of the provisions of s. 19(2) of the *Human Rights Code*, which are set out hereunder:

> 19(2) The right under section 1 to equal treatment with respect to services and facilities is not infringed where membership in an athletic organization or participation in an athletic activity is restricted to persons of the same sex.

In the Supreme Court of Ontario it was claimed that s. 19(2) of the *Human Rights Code* was contrary to s. 15(1) of the *Charter* and that it was accordingly void. The application was dismissed. In the Court of Appeal, the appeal was allowed....Dubin J.A. writing for the majority, stated the issue in these terms...:

> Indeed, it was on the premise that the ruling of the Ontario Human Rights Commission was correct that these proceedings were launched and which afforded the status to the applicant to complain now that, by reason of s. 19(2) of the *Human Rights Code*, she is being denied the equal protection and equal benefit of the *Human Rights Code* by reason of her sex, contrary to the provision of s. 15(1) of the *Canadian Charter of Rights and Freedoms*.

He concluded that the provisions of s. 19(2) were in contradiction of the *Charter* and hence of no force or effect. In the *Blainey* case, a lawsuit between private parties, the *Charter* was applied because one of the parties acted on the authority of a statute, i.e., s. 19(2) of the Ontario *Human Rights Code*, which infringed the *Charter* rights of another. *Blainey* then affords an illustration of the manner in which

Charter rights of private individuals may be enforced and protected by the courts, that is, by measuring legislation – government action – against the *Charter*.

As has been noted above, it is difficult and probably dangerous to attempt to define with narrow precision that element of governmental intervention which will suffice to permit reliance on the *Charter* by private litigants in private litigation. Professor Hogg has dealt with this question:

> ...the *Charter* would apply to a private person exercising the power of arrest that is granted to "any one" by the Criminal Code, and to a private railway company exercising the power to make by-laws (and impose penalties for their breach) that is granted to a "railway company" by the Railway Act; all action taken in exercise of a statutory power is covered by the *Charter* by virtue of the references to "Parliament" and "legislature" in s. 32. The *Charter* would also apply to the action of a commercial corporation that was an agent of the Crown, by virtue of the reference to "government" in s. 32.

It would also seem that the *Charter* would apply to many forms of delegated legislation, regulations, orders in council, possibly municipal by-laws, and by-laws and regulations of other creatures of Parliament and the Legislatures. It is not suggested that this list is exhaustive. Where such exercise of, or reliance upon, governmental action is present and where one private party invokes or relies upon it to produce an infringement of the *Charter* rights of another, the *Charter* will be applicable. Where, however, private party "A" sues private party "B" relying on the common law and where no act of government is relied upon to support the action, the *Charter* will not apply. I should make it clear, however, that this is a distinct issue from the question whether the judiciary ought to apply and develop the principles of the common law in a manner consistent with the fundamental values enshrined in the Constitution. The answer to this question must be in the affirmative. In this sense, then, the *Charter* is far from irrelevant to private litigants whose disputes fall to be decided at common law. But this is different from the proposition that one private party owes a constitutional duty to another, which proposition underlies the purported assertion of *Charter* causes of action or *Charter* defences between individuals.

Can it be said in the case at bar that the required element of government intervention or intrusion may be found? In *Blainey*, s. 19(2) of the Ontario *Human Rights Code*, an Act of a legislature, was the factor which removed the case from the private sphere. If in our case one could point to a statutory provision specifically outlawing secondary picketing of the nature contemplated by the appellants, the case – assuming for the moment an infringement of the *Charter* – would be on all fours with *Blainey* and, subject to s. 1 of the *Charter*, the statutory provision could be struck down. In neither case, would it be, as Professor Hogg would have it, the order of a court which would remove the case from the private sphere. It would be the result of one party's reliance on a statutory provision violative of the *Charter*.

In the case at bar, however, we have no offending statute. We have a rule of the common law which renders secondary picketing tortious and subject to injunctive restraint, on the basis that it induces a breach of contract. While, as we have found, the *Charter* applies to the common law, we do not have in this litigation between purely private parties any exercise of or reliance upon governmental action which would invoke the *Charter*. It follows then that the appeal must fail.

R. V. OAKES

Supreme Court of Canada

[1986] 1 S.C.R. 103

A unique feature of Canada's constitutional framework for the protection of rights and freedoms is section 1 of the *Charter*. This section reads: "The *Canadian Charter of Rights and Freedoms* guarantees the rights and freedoms set out in it subject only to such reasonable limits prescribed by law as can be demonstrably justified in a free and democratic society." In effect, section 1 asserts that sometimes a law or state action that violates rights or freedoms may nonetheless be constitutionally acceptable. When are limits on our rights and freedoms "reasonable" and when can they be "demonstrably justified"?

In the *Oakes* case Chief Justice Dickson attempted to answer these questions by offering a sophisticated test for the application of section 1. David Oakes had been charged with unlawful possession of a narcotic for the purpose of trafficking. In the course of his trial, he challenged the constitutionality of the "reverse onus" provision of section 8 of the *Narcotic Control Act*. That section provided that once the court found that Oakes was in possession of the narcotic, he was presumed to be in possession for the purposes of trafficking (a much more serious offence), and that it was up to him to prove otherwise. The Supreme Court of Canada quickly found that this provision violated Oakes' *Charter* section 11(d) right to be presumed innocent until proven guilty. But the question remained whether, given that drug trafficking is a serious social problem, this infringement of Oakes' rights could be justified in a "free and democratic society." Chief Justice Dickson's analysis of the application of section 1 has had a profound effect on *Charter* jurisprudence. As many of the *Charter* cases found in this book indicate, a substantial part of our constitutional jurisprudence now involves section 1 and the *Oakes* test.

* * * *

Chief Justice Dickson:

The Crown submits that even if s. 8 of the *Narcotic Control Act* violates s. 11(d) of the *Charter*, it can still be upheld as a reasonable limit under s. 1 which...provides:

> 1. The *Canadian Charter of Rights and Freedoms* guarantees the rights and freedoms set out in it subject only to such reasonable limits prescribed by law as can be demonstrably justified in a free and democratic society."

It is important to observe at the outset that s. 1 has two functions: first, it constitutionally guarantees the rights and freedoms set out in the provisions which follow; and, second, it states explicitly the exclusive justificatory criteria (outside of s. 33 of the *Constitution Act, 1982*) against which limitations on those rights and freedoms must be measured. Accordingly, any s. 1 inquiry must be premised on an understanding that the impugned limit violates constitutional rights and freedoms – rights and freedoms which are part of the supreme law of Canada. As Wilson J. stated in *Singh v. Minister of Employment and Immigration* (1985): "...it is important to remember that the courts are conducting this inquiry in light of a commitment to uphold the rights and freedoms set out in the other sections of the *Charter*."

A second contextual element of interpretation of s. 1 is provided by the words "free and democratic society". Inclusion of these words as the final standard of justification for limits on rights and freedoms refers the Court to the very purpose for which the *Charter* was originally entrenched in the Constitution: Canadian society is to be free and democratic. The Court must be guided by the values and principles essential to a free and democratic society which I believe embody, to name but a few, respect for the inherent dignity of the human person, commitment to social justice and equality, accommodation of a wide variety of beliefs, respect for cultural and group identity, and faith in social and political institutions which enhance the participation of individuals and groups in society. The underlying values and principles of a free and democratic society are the genesis of the rights and freedoms guaranteed by the *Charter* and the ultimate standard against which a limit on a right or freedom must be shown, despite its effect, to be reasonable and demonstrably justified.

The rights and freedoms guaranteed by the *Charter* are not, however, absolute. It may become necessary to limit rights and freedoms in circumstances where their exercise would be inimical to the realization of collective goals of fundamental importance. For this reason, s. 1 provides criteria of justification for limits on the rights and freedoms guaranteed by the *Charter* in circumstances where their exercise would be inimical to the realization of collective goals of fundamental importance. These criteria impose a stringent standard of justification, especially when understood in terms of the two contextual considerations discussed above, namely, the violation of a constitutional guaranteed right or freedom and the fundamental principles of a free and democratic society.

The onus of proving that a limit on a right and freedom guaranteed by the *Charter* is reasonable and demonstrably justified in a free and democratic society rests upon the party seeking to uphold the limitation. It is clear from the text of s. 1 that limits on the rights and freedoms enumerated in the *Charter* are exceptions to their general guarantee. The presumption is that the rights and freedoms are guaranteed unless the party invoking s. 1 can bring itself within the exceptional criteria which justify their being limited. This is further substantiated by the use of the word "demonstrably" which clearly indicates that the onus of justification is on the party seeking to limit....

The standard of proof under s. 1 is the civil standard, namely, proof by a preponderance of probability. The alternative criminal standard, proof beyond a reasonable doubt, would, in my view, be unduly onerous on the party seeking to limit. Concepts such as "reasonableness", "justifiability" and "free and democratic society" are simply not amenable to such a standard. Nevertheless, the preponderance of probability test must be applied rigorously. Indeed, the phrase "demonstrably justified" in s. 1 of the *Charter* supports this conclusion....

Having regard to the fact that s. 1 is being invoked for the purpose of justifying a violation of the constitutional rights and freedoms the *Charter* was designed to protect, a very high degree of probability will be, in the words of Lord Denning, "commensurate with the occasion". Where evidence is required in order to prove the constituent elements of a s. 1 inquiry, and this will generally be the case, it should be cogent and persuasive and make clear to the Court the consequences of imposing or not imposing the limit....A court will also need to know what alternative measures for implementing the objective were available to the legislators when they made their decisions. I should add, however, that there may be cases where certain elements of the s. 1 analysis are obvious or self-evident.

To establish that a limit is reasonable and demonstrably justified in a free and democratic society, two central criteria must be satisfied.

First, the objective, which the measures responsible for a limit on a *Charter* right and freedom are designed to serve, must be "of sufficient importance to warrant overriding a constitutionally protected right or freedom": *R. v. Big M Drug Mart Ltd* (1985). The standard must be high in order to ensure that objectives which are trivial or discordant with the principles integral to a free and democratic society do not gain s. 1 protection. It is necessary, at a minimum, that an objective relate to concerns which are pressing and substantial in a free and democratic society before it can be characterized as sufficiently important.

Second, once a sufficiently significant objective is recognized, then the party invoking s. 1 must show that the means chosen are reasonable and demonstrably justified. This involves "a form of proportionality test": *R. v. Big M Drug mart Ltd.* (1985). Although the nature of the proportionality test will vary depending on the circumstances, in each case courts will be required to balance the interests of society with those of individuals and groups. There are, in my view, three important components of a proportionality test. First, the measures adopted must be carefully designed to achieve the objective in question. They must not be arbitrary, unfair or based on irrational considerations. In short, they must be rationally connected to the objective. Second, the means, even if rationally connected to the objective in this first sense, should impair "as little as possible" the right or freedom in question: *R. v. Big M Drug Mart Ltd.* (1985). Third, there must be a proportionality between the *effects* of the measures which are responsible for limiting the *Charter* right or freedom, and the objective which has been identified as of "sufficient importance".

With respect to the third component, it is clear that the general effect of any measure impugned under s. 1 will be the infringement of a right or freedom guaranteed by the *Charter*; this is the reason why resort to s. 1 is necessary. The inquiry into effects must, however, go further. A wide range of rights and freedoms are guaranteed by the *Charter*, and an almost infinite number of factual situations may arise in respect of these. Some limits on rights and freedoms protected by the *Charter* will be more serious than others in terms of the nature of the right or freedom violated, the extent of the violation, and the degree to which the measures which impose the limit trench upon the integral principles of a free and democratic society. Even if an objective is of sufficient importance, and the first two elements of the proportionality test are satisfied, it is still possible that, because of the severity of the deleterious effects of a measure on individuals or groups, the measure will not be justified by the purposes it is intended to serve. The more severe the deleterious effects of a measure, the more important the objective must be if the measure is to be reasonable and demonstrably justified in a free and democratic society.

Having outlined the general principles of a s. 1 inquiry, we must apply them to s. 8 of the *Narcotic Control Act*. Is the reverse onus provision in s. 8 a reasonable limit on the right to be presumed innocent until proven guilty beyond a reasonable doubt as can be demonstrably justified in a free and democratic society?

The starting point for formulating a response to this question is, as stated above, the nature of Parliament's interest or objective which accounts for the passage of s. 8 of the *Narcotic Control Act*. According to the Crown, s. 8 of the *Narcotic Control Act* is aimed at curbing drug trafficking by facilitating the conviction of drug traffickers. In my opinion, Parliament's concern that drug trafficking be decreased can be characterized as substantial and pressing. The problem of drug trafficking has been increasing since the 1950's at which time there was already considerable concern....Throughout this period, numerous measures were adopted by free and democratic societies, at both the international and national levels....

The objective of protecting our society from the grave ills associated with drug trafficking, is, in my view, one of sufficient importance to warrant overriding a constitutionally protected right or freedom in certain cases. Moreover, the degree of seriousness of drug trafficking makes its acknowledgement as a sufficiently important objective for the purposes of s. 1, to a large extent, self-evident. The first criterion of a s. 1 inquiry, therefore, has been satisfied by the Crown.

The next stage of inquiry is a consideration of the means chosen by Parliament to achieve its objective. The means must be reasonable and demonstrably justified in a free and democratic society. As outlined above, this proportionality test should begin with a consideration of the rationality of the provision: is the reverse onus clause in s. 8 rationally related to the objective of curbing drug trafficking? At a minimum, this requires that s. 8 be internally rational; there must be a rational connection between the basic fact of possession and the presumed fact of possession for the purpose of trafficking. Otherwise, the reverse onus clause could give rise to unjustified and erroneous convictions for drug trafficking of persons guilty only of possession of narcotics.

In my view, s. 8 does not survive this rational connection test. As Martin J.A. of the Ontario Court of Appeal concluded, possession of a small or negligible quantity of narcotics does not support the inference of trafficking. In other words, it would be irrational to infer that a person had an intent to traffic on the basis of his or her possession of a very small quantity of narcotics. The presumption required under s. 8 of the *Narcotic Control Act* is over-inclusive and could lead to results in certain cases which would defy both rationality and fairness. In light of the seriousness of the offence in question, which carries with it the possibility of imprisonment for life, I am further convinced that the first component of the proportionality test has not been satisfied by the Crown.

Having concluded that s. 8 does not satisfy this first component of proportionality, it is unnecessary to consider the other two components.

[Therefore, s. 8 of the *Narcotic Control Act* is inconsistent with s. 11(d) of the *Charter* and thus is of no force and effect.]

> does it have to apply to all cases.
> does -the intent not change when
> their is an extreme amount of
> narcotics in question?

SCHACHTER V. CANADA

Supreme Court of Canada

[1992] 2 S.C.R. 679

If a complainant has successfully proven that a right or freedom set out in the *Charter* has been violated, and if that violation can not be "saved" by an appeal to section 1 of the *Charter*, what is the court empowered to do by way of remedy? The *Charter* contains two remedial or enforcement provisions, sections 24 and 52. Both of these are very broadly worded. But the question remains: what do these remedial powers entail, in practice?

In this important and controversial case, the natural father of a newborn child was denied 15 weeks of paternity benefits under section 32 of the *Unemployment Insurance Act* because these benefits were only available for adoptive parents. Section 32 was successfully challenged as a denial of equality, as guaranteed under section 15 of the *Charter*. The issue then became, what can, and should, the court do by way of remedy, given that whatever it does will have a wide range of consequences. The court surveyed a wide variety of remedial approaches and attempted to provide a mechanism, based in part on the *Oakes* case, for deciding when each is appropriate. One of the issues addressed here is when it is legitimate for a court to take active steps to reconstruct new legislative provisions – or in the jargon, to "read in" new provisions of existing laws in order to repair their unconstitutionality.

* * * *

Chief Justice Lamer, and Mr. Justices Sopinka, Gonthier, Cory and Madame Justice McLachlin:

I. Reading in as a remedial option under section 52

A court has flexibility in determining what course of action to take following a violation of the *Charter* which does not survive s. 1 scrutiny. Section 52 of the *Constitution Act, 1982* mandates the striking down of any law that is inconsistent with the provisions of the Constitution, but only "to the extent of the inconsistency". Depending upon the circumstances, a court may simply strike down, it may strike down and temporarily suspend the declaration of invalidity, or it may resort to the techniques of reading down or reading in. In addition, s. 24 of the *Charter* extends to any court of competent jurisdiction the power to grant an "appropriate and just" remedy to "[a]nyone whose [*Charter*] rights and freedoms...have been infringed or denied". In choosing how to apply s. 52 or s. 24 a court will determine its course of action with reference to the nature of the violation and the context of the specific legislation under consideration.

A. *The Doctrine of Severance*

The flexibility of the language of s. 52 is not a new development in Canadian constitutional law. The courts have always struck down laws only to the extent of the inconsistency by using the doctrine of severance or "reading down". Severance is used by the courts so as to interfere with the laws adopted by the Legislature as little as possible. Generally speaking, when only a part of a statute or provision violates the Constitution, it is common sense that only the offending portion should be declared to be of no force or effect, and the rest should be spared.

Far from being an unusual technique, severance is an ordinary and everyday part of constitutional adjudication. For instance if a single section of a statute violates the Constitution, normally that section may be severed from the rest of the statute so that the whole statute need not be struck down. To refuse to sever the offending part, and therefore declare inoperative parts of a legislative enactment which do not themselves violate the Constitution, is surely the more difficult course to justify....

Where the offending portion of a statute can be defined in a limited manner it is consistent with legal principles to declare inoperative only that limited portion. In that way, as much of the legislative purpose as possible may be realized. However, there are some cases in which to sever the offending portion would actually be more intrusive to the legislative purpose than the alternate course of striking down provisions which are not themselves offensive but which are closely connected with those that are....

Therefore, the doctrine of severance requires that a court define carefully the extent of the inconsistency between the statute in question and the requirements of the Constitution, and then declare inoperative (a) the inconsistent portion, and (b) such part of the remainder of which it cannot be safely assumed that the Legislature would have enacted it without the inconsistent portion.

B. Reading In as Akin to Severance

This same approach should be applied to the question of reading in since extension by way of reading in is closely akin to the practice of severance. The difference is the manner in which the extent of the inconsistency is defined. In the usual case of severance the inconsistency is defined as something improperly included in the statute which can be severed and struck down. In the case of reading in the inconsistency is defined as what the statue wrongly *excludes* rather than what it wrongly *includes*. Where the inconsistency is defined as what the statute excludes, the logical result of declaring inoperative that inconsistency may be to include the excluded group within the statutory scheme. This has the effect of extending the reach of the statute by way of reading in rather than reading down.

A statute may be worded in such a way that it gives a benefit or right to one group (inclusive wording) or it may be worded to give a right or benefit to everyone except a certain group (exclusive wording). It would be an arbitrary distinction to treat inclusively and exclusively worded statutes differently. To do so would create a situation where the style of drafting would be the single critical factor in the determination of a remedy. This is entirely inappropriate....

There is nothing in s. 52 of the *Constitution Act, 1982* to suggest that the court should be restricted to the verbal formula employed by the legislature in defining the inconsistency between a statute and the Constitution. Section 52 does not say that the *words* expressing a law are of no force or effect to the extent that they are inconsistent with the Constitution. It says that a *law* is of no force or effect to the extent of the inconsistency. Therefore, the inconsistency can be defined as what is left out of the verbal formula as well as what is wrongly included.

C. The Purposes of Reading In and Severance

(i) Respect for the Role of the Legislature

The logical parallels between reading in and severance are mirrored by their parallel purposes. Reading in is as important a tool as severance in avoiding undue intrusion into the legislative sphere. As with severance, the purpose of reading in is to be as faithful as possible within the requirements of the Constitution to the scheme enacted by the Legislature....

Of course, reading in will not always constitute the lesser intrusion for the same reason that severance sometimes does not. In some cases, it will not be a safe assumption that the Legislature would have enacted the constitutionally permissible part of its enactment without the impermissible part. For example, in a benefits case, it may not be a safe assumption that the Legislature would have enacted a benefits scheme if it were impermissible to exclude particular parties from entitlement under that scheme.

a better ex. of the exclusion of the group.

(ii) Respect for the Purposes of the Charter

Just as reading in is sometimes required to respect the purposes of the Legislature, it is also sometimes required in order to respect the purposes of the *Charter*. The absolute unavailability of reading in would mean that the standards developed under the *Charter* would have to be applied in certain cases in ways which would derogate from the deeper social purposes of the *Charter*....

This is best illustrated by the case of *Nova Scotia (Attorney General) v. Phillips* (1986). In that case, a form of welfare benefit was available to single mothers but not single fathers. This was held to violate s. 15 of the *Charter* since benefits should be available to single mothers and single fathers equally. However, the court held that s. 15 merely required equal benefit, so that the *Charter* would be equally satisfied whether the benefit was available to both mothers and fathers or to neither. Given this and the court's conclusion that it could not extend benefits, the only available course was to nullify the benefits to single mothers. The irony of this result is obvious.

Perhaps in some cases s. 15 does simply require relative equality and is just as satisfied with equal graveyards as equal vineyards, as it has sometimes been put....Yet the nullification of benefits to single mothers does not sit well with the overall purpose of s.15 of the *Charter* and for s. 15 to have such a result clearly amounts to "equality with a vengeance" as [Women's Legal Education and Action Fund], one of the interveners in this case, has suggested. While s. 15 may not absolutely require that benefits be available to single mothers, surely it at least encourages such action to relieve the disadvantaged position of persons in those circumstances. In cases of this kind, reading in allows the courts to act in a manner more consistent with the basic purposes of the *Charter*.

Reading in should therefore be recognized as a legitimate remedy akin to severance and should be available under s. 52 in cases where it is an appropriate technique to fulfil the purposes of the *Charter* and at the same time minimize the interference of the court with the parts of legislation that do not themselves violate the *Charter*.

II. Choice of Remedial Options under Section 52

A. Defining the Extent of the Inconsistency

The first step in choosing a remedial course under s. 52 is defining the extent of the inconsistency which must be struck down. Usually, the manner in which the law violates the *Charter* and the manner in which it fails to be justified under s. 1 will be critical to this determination....

It is useful at this point to set out the two stage s. 1 test developed by this court in *R. v. Oakes* (1986):

1. Is the legislative objective which the measures limiting an individual's rights or freedoms are designed to serve sufficiently pressing and substantial to justify the limitation of those rights or freedoms?

2. Are the measures chosen to serve that objective proportional to it, that is: (a) Are the measures rationally connected to the objective? (b) Do the measures impair as little as possible the right and freedom in question? and, (c) Are the effects of the measures proportional to the objective identified above?

(i) The Purpose Test

In some circumstances, s. 52(1) mandates defining the inconsistent portion which must be struck down very broadly. This will almost always be the case where the legislation or legislative provision does not meet the first part of the *Oakes* test, in that the purpose is not sufficiently pressing or substantial to warrant overriding a *Charter* right....The [*R. v. Big M Drug Mart Ltd.* (1985)] case stands as authority for the proposition that where the purpose of the legislation is itself unconstitutional, the legislation should be struck down in its entirety. Indeed, it is difficult to imagine anything less being appropriate where the purpose of the legislation is deemed unconstitutional; however, I do not wish to foreclose that possibility prematurely.

(ii) The Rational Connection Test

Where the purpose of the legislation or legislative provision is deemed to be pressing and substantial, but the means used to achieve this objective are found not to be rationally connected to it, the inconsistency to be struck down will generally be the whole of the portion of the legislation which fails the rational connection test....It matters not how pressing or substantial the objective of the legislation may be; if the means used to achieve the objective are not rationally connected to it, then the objective will not be furthered by somehow upholding the legislation as it stands.

(iii) The Minimal Impairment/Effects Test

Where the second and/or third elements of the proportionality test are not met, there is more flexibility in defining the extent of the inconsistency. For instance, if the legislative provision fails because it is not carefully tailored to be a minimal intrusion, or because it has effects disproportionate to its purpose, the inconsistency could be defined as being the provisions left out of the legislation which would carefully tailor it, or would avoid a disproportionate effect. According to the logic outlined above, such an inconsistency could be declared inoperative with the result that the statute was extended by way of reading in. Striking down, severing or reading in may be appropriate in cases where the second and/or third elements of the proportionality test are not met....

D. Summary

It is valuable to summarize the above propositions with respect to the operation of s. 52 of the *Constitution Act, 1982* before turning to the question of the independent availability of remedies pursuant to s. 24(1) of the *Charter*. Section 52 is engaged when a law is itself held to be unconstitutional, as opposed to simply a particular action taken under it. Once s. 52 is engaged, three questions must be answered. First, what is the extent of the inconsistency? Second, can that inconsistency be dealt with alone, by way of severance or reading in, or are other parts of the legislation inextricably linked to it? Third, should the declaration of invalidity be temporarily suspended? The factors to be considered can be summarized as follows:

(i) The Extent of the Inconsistency

The extent of the inconsistency should be defined:

A. broadly where the legislation in question fails the first branch of the *Oakes* test in that its purpose is held not to be sufficiently pressing or substantial to justify infringing a *Charter* right or, indeed, if the purpose is itself held to be unconstitutional – perhaps the legislation in its entirety;

B.   more narrowly where the purpose is held to be sufficiently pressing and substantial, but the legislation fails the first element of the proportionality branch of the *Oakes* test in that the means used to achieve that purpose are held not to be rationally connected to it – generally limited to the particular portion which fails the rational connection test; or,

C.   flexibly where the legislation fails the second or third element of the proportionality branch of the *Oakes* test.

(ii) Severance/Reading In

Severance or reading in will be warranted only in the clearest of cases, that is, where each of the following criteria is met:

A.   the legislative objective is obvious, or it is related through the evidence offered pursuant to the failed s. 1 argument, and severance or reading in would further that objective, or constitute a lesser interference with that objective than would striking down;

B.   the choice of means used by the legislature to further that objective is not so unequivocal that severance/reading in would constitute an unacceptable intrusion into the legislative domain; and,

C.   severance or reading in would not involve an intrusion into legislative budgetary decisions so substantial as to change the nature of the legislative scheme in question.

(iii) Temporarily Suspending the Declaration of Invalidity

Temporarily suspending the declaration of invalidity to give Parliament or the provincial Legislature in question an opportunity to bring the impugned legislation or legislative provision into line with its constitutional obligations will be warranted even where striking down has been deemed the most appropriate option on the basis of one of the above criteria if:

A.   striking down the legislation without enacting something in its place would pose a danger to the public;

B. striking down the legislation without enacting something in its place would threaten the rule of law; or,

C. the legislation was deemed unconstitutional because of under-inclusiveness rather than overbreadth, and therefore striking down the legislation would result in the deprivation of benefits from deserving persons without thereby benefiting the individual whose rights have been violated.

I should emphasize before I move on that the above propositions are intended as guidelines to assist courts in determining what action under s. 52 is most appropriate in a given case, not as hard and fast rules to be applied regardless of factual context.

III. Section 24(1)

A. Section 24(1) Alone

Where s. 52 of the *Constitution Act, 1982* is not engaged, a remedy under s. 24(1) of the *Charter* may nonetheless be available. This will be the case where the statute or provision in question is not in and of itself unconstitutional, but some action taken under it infringes a person's *Charter* rights. Section 24(1) would there provide for an individual remedy for the person whose rights have been so infringed.

This course of action has been described as "reading down as an interpretive technique", but it is not reading down in any real sense and ought not to be confused with the practice of reading down as referred to above. It is, rather, founded upon a presumption of constitutionality. It comes into play when the text of the provision in question supports a constitutional interpretation and the violative action taken under it thereby falls outside the jurisdiction conferred by the provision....

B. Section 24(1) in Conjunction with Section 52

An individual remedy under s. 24(1) of the *Charter* will rarely be available in conjunction with an action under s. 52 of the *Constitution Act, 1982*. Ordinarily, where a provision is declared unconstitutional and immediately struck down pursuant to s. 52, that will be the end of the matter. It follows that where the declaration of invalidity is temporarily suspended, a s. 24 remedy will not often be available either. To allow for s. 24 remedies during the period of suspension would be tantamount to giving the declaration of invalidity retroactive effect. Finally, if a court takes the course of reading down or in, a s. 24 remedy would probably only duplicate the relief flowing from the action that court has already taken.

IV. Remedial Options Appropriate to this Case

A. The Nature of the Right Involved

The right which was determined to be violated here is a positive right: the right to equal *benefit* of the law. Positive rights by their very nature tend to carry with them special considerations in the remedial context. It will be a rare occasion when a benefit conferring scheme is found to have an unconstitutional purpose. Cases involving positive rights are more likely to fall into the remedial classifications of reading down/reading in or striking down and suspending the operation of the declaration of invalidity than to mandate an immediate striking down. Indeed, if the benefit which is being conferred is itself constitutionally guaranteed (for example, the right to vote), reading in may be mandatory. For a court to deprive persons of a constitutionally guaranteed right by striking down under-inclusive legislation would be absurd. Certainly the intrusion into the legislative sphere of extending a constitutionally guaranteed benefit is warranted when the benefit was itself guaranteed by the legislature through constitutional amendment.

Other rights will be more in the nature of "negative" rights, which merely restrict the government. However, even in those cases, the rights may have certain positive aspects. For instance, the right to life, liberty and security of the person is in one sense a negative right, but the requirement that the government respect the "fundamental principles of justice" may provide a basis for characterizing s. 7 as a positive right in some circumstances. Similarly, the equality right is a hybrid of sorts since it is neither purely positive nor purely negative. In some contexts it will be proper to characterize s. 15 as providing positive rights.

II FUNDAMENTAL FREEDOMS

The reliance upon law for the protection of rights and freedoms within a social structure is a fundamental feature of our legal tradition, as basic as the rule of law itself. Part I, Schedule B of the *Constitution Act, 1982* – better known as the *Charter of Rights and Freedoms* – sets out the traditional and familiar rights and freedoms of a liberal constitutional order. Since 1982 our courts have cautiously crafted a jurisprudence of rights and freedoms. Despite the immense gravitational force from the United States, which has a two-hundred year jurisprudence to draw upon, distinctive features of the Canadian jurisprudence are emerging.

Section 2 of the *Charter* sets out the four basic liberal freedoms: freedom of conscience and religion; freedom of thought and expression; freedom of peaceful assembly; and freedom of association. The first two of these classic freedoms have been the most heavily litigated in recent years, which has given the Supreme Court of Canada the opportunity to refine the law in this area. The court's treatment of religious freedom appears to follow traditional lines, as the *Big M Drug Mart* case indicates (see, as well, the *Simpson Sears* case in Part III and the *B.(R.)* case in Part IV). The cases involving freedom of expression, on the other hand, suggest that Canadian courts are struggling to perfect a novel conception of the moral and political purpose of section 2 of the *Charter*.

Does freedom of expression demand that we put up with pornography and anti-Semitism? (*Butler* and *Keegstra*) Even when the perpetrator teaches young children? (*Attis*) Do corporations enjoy freedom of expression when they advertise, even if the product they are selling injures and kills its customers? (*RJR-MacDonald Inc.*) As the cases in this Part make clear, in *Charter* terms, most of the judicial reasoning about freedom of expression has focused on the application of the *Oakes* test for section 1 of the *Charter*. The issue in all these cases is not whether the state has infringed freedom of expression, but whether it is justified in doing so.

A very different issue involving freedom of speech is raised by the last case in this Part (*Native Women's Association*). We normally think of freedom of expression as a right to speak or write without interference from the state. But is our freedom of expression also hindered if the state does not give us the opportunity, and the means, to express our views?

R. V. BIG M DRUG MART LTD.

Supreme Court of Canada

[1985] 1 S.C.R. 295

Federal and provincial legislation declaring Sundays to be the official "day of rest" for business purposes has frequently come before Canadian courts, but this case gave the Supreme Court of Canada the opportunity to test this legislation against the *Charter*. As in earlier cases, the government insists that its "Lord's Day" legislation is not intended to put into law the dictates of any particular religion. It is argued, though, that even if the legislation's purpose is not the religious one of compelling sabbatical observance, the effect is to attach an economic penalty to those who close on Saturdays for religious reasons since they are required to be closed two days in a week rather than one. In response, the government insists that the point of the legislation is to insure that workers have at least one day off to enjoy social and leisure activities with family and friends.

Before tackling these arguments, Chief Justice Dickson had to address the question whether the plaintiff in this case had the right to bring the action in the first place – the legal issue of "standing". The problem is that the plaintiff in this case is a corporation, not an individual human being. Does it make sense for a corporation, or some other artificial, legal person, to complain that its freedom of religion is being infringed? Do corporations have constitutional rights?

* * * *

Chief Justice Dickson and Justices Beetz, McIntyre, Chouinard and Lamer:

As a preliminary issue the Attorney-General for Alberta challenges the standing of Big M to raise the question of a possible infringement of the guarantee of freedom of conscience and religion and the jurisdiction of the provincial court to declare the *Lord's Day Act* inoperative.

As best I understand the first submission, the assertion is that Big M is not entitled to any relief pursuant to s. 24(1) of the *Charter*. It is urged that freedom of religion is a personal freedom and that a corporation, being a statutory creation, cannot be said to have a conscience or hold a religious belief. It cannot, therefore, be protected by s. 2(a) of the *Charter*, nor can its rights and freedoms have been infringed or denied under s. 24(1); Big M's application under that section must consequently fail....

Any accused, whether corporate or individual, may defend a criminal charge by arguing that the law under which the charge is brought is constitutionally invalid. Big M is urging that the law under which it has been charged is inconsistent with s. 2(a) of the *Charter* and by reason of s. 52 of the *Constitution Act, 1982*, it is of no force or effect.

Whether a corporation can enjoy or exercise freedom of religion is therefore irrelevant. The respondent is arguing that the legislation is constitutionally invalid because it impairs freedom of religion – if the law impairs freedom of religion it does not matter whether the company can possess religious belief. An accused atheist would be equally entitled to resist a charge under the Act. The only way this question might be relevant would be if s. 2(a) were interpreted as limited to protecting only those persons who could prove a genuinely held religious belief. I can see no basis to so limit the breadth of s. 2(a) in this case.

The argument that the respondent, by reason of being a corporation, is incapable of holding religious belief and therefore incapable of claiming rights under s. 2(a) of the *Charter*, confuses the nature of this appeal. A law which itself infringes religious freedom is, by that reason alone, inconsistent with s. 2(a) of the *Charter* and it matters not whether the accused is a Christian, Jew, Muslim, Hindu, Buddhist, atheist, agnostic or whether an individual or a corporation. It is the nature of the law, not the status of the accused, that is in issue....

There are obviously two possible ways to characterize the purpose of Lord's Day legislation, the one religious, namely, securing public observance of the Christian institution of the Sabbath and the other secular, namely, providing a uniform day of rest from labour. It is undoubtedly true that both elements may be present in any given enactment, indeed it is almost inevitable that they will be, considering that such laws combine a prohibition of ordinary employment for one day out of seven with a specification that this day of rest shall be the Christian Sabbath – Sunday....

A finding that the *Lord's Day Act* has [only] a secular purpose is, on the authorities, simply not possible. Its religious purpose, in compelling sabbatical observance, has been long-established and consistently maintained by the courts of this country.

The Attorney-General for Alberta concedes that the Act is characterized by this religious purpose. He contends, however, that it is not the purpose but the effects of the Act which are relevant. In his submission, *Robertson and Rosetanni v. The Queen* (1963) is support for the proposition that it is effects alone which must be assessed in determining whether legislation violates a constitutional guarantee of freedom of religion.

I cannot agree. In my view, both purpose and effect are relevant in determining constitutionality; either an unconstitutional purpose or an unconstitutional effect can invalidate legislation. All legislation is animated by an object the legislature intends to achieve. This object is realized through the impact produced by the operation and application of the legislation. Purpose and effect respectively, in the sense of the legislation's object and its ultimate impact, are clearly linked, if not indivisible. Intended and actual effects have often been looked to for guidance in assessing the legislation's object and thus, its validity.

Moreover, consideration of the object of legislation is vital if rights are to be fully protected. The assessment by the courts of legislative purpose focuses scrutiny upon the aims and objectives of the legislature and ensures they are consonant with the guarantees enshrined in the *Charter*. The declaration that certain objects lie outside the legislature's power checks governmental action at the first stage of unconstitutional conduct. Further, it will provide more ready and more vigorous protection of constitutional rights by obviating the individual litigant's need to prove effects violative of *Charter* rights. It will also allow courts to dispose of cases where the object is clearly improper, without inquiring into the legislation's actual impact....

If the acknowledged purpose of the *Lord's Day Act*, namely, the compulsion of sabbatical observance, offends freedom of religion, it is then unnecessary to consider the actual impact of Sunday closing upon religious freedom. Even if such effects were found inoffensive, as the Attorney-General of Alberta urges, this could not save legislation whose purpose has been found to violate the *Charter*'s guarantees. In any event, I would find it difficult to conceive of legislation with an unconstitutional purpose, where the effects would not also be unconstitutional....

While the effect of such legislation as the *Lord's Day Act* may be more secular today than it was in 1677 or in 1906, such a finding cannot justify a conclusion that its purpose has similarly changed. In result, therefore, the *Lord's Day Act* must be characterized as it has always been, a law the primary purpose of which is the compulsion of sabbatical observance.

A truly free society is one which can accommodate a wide variety of beliefs, diversity of tastes and pursuits, customs and codes of conduct. A free society is one which aims at equality with respect to the enjoyment of fundamental freedoms and I say this without any reliance upon s. 15 of the *Charter*. Freedom must surely be founded in respect for the inherent dignity and the inviolable rights of the human person. The essence of the concept of freedom of religion is the right to entertain such religious beliefs as a person chooses, the right to declare religious beliefs openly and without fear of hindrance or reprisal, and the right to manifest belief by worship and practice or by teaching and dissemination. But the concept means more than that.

Freedom can primarily be characterized by the absence of coercion or constraint. If a person is compelled by the State or the will of another to a course of action or inaction which he would not otherwise have chosen, he is not acting of his own violation and he cannot be said to be truly free. One of the major purposes of the *Charter* is to protect, within reason, from compulsion or restraint. Coercion includes not only such blatant forms of compulsion as direct commands to act or refrain from acting on pain of sanction, coercion includes indirect forms of control which determine or limit alternative courses of conduct available to others. Freedom in a broad sense embraces both the absence of coercion and constraint, and the right to manifest beliefs and practices. Freedom means that, subject to such limitations as are necessary to protect public safety, order, health, or morals or the fundamental rights and freedoms of others, no one is to be forced to act in a way contrary to his beliefs or his conscience.

What may appear good and true to a majoritarian religious group, or to the state acting at their behest, may not, for religious reasons, be imposed upon citizens who take a contrary view. The *Charter* safeguards religious minorities from the threat of "the tyranny of the majority".

To the extent that it binds all to a sectarian Christian ideal, the *Lord's Day Act* works a form of coercion inimical to the spirit of the *Charter* and the dignity of all non-Christians. In proclaiming the standards of the Christian faith, the Act creates a climate hostile to, and gives the appearance of discrimination against, non-Christian Canadians. It takes religious values rooted in Christian morality and, using the force of the state, translates them into a positive law binding on believers and non-believers alike. The theological content of the legislation remains as a subtle and constant reminder to religious minorities within the country of their differences with, and alienation from, the dominant religious culture.

Non-Christians are prohibited for religious reasons from carrying out activities which are otherwise lawful, moral and normal. The arm of the state requires all to remember the Lord's day of the Christians and to keep it holy. The protection of one religion and the concomitant non-protection of others imports disparate impact destructive of the religious freedom of the collectivity.

I agree with the submission of the respondent that to accept that Parliament retains the right to compel universal observance of the day of rest preferred by one religion is not consistent with the preservation and enhancement of the multicultural heritage of Canadians. To do so is contrary to the expressed provisions of s. 27....

If I am a Jew or a Sabbatarian or a Muslim, the practice of my religion at least implies my right to work on a Sunday if I wish. It seems to me that any law purely religious in purpose, which denies me that right, must surely infringe my religious freedom....

What unites enunciated freedoms in the American First Amendment, s. 2(a) of the *Charter* and in the provisions of other human rights documents in which they are associated is the notion of the centrality of individual conscience and the inappropriateness of governmental intervention to compel or to constrain its manifestation. In *Hunter v. Southam Inc.* (1984), the purpose of the *Charter* was identified as "the unremitting protection of individual rights and liberties". It is easy to see the relationship between respect for individual conscience and the valuation of human dignity that motivates such unremitting protection.

It should also be noted, however, that an emphasis on individual judgment also lies at the heart of our democratic political tradition. The ability of each citizen to make free and informed decisions is the absolute prerequisite for the legitimacy, acceptability, and efficacy of our system of self government. It is because of the centrality of the rights associated with freedom of individual conscience both to basic beliefs about human worth and dignity and to a free and democratic political system that American jurisprudence has emphasized the primacy or "firstness" of the First Amendment. It is this same centrality that in my view underlies their designation in the *Canadian Charter of Rights and Freedoms* as "fundamental". They are the *sine qua non* of the political tradition underlying the *Charter*.

Viewed in this context, the purpose of freedom of conscience and religion becomes clear. The values that underlie our political and philosophic traditions demand that every individual be free to hold and to manifest whatever beliefs and opinions his or her conscience dictates, provided, *inter alia*, only that such manifestations do not injure his or her neighbours or their parallel rights to hold and manifest beliefs and opinions of their own. Religious belief and practice are historically prototypical and, in many ways, paradigmatic of conscientiously held beliefs and manifestations and are therefore protected by the *Charter*. Equally protected, and for the same reasons, are expressions and manifestations of religious non-belief and refusals to participate in religious practice. It may perhaps be that freedom of conscience and religion extends beyond these principles to prohibit other sorts of governmental involvement in matters having to do with religion. For the present case it is sufficient in my opinion to say that whatever else freedom of conscience and religion may mean, it must at the very least mean this: government may not coerce individuals to affirm a specific religious belief or to manifest a specific religious practice for a sectarian purpose. I leave to another case the degree, if any, to which the government may, to achieve a vital interest or objective, engage in coercive action which s. 2(a) might otherwise prohibit.

R. V. KEEGSTRA

Supreme Court of Canada

[1990] 3 S.C.R. 697

Section 319 of the *Criminal Code* prohibits the wilful promotion of hatred, other than in private conversation, towards any section of the public distinguished by colour, race, religion, or ethnic origin. It is one of the few explicit, statutory limitations of freedom of speech in Canada, and the Supreme Court had no difficulty finding it to infringe section 2(b) of the *Charter*. The real question, though, was whether this kind of infringement is justifiable as a reasonable limit in a free and democratic society under section 1 of the *Charter*. In deciding that it was, Chief Justice Dickson found it necessary to explore the meaning and rationale of freedom of speech.

* * * *

Chief Justice Dickson and Justices Wilson, L'Heureux-Dubé, and Gonthier:

I now turn to the specific requirements of the *Oakes* approach in deciding whether the infringement of s. 2(b) occasioned by s. 319(2) is justifiable in a free and democratic society. According to *Oakes*, the first aspect of the s. 1 analysis is to examine the objective of the impugned legislation....

...[T]he presence of hate propaganda in Canada is sufficiently substantial to warrant concern. Disquiet caused by the existence of such material is not simply the product of its offensiveness, however, but stems from the very real harm which it causes. Essentially, there are two sorts of injury caused by hate propaganda. First, there is harm done to members of the target group. It is indisputable that the emotional damage caused by words may be of grave psychological and social consequence. In the context of sexual harassment, for example, this Court has found that words can in themselves constitute harassment. In a similar manner, words and writings that wilfully promote hatred can constitute a serious attack on persons belonging to a racial or religious group....

A second harmful effect of hate propaganda which is of pressing and substantial concern is its influence upon society at large....It is...not inconceivable that the active dissemination of hate propaganda can attract individuals to its cause, and in the process create serious discord between various cultural groups in society. Moreover, the alteration of views held by the recipients of hate propaganda may occur subtly, and is not always attendant upon conscious acceptance of the communicated ideas. Even if the message of hate propaganda is outwardly rejected, there is evidence that its premise of racial or religious inferiority may persist in a recipient's mind as an idea that holds some truth, an incipient effect not to be entirely discounted....

In my opinion, it would be impossible to deny that Parliament's objective in enacting s. 319(2) is of the utmost importance. Parliament has recognized the substantial harm that can flow from hate propaganda, and in trying to prevent the pain suffered by target group members and to reduce racial, ethnic and religious tension in Canada has decided to suppress the wilful promotion of hatred against identifiable groups. The nature of Parliament's objective is supported not only by the work of numerous study groups, but also by our collective historical knowledge of the potentially catastrophic effects of the promotion of hatred. Additionally, the international commitment to eradicate hate propaganda and the stress placed upon equality and multiculturalism in the *Charter* strongly buttress the importance of this objective. I consequently find that the first part of the test under s. 1 of the *Charter* is easily satisfied and that a powerfully convincing legislative objective exists such as to justify some limit on freedom of expression.

The second branch of the *Oakes* test – proportionality – poses the most challenging questions with respect to the validity of s. 319(2) as a reasonable limit on freedom of expression in a free and democratic society. It is therefore not surprising to find most commentators, as well as the litigants in the case at bar, agreeing that the objective of the provision is of great importance, but to observe considerable disagreement when it comes to deciding whether the means chosen to further the objective are proportional to the ends....

From the outset, I wish to make clear that in my opinion the expression prohibited by s. 319(2) is not closely linked to the rationale underlying s. 2(b)....

At the core of freedom of expression lies the need to ensure that truth and the common good are attained, whether in scientific and artistic endeavors or in the process of determining the best course to take in our political affairs. Since truth and the ideal form of political and social organization can rarely, if at all, be identified with absolute certainty, it is difficult to prohibit expression without impeding the free exchange of potentially valuable information. Nevertheless, the argument from truth does not provide convincing support for the protection of hate propaganda. Taken to its extreme, this argument would require us to permit the communication of all expression, it being impossible to know with absolute certainty which factual statements are true, or which ideas obtain the greatest good. The problem with this extreme position, however, is that the greater the degree of certainty that a statement is erroneous or mendacious, the less its value in the quest for truth. Indeed, expression can be used to the detriment of our search for truth; the state should not be the sole arbiter of truth, but neither should we overplay the view that rationality will overcome all falsehoods in the unregulated market-place of ideas. There is very little chance that statements intended to promote hatred against an identifiable group are true, or that their vision of society will lead to a better world. To portray such state-ments as crucial to truth and the betterment of the political and social milieu is therefore misguided.

Another component central to the rationale underlying s. 2(b) concerns the vital role of free expression as a means of ensuring indi-viduals the ability to gain self-fulfillment by developing and articulat-ing thoughts and ideas as they see fit. It is true that s. 319(2) inhibits this process among those individuals whose expression it limits, and hence arguably works against freedom of expression values. On the other hand, such self-autonomy stems in large part from one's abili-ty to articulate and nurture an identity derived from membership in a cultural or religious group. The message put forth by individuals who fall within the ambit of s. 319(2) represents a most extreme opposition to the idea that members of identifiable groups should enjoy this aspect of the s. 2(b) benefit. The extent to which the unhindered promotion of this message furthers free expression val-ues must therefore be tempered insofar as it advocates with inordi-nate vitriol an intolerance and prejudice which views as execrable the process of individual self development and human flourishing among all members of society.

Moving on to a third strain of thought said to justify the protection of free expression, one's attention is brought specially to the political realm. The connection between freedom of expression and the polit-ical process is perhaps the linchpin of the s. 2(b) guarantee, and the nature of this connection is largely derived from the Canadian com-mitment to democracy. Freedom of expression is a crucial aspect of the democratic commitment, not merely because it permits the best policies to be chosen from among a wide array of proffered options, but additionally because it helps to ensure that participation in the political process is open to all persons. Such open participation must involve to a substantial degree the notion that all persons are equal-ly deserving of respect and dignity. The state therefore cannot act to hinder or condemn a political view without to some extent harming the openness of Canadian democracy and its associated tenet of equality for all.

The suppression of hate propaganda undeniably muzzles the participation of a few individuals in the democratic process, and hence detracts somewhat from free expression values, but the degree of this limitation is not substantial. I am aware that the use of strong language in political and social debate – indeed, perhaps even language intended to promote hatred – is an unavoidable part of the democratic process. Moreover, I recognize that hate propaganda is expression of a type which would generally be categorized as "political", thus putatively placing it at the very heart of the principle extolling freedom of expression as vital to the democratic process. Nonetheless, expression can work to undermine our commitment to democracy where employed to propagate ideas anathemic to democratic values. Hate propaganda works in just such a way, arguing as it does for a society in which the democratic process is subverted and individuals are denied respect and dignity simply because of racial or religious characteristics. This brand of expressive activity is thus wholly inimical to the democratic aspirations of the free expression guarantee.

Indeed, one may quite plausibly contend that it is through rejecting hate propaganda that the state can best encourage the protection of values central to freedom of expression, while simultaneously demonstrating dislike for the vision forwarded by hate-mongers. In this regard, the reaction to various types of expression by a democratic government may be perceived as meaningful expression on behalf of the vast majority of citizens. I do not wish to be construed as saying that an infringement of s. 2(b) can be justified under s. 1 merely because it is the product of a democratic process; the *Charter* will not permit even the democratically elected legislature to restrict the rights and freedoms crucial to a free and democratic society. What I do wish to emphasize, however, is that one must be careful not to accept blindly that the suppression of expression must always and unremittingly detract from values central to freedom of expression.

I am very reluctant to attach anything but the highest importance to expression relevant to political matters. But given the unparalleled vigour with which hate propaganda repudiates and undermines democratic values, and in particular its condemnation of the view that all citizens need be treated with equal respect and dignity so as to make participation in the political process meaningful, I am unable to see the protection of such expression as integral to the democratic ideal so central to the s. 2(b) rationale. Together with my comments as to the tenuous link between communications covered by s. 319(2) and other values at the core of the free expression guarantee, this conclusion leads me to disagree with the opinion of McLachlin J. [in dissent] that the expression at stake in this appeal mandates the most solicitous degree of constitutional protection. In my view, hate propaganda should not be accorded the greatest of weight in the s. 1 analysis.

As a caveat, it must be emphasized that the protection of extreme statements, even where they attack those principles underlying the freedom of expression, is not completely divorced from the aims of s. 2(b) of the *Charter*. As noted already, suppressing the expression covered by s. 319(2) does to some extent weaken these principles. It can also be argued that it is partly through a clash with extreme and erroneous views that truth and the democratic vision remain vigorous and alive. In this regard, judicial pronouncements strongly advocating the importance of free expression values might be seen as helping to expose prejudiced statements as valueless even while striking down legislative restrictions that proscribe such expression. Additionally, condoning a democracy's collective decision to protect itself from certain types of expression may lead to a slippery slope on which encroachments on expression central to s. 2(b) values are permitted. To guard against such a result, the protection of communications virulently unsupportive of free expression values may be necessary in order to ensure that expression more compatible with these values is never unjustifiably limited.

None of these arguments is devoid of merit, and each must be taken into account in determining whether an infringement of s. 2(b) can be justified under s. 1. It need not be, however, that they apply equally or with the greatest of strength in every instance. As I have said already, I am of the opinion that hate propaganda contributes little to the aspirations of Canadians or Canada in either the quest for truth, the promotion of individual self-development or the protection and fostering of a vibrant democracy where the participation of all individuals is accepted and encouraged. While I cannot conclude that hate propaganda deserves only marginal protection under the s. 1 analysis, I can take cognizance of the fact that limitations upon hate propaganda are directed at a special category of expression which strays some distance from the spirit of s. 2(b), and hence conclude that "restrictions on expression of this kind might be easier to justify than other infringements of s. 2(b)"....

Having made some preliminary comments as to the nature of the expression at stake in this appeal, it is now possible to ask whether s.

319(2) is an acceptably proportional response to Parliament's valid objective. As stated above, the proportionality aspect of the *Oakes* test requires the Court to decide whether the impugned state action: i) is rationally connected to the objective; ii) minimally impairs the *Charter* right or freedom at issue; and iii) does not produce effects of such severity so as to make the impairment unjustifiable....

Section 319(2) makes the wilful promotion of hatred against identifiable groups an indictable offence, indicating Parliament's serious concern about the effects of such activity. Those who would uphold the provision argue that the criminal prohibition of hate propaganda obviously bears a rational connection to the legitimate Parliamentary objective of protecting target group members and fostering harmonious social relations in a community dedicated to equality and multiculturalism. I agree, for in my opinion it would be difficult to deny that the suppression of hate propaganda reduces the harm such expression does to individuals who belong to identifiable groups and to relations between various cultural and religious groups in Canadian society.

Doubts have been raised, however, as to whether the actual effect of s. 319(2) is to undermine any rational connection between it and Parliament's objective. As stated in the reasons of McLachlin J., there are three primary ways in which the effect of the impugned legislation might be seen as an irrational means of carrying out the Parliamentary purpose. First, it is argued that the provision may actually promote the cause of hate-mongers by earning them extensive media attention. In this vein, it is also suggested that persons accused of intentionally promoting hatred often see themselves as martyrs, and may actually generate sympathy from the community in the role of underdogs engaged in battle against the immense powers of the state. Second, the public may view the suppression of expression by the government with suspicion, making it possible that such expression – even if it is hate propaganda – is perceived as containing an element of truth. Finally, it is often noted...that Germany of the 1920s and 1930s possessed and used hate propaganda laws similar to those existing in Canada, and yet these laws did nothing to stop the triumph of a racist philosophy under the Nazis.

If s. 319(2) can be said to have no impact in the quest to achieve Parliament's admirable objectives, or in fact works in opposition to these objectives, then I agree that the provision could be described as "arbitrary, unfair or based on irrational considerations". In my view, however, the position that there is no strong and evident connection between the criminalization of hate propaganda and its suppression is unconvincing. I come to this conclusion for a number of reasons, and will elucidate these by answering in turn the three arguments just mentioned.

It is undeniable that media attention has been extensive on those occasions when s. 319(2) has been used. Yet from my perspective, s. 319(2) serves to illustrate to the public the severe reprobation with which society holds messages of hate directed towards racial and religious groups. The existence of a particular criminal law, and the process of holding a trial when that law is used, is thus itself a form of expression, and the message sent out is that hate propaganda is harmful to target group members and threatening to a harmonious society....

In this context, it can also be said that government suppression of hate propaganda will not make the expression attractive and hence increase acceptance of its content. Similarly, it is very doubtful that Canadians will have sympathy for either propagators of hatred or their ideas. Governmental disapproval of hate propaganda does not invariably result in dignifying the suppressed ideology. Pornography is not dignified by its suppression, nor are defamatory statements against individuals seen as meritorious because the common law lends its support to their prohibition....

As for the use of hate propaganda laws in pre-World War Two Germany, I am skeptical as to the relevance of the observation that legislation similar to s. 319(2) proved ineffective in curbing the racism of the Nazis. No one is contending that hate propaganda laws can in themselves prevent the tragedy of a Holocaust; conditions particular to Germany made the rise of Nazi ideology possible despite the existence and use of these laws. Rather, hate propaganda laws are one part of a free and democratic society's bid to prevent the spread of racism, and their rational connection to this objective must be seen in such a context....

...In light of the great importance of Parliament's objective and the discounted value of the expression at issue I find that the terms of s. 319(2) create a narrowly confined offence which suffers from neither overbreadth nor vagueness. This interpretation stems largely from my view that the provision possesses a stringent *mens rea* requirement, necessitating either an intent to promote hatred or knowledge of the substantial certainty of such, and is also strongly supported by the conclusion that the meaning of the word "hatred" is restricted to the most severe and deeply-felt form of opprobrium. Additionally, however, the conclusion that s. 319(2) represents a minimal impairment of the freedom of expression gains credence through the exclusion of private conversation from its scope, the need for the promotion of hatred to focus upon an identifiable group and the presence of the s. 319(3) defences [these are: (a) truth; (b) good faith opinion on a religious matter; (c) public interest; (d) good faith attempt to point out, so as to remove, matters producing feelings of hatred toward an identifiable group.] As for the argument that other modes of combating hate propaganda eclipse the need for a criminal provision, it is eminently reasonable to utilize more than one type of legislative tool in working to prevent the spread of racist expression and its resultant harm....

The third branch of the proportionality test entails a weighing of the importance of the state objective against the effect of limits imposed upon a *Charter* right or guarantee. Even if the purpose of the limiting measure is substantial and the first two components of the proportionality test are satisfied, the deleterious effects of a limit may be too great to permit the infringement of the right or guarantee in issue.

I have examined closely the significance of the freedom of expression values threatened by s. 319(2) and the importance of the objective which lies behind the criminal prohibition. It will by now be quite clear that I do not view the infringement of s. 2(b) by s. 319(2) as a restriction of the most serious kind. The expressive activity at which this provision aims is of a special category, a category only tenuously connected with the values underlying the guarantee of freedom of speech. Moreover, the narrowly drawn terms of s. 319(2) and its defences prevent the prohibition of expression lying outside of this narrow category. Consequently, the suppression of hate propaganda affected by s. 319(2) represents an impairment of the individual's freedom of expression which is not of a most serious nature.

It is also apposite to stress yet again the enormous importance of the objective fueling s. 319(2), an objective of such magnitude as to support even the severe response of criminal prohibition. Few concerns can be as central to the concept of a free and democratic society as the dissipation of racism, and the especially strong value which Canadian society attaches to this goal must never be forgotten in assessing the effects of an impugned legislative measure. When the purpose of s. 319(2) is thus recognized, I have little trouble in finding that its effects, involving as they do the restriction of expression largely removed from the heart of free expression values, are not of such a deleterious nature as to outweigh any advantage gleaned from the limitation of s. 2(b).

ATTIS V. THE BOARD OF SCHOOL TRUSTEES, DISTRICT NO. 15

Supreme Court of Canada

(1996) 195 N.R. 81

For many years, Malcolm Ross has argued, in published writings and in public appearances, that Christian civilization was being destroyed by an international Jewish conspiracy. He was also a teacher at the Magnetic Hill School, Moncton, New Brunswick. Mr. Attis, a Moncton resident and Jew, filed a complaint against the school board with the Human Rights Commission of New Brunswick alleging that the school board, by failing to discipline Ross meaningfully, had discriminated against Attis and his children in the provision of public services. The Human Rights Board of Inquiry found that there was no evidence that Ross' views were expressed in the classroom, but argued that his off-duty comments denigrated the Jewish faith and Jewish people, and that these comments were so notorious that it would be appropriate to infer that they must have resulted in a "poisoned educational environment". The Board of Inquiry issued an order to the school board that split into two parts: First (in Clauses 2 (a), (b) and (c)), the school board was required to place Mr. Ross on a leave of absence without pay for 18 months, and then to appoint him to a non-teaching position, if one became open, or if not, to terminate his employment. Second (Clause 2 (d)), the order directed the school board to terminate Mr. Ross' employment immediately if, during his leave of absence or afterwards, he published or wrote "anything that mentions a Jewish or Zionist conspiracy, or attacks followers of the Jewish religion".

The Supreme Court of Canada had to decide the extent to which Ross' expression was protected by s. 2(b) of the *Charter*. The legal debate, as always, is at the level of section 1 of the *Charter*, and, in particular, whether the Board of Inquiry's order, in the circumstances, only "minimally impaired" his constitutional freedoms.

* * * *

Mr. Justice La Forest:

This appeal concerns the obligation imposed upon a public school board pursuant to provincial human rights legislation to provide discrimination-free educational services. It further involves the fundamental freedom of an individual teacher to publicly express his views and to exercise his religious beliefs during his off-duty time. The main issues raised by this appeal are whether a school board, which employs a teacher who publicly makes invidiously discriminatory statements, discriminates with respect to services it offers to the public...and whether an order to rectify the discrimination, which seeks to remove the teacher from his teaching position, infringes upon the teacher's freedom of expression and freedom of religion guaranteed under ss. 2(a) and 2(b) of the *Canadian Charter of Rights and Freedoms*....

...the argument of the appellant Attis is essential this: the Board of Inquiry was correct in finding that the respondent [Ross'] continued employment as a teacher constituted discrimination under s. 5(1) of the New Brunswick *Human Rights Act*. The finding of discrimination, he continues, was made in light of the respondent's off-duty conduct, which poisoned the educational environment at the school and created an environment in which Jewish students were forced to confront racist sentiment. His continued employment signalled the school board's toleration of his anti-Semitic conduct and compromised its ability to provide discrimination-free educational services....

The respondent does not contest the [Board of Inquiry's] findings in relation to his off-duty conduct and publications, or in relation to anti-Semitic incidents in the school district. His point is that there is no direct evidence linking these two findings. I am unable to agree with this contention. For the following reasons, I am of the view that the finding of discrimination against the school board must stand.

A school is a communication centre for a whole range of values and aspirations of a society. In large part, it defines the values that transcend society through the educational medium. The school is an arena for the exchange of ideas and must, therefore, be premised upon principles of tolerance and impartiality so that all persons within the school environment feel equally free to participate. As the Board of Inquiry stated, a school board has a duty to maintain a positive school environment for all persons served by it.

Teachers are inextricably linked to the integrity of the school system. Teachers occupy positions of trust and confidence, and exert considerable influence over their students as a result of their positions. The conduct of a teacher bears directly upon the community's perception of the ability of the teacher to fulfill such a position of trust and influence, and upon the community's confidence in the public school system as a whole....

By their conduct, teachers as "medium" must be perceived to uphold the values, beliefs and knowledge sought to be transmitted by the school system. The conduct of a teacher is evaluated on the basis of his or her position, rather than whether the conduct occurs within the classroom or beyond. Teachers are seen by the community to be the medium for the educational message and because of the community position they occupy, they are not able to "choose which hat they will wear on what occasion"...teachers do not necessarily check their teaching hats at the school-yard gate and may be perceived to be wearing their teaching hats even off duty....

It is on the basis of the position of trust and influence that we hold the teacher to high standards both on and off duty, and it is an erosion of these standards that may lead to a loss in the community of confidence in the public school system. I do not wish to be understood as advocating an approach that subjects the entire lives of teachers to inordinate scrutiny on the basis of more onerous moral standards of behaviour. This could lead to a substantial invasion of the privacy rights and fundamental freedoms of teachers. However, where a "poisoned" environment within the school system is traceable to the off-duty conduct of a teacher that is likely to produce a corresponding loss of confidence in the teacher and the system as a whole, then the off-duty conduct of the teacher is relevant.

In the present case, I note that the Board was presented with evidence from Ernest Hodgson on the likely effects of the respondent's conduct. He stated that the Jewish students having a general knowledge of the respondent could be fearful of him. Indeed, this is borne out in Yona Attis' testimony, and is supported by the pervasive awareness of the respondent's conduct throughout the community. Ernest Hodgson gave further evidence that it was possible that Jewish students would be negatively influenced by the respondent and that they would see themselves as the subject of suspicion, distrust and isolation. He considered that there might be a reluctance on the part of Jewish parents to become involved in the school system that might deter other Jewish families from moving to Moncton.

Pursuant to a television interview given by the respondent in 1989, the school board itself characterized the effect produced by the respondent's conduct in this manner:

> ...the climate created by this aggressive approach creates hostility that permeates and interferes with the desired tolerance required

by the school system to show respect for the rights of all students and their families to practice their religious faith.

As to whether there is impairment on a broader scale, I conclude...that a reasonable inference is sufficient in this case to support a finding that the continued employment of the respondent impaired the educational environment generally in creating a "poisoned" environment characterized by a lack of equality and tolerance. The respondent's off-duty conduct impaired his ability to be impartial and impacted upon the educational environment in which he taught.

The Board found that School District 15 discriminated contrary to s. 5 of the [*Human Rights Act*]. It found the school board had been reluctant to take disciplinary action against the respondent, notwithstanding the publicity his conduct received and the awareness on the part of the school board of the situation in the community at large. In effect, its passivity signalled a silent condonation of, and support for the respondent's view. The Board found an obligation within the school community "to work towards the creation of an environment in which students of all backgrounds will feel welcomed and equal". It stated:

> In such situations it is not sufficient for a school board to take a passive role. A school board has a duty to maintain a positive school environment for all persons served by it and it must be ever vigilant of anything that might interfere with this duty.

I am in complete agreement with this statement, and I refer to the findings of the Board that the school board failed to maintain a positive environment....The finding of discrimination against the school board is supported by the evidence and I accordingly see no error in this finding of the Board of Inquiry.

A finding of discrimination does not end the analysis, however. The respondent also raises the issue of the validity of the order [issued by the Board of Inquiry]...the important question in relation to the validity of the order is whether it is constitutionally sound. The respondent submits that his freedom of expression and freedom of religion have been infringed. I turn now to these constitutional issues.

Freedom of expression

The expression in question in this appeal concerns the respondent's writings, publications and statements....The gist of the respondent's message is that Jews are heading a "conspiracy" or a "great Satanic movement" against Christians with a view to destroying the Christian faith and civilization. The respondent attributes many of the "evils in our land" to the fact that Christians have permitted "those 'who hate the Lord' to rule over (them)". The board referred to the contents of the letter and found within it encouragement to others to condemn all Jews and to throw off the "yoke of Jewish domination"....

The writings, publications and statements of Malcolm Ross constitute expression within the meaning of s. 2(b). They clearly convey meaning. The truth or falsehood of their contents is not a matter to be considered in the context of determining whether they fall within the guarantee of freedom of expression; nor is the unpopularity of the views espoused within them....

In the present case, the purpose of the Board's order, while intended to remedy the discrimination with respect to services available to the public, is to prevent the respondent from publicly espousing his views while he is employed as a public school teacher. On its face the purpose of the order is to restrict the respondent's expression; it has a direct effect on the respondent's freedom of expression, and so violates s. 2(b) of the *Charter*.

Freedom of religion

The respondent's expression in this case is of a religious nature. He, therefore, submits that his freedom of religion has also been infringed....

In arguing that the order does infringe his freedom of religion, the respondent submits that the Act is being used as a sword to punish individuals for expressing their discriminating religious beliefs. He maintains that "[a]ll of the invective and hyperbole about anti-Semitism is really a smoke screen for imposing an officially sanctioned religious belief on society as a whole which is not the function of courts or Human Rights Tribunals in a free society"....

I agree with his statement about the role of the court. In *R. v. Jones* I stated that, assuming the sincerity of an asserted religious belief, it was not open to the court to question its validity. It was sufficient to trigger constitutional scrutiny if the effect of the impugned act or provision interfered with an individual's religious activities or convictions.

Indeed, this court has affirmed that freedom of religion ensures that every individual must be free to hold and to manifest without state interference those beliefs and opinions dictated by one's conscience. This freedom is not unlimited, however, and is restricted by the right of others to hold and to manifest beliefs and opinions of their own, and to be free from injury from the exercise of the freedom of religion of others. Freedom of religion is subject to such limitations as are necessary to protect public safety, order, health or morals and the fundamental rights and freedoms of others.

Section 1 of the Charter

There can be no doubt that the attempt to foster equality, respect and tolerance in the Canadian educational system is a laudable goal. But the additional driving factor in this case is the nature of the educational services in question: we are dealing here with the education of young children. While the importance of education of all ages is acknowledged, of principal importance is the education of the young....Young children are especially vulnerable to the messages conveyed by their teachers. They are less likely to make an intellectual distinction between comments a teacher makes in the school and those the teacher makes outside the school. They are, therefore, more likely to feel threatened and isolated by a teacher who makes comments that denigrate personal characteristics of a group to which they belong. Furthermore, they are unlikely to distinguish between falsehoods and truth and more likely to accept derogatory views espoused by a teacher. The importance of ensuring an equal and discrimination-free educational environment, and the perception of fairness and tolerance in the classroom are paramount in the education of young children. This helps foster self-respect and acceptance by others.

It is this context that must be invoked when balancing the respondent's freedom to make discriminatory statements against the right of the children in the school board "to be educated in a school system that is free from bias, prejudice and intolerance"....

In *Keegstra*...Dickson C.J.C. recognized that some forms of expression can undermine our commitment to democracy and found that "[h]ate propaganda works in just such a way, arguing as it does for a society in which the democratic process is subverted and individuals are denied respect and dignity simply because of racial or religious characteristics"....Dickson C.J.C. concluded that expression that promotes the hatred of identifiable groups is of limited importance as measured against freedom of expression values.

Similarly any restrictions imposed by the order upon the respondent's freedom of expression should, in my view, attract a less "searching degree of scrutiny" and be easier to justify under s. 1....

In relation to the protection of individual autonomy and self-development, a value said to underlie s. 2(b), expression that incites contempt for Jewish people on the basis of an "international Jewish conspiracy" hinders the ability of Jewish people to develop a sense of self-identity and belonging....

In relation to freedom of religion, any religious belief that denigrates and defames the religious beliefs of others erodes the very basis of the guarantee in s. 2(a) – a basis that guarantees that every individual is free to hold and to manifest the beliefs dictated by one's conscience. The respondent's religious views serve to deny Jews respect for dignity and equality said to be among the fundamental guiding values of a court undertaking a s. 1 analysis. Where the manifestations of an individual's right or freedom are incompatible with the very values sought to be upheld in the process of undertaking a s. 1 analysis, then, an attenuated level of s. 1 justification is appropriate....

In arriving at its order, the Board considered the alternatives available to remedy the discrimination. It concluded that the removal of the respondent from the classroom was "the only viable solution". In the course of examining alternative solutions, the Board found that the situation could not be corrected through an apology and renunciation of his views by the respondent. Nor could it be corrected through continual monitoring of the respondent's classroom, as the Board considered the influence of a teacher to be "so much more complex than the formal content of any subject matter taught by the teacher". The Board also rejected the exclusion of Jewish children from the respondent's class or school, emphasizing the importance of accessibility to schools within a public school system. Finally, it concluded that the situation could not be dealt with through monetary compensation to Attis for pain and suffering....

The order, in cls. 2(a), (b) and (c) [which removed Malcolm Ross from the classroom], was carefully tailored to accomplish its specific objective, i.e., "to remedy the discriminatory situation in School District 15 created through the writings and publications of Malcolm Ross"....In my view, *cls.* 2(a), (b) and (c) minimally impair the respondent's freedom of expression and freedom of religion [and so are justified under s. 1 of the *Charter*]....

In relation to cl. 2(d), however, I arrive at a different conclusion. [Clause 2(d) states that the school board]:

> (d) terminate Malcolm Ross' employment with the School Board immediately if, at any time during the eighteen month leave of absence or if at any time during his employment in a non-teaching position, he:

(i) publishes or writes for the purpose of publication, anything that mentions a Jewish or Zionist conspiracy, or attacks followers of the Jewish religion....

It may be that the continued presence of the respondent in the school board produces a residual poisoned effect, even after he is removed from a teaching position, and it may be that this is what cl. 2(d) seeks to address. Given the respondent's high profile and long teaching career, I acknowledge that the problem in the school district could remain for some time. However, the evidence does not support the conclusion that the residual poisoned effect would last indefinitely once Ross has been placed in a non-teaching role. For that reason, cl. 2(d) which imposes a permanent ban does not minimally impair the respondent's constitutional freedom. Clause 2(d) is not justified under s. 1

[Conclusion]

In my assessment, the evidence reveals that the school board discriminated within the meaning of s. 5(1) of the Act, with respect to educational services available to the public. The continued employment of the respondent contributed to an invidiously discriminatory or "poisoned" educational environment, as established by the evidence and the board's finding that it was "reasonable to anticipate" that the respondent's writings and statements influenced the anti-Semitic sentiment. In my opinion, this finding is necessarily linked to the finding that the respondent's statements are "highly public" and that he is a notorious anti-Semite, as well as the supported view that public school teachers assume a position of influence and trust over their students and must be seen to be impartial and tolerant.

I have concluded that cls. 2(a), (b) and (c) of the Board of Inquiry's order are properly made...any resulting infringement of the respondent's freedom of expression or freedom or religion is a justifiable infringement. Clause 2(d) of the order is not a justifiable infringement of the respondent's fundamental freedoms and is accordingly struck from the remainder of the order.

R. V. BUTLER

Supreme Court of Canada

[1992] 1 S.C.R. 452

Section 163 of the *Criminal Code* makes it an offence to make, publish or sell obscene material, defined as "any publication a dominant characteristic of which is the undue exploitation of sex, or of sex and...crime, horror, cruelty and violence". Manitoba sex shop owner Donald Butler had no trouble convincing the Supreme Court of Canada that section 163 violates his *Charter* section 2(b) right of freedom of expression. But, in this ground-breaking decision, the court unanimously agreed that section 163 constitutes a reasonable limit on this freedom. In coming to this conclusion, the court argued that the objective of Canada's anti-obscenity provision is not to express moral disapprobation about sexual behaviour, but to avoid the harm to society's basic values that is involved in portraying women as a class as objects for sexual exploitation and abuse.

* * * * *

Mr. Justice Sopinka and Chief Justice Lamer and Justices La Forest, Cory, McLachlin, Stevenson and Iacobucci:

Is section 163 justified under section 1 of the Charter?

(1) Objective

The respondent [the Crown] argues that there are several pressing and substantial objectives which justify overriding the freedom to distribute obscene materials. Essentially, these objectives are the avoidance of harm resulting from antisocial attitudinal changes that exposure to obscene material causes and the public interest in maintaining a "decent society". On the other hand, the appellant [Butler] argues that the objective of s. 163 is to have the state act as "moral custodian" in sexual matters and to impose subjective standards of morality.

The obscenity legislation and jurisprudence prior to the enactment of s. 163 were evidently concerned with prohibiting the "immoral influences" of obscene publications and safeguarding the morals of individuals into whose hands such works could fall. The

Hicklin (1868) philosophy posits that explicit sexual depictions, particularly outside the sanctioned contexts of marriage and procreation, threatened the morals or the fabric of society. In this sense, its exclusive purpose was to advance a particular conception of morality. Any deviation from such morality was considered to be inherently undesirable, independently of any harm to society. As Judson J. described the test in *Brodie* (1962):

> [The work under attack] has none of the characteristics that are often described in judgments dealing with obscenity – dirt for dirt's sake, the leer of the sensualist, depravity in the mind of an author with an obsession for dirt, pornography, an appeal to a prurient interest, etc.

I agree with Twaddle J.A. of the Court of Appeal that this particular objective is no longer defensible in view of the *Charter*. To impose a certain standard of public and sexual morality, solely because it reflects the conventions of a given community, is inimical to the exercise and enjoyment of individual freedoms, which form the basis of our social contract. David Dyzenhaus, "Obscenity and the Charter; Autonomy and Equality" (1991) refers to this as "legal moralism", of a majority deciding what values should inform individual lives and then coercively imposing those values on minorities. The prevention of "dirt for dirt's sake" is not a legitimate objective which would justify the violation of one of the most fundamental freedoms enshrined in the *Charter*.

On the other hand, I cannot agree with the suggestion of the appellant that Parliament does not have the right to legislate on the basis of some fundamental conception of morality for the purposes of safeguarding the values which are integral to a free and democratic society. As Dyzenhaus writes: "Moral disapprobation is recognized as an appropriate response when it has its basis in *Charter* values."

As the respondent and many of the interveners have pointed out, much of the criminal law is based on moral conceptions of right and wrong and the mere fact that a law is grounded in morality does not automatically render it illegitimate. In this regard, criminalizing the proliferation of materials which undermine another basic *Charter* right may indeed be a legitimate objective.

In my view, however, the overriding objective is not moral disapprobation but the avoidance of harm to society. In *R. v. Towne Cinema Theatres Ltd.* (1985), Dickson C.J.C. stated: "It is harm to society from undue exploitation that is aimed at by the section, not simply lapses in propriety or good taste."

The harm was described in the following way in the *Report on Pornography* by the Standing Committee on Justice and Legal Affairs (MacGuigan Report) (1978):

The clear and unquestionable danger of this type of material is that it reinforces some unhealthy tendencies in Canadian society. The effect of this type of material is to reinforce male-female stereotypes to the detriment of both sexes. It attempts to make degradation, humiliation, victimization, and violence in human relationships appear normal and acceptable. A society which holds that egalitarianism, non-violence, consensualism, and mutuality are basic to any human interaction, whether sexual or other, is clearly justified in controlling and prohibiting any medium of depiction, description or advocacy which violates these principles....

This being the objective, is it pressing and substantial? Does the prevention of the harm associated with the dissemination of certain obscene materials constitute a sufficiently pressing and substantial concern to warrant a restriction on the freedom of expression? In this regard, it should be recalled that in *R. v. Keegstra* (1990), this court unanimously accepted that the prevention of the influence of hate propaganda on society at large was a legitimate objective....

This court has thus recognized that the harm caused by the proliferation of materials which seriously offend the values fundamental to our society is a substantial concern which justifies restricting the otherwise full exercise of the freedom of expression. In my view, the harm sought to be avoided in the case of the dissemination of obscene materials is similar. In the words of Nemetz C.J.B.C. in *R. v. Red Hot Video Ltd.* (1985), there is a growing concern that the exploitation of women and children, depicted in publications and films can, in certain circumstances, lead to "abject and servile victimization". As Anderson J.A. also noted in that same case, if true equality between male and female persons is to be achieved, we cannot ignore the threat to equality resulting from exposure to audiences of certain types of violent and degrading material. Materials portraying women as a class as objects for sexual exploitation and abuse have a negative impact on "the individual's sense of self-worth and acceptance"....

Finally, it should be noted that the burgeoning pornography industry renders the concern even more pressing and substantial than when the impugned provisions were first enacted. I would therefore conclude that the objective of avoiding the harm associated with the dissemination of pornography in this case is sufficiently pressing and substantial to warrant some restriction on full exercise of the right to freedom of expression. The analysis of whether the measure is proportional to the objective must, in my view, be undertaken in light of the conclusion that the objective of the impugned section is valid only insofar as it relates to the harm to society associated with obscene materials. Indeed, the section as interpreted in previous decisions and in these reasons is fully consistent with that objective. The objective of maintaining conventional standards of propriety, independently of any harm to society, is no longer justified in light of the values of individual liberty which underlie the *Charter*. This, then, being the objective of s. 163, which I have found to be pressing and substantial, I must now determine whether the section is rationally connected and proportional to this objective. As outlined above, s. 163(8) criminalizes the exploitation of sex and sex and violence, when, on the basis of the community test, it is undue. The determination of when such exploitation is undue is directly related to the immediacy of a risk of harm to society which is reasonably perceived as arising from its dissemination.

(2) Proportionality

(i) General

The values which underlie the protection of freedom of expression relate to the search for truth, participation in the political process, and individual self-fulfilment. The Attorney-General for Ontario [one of the interveners] argues that of these, only "individual self-fulfilment", and only in its most base aspect, that of physical arousal, is engaged by pornography. On the other hand, the civil liberties groups argue that pornography forces us to question conventional notions of sexuality and thereby launches us into an inherently political discourse. In their factum, the British Columbia Civil Liberties Association adopts a passage from R. West, "The Feminist-Conservative Anti-Pornography Alliance and the 1986 Attorney General's Commission on Pornography Report" (1987):

> Good pornography has value because it validates women's will to pleasure. It celebrates female nature. It validates a range of female sexuality that is wider and truer than that legitimate by the non-pornographic culture. Pornography when it is good celebrates both female pleasure and male rationality.

A proper application of the test should not suppress what West refers to as "good pornography". The objective of the impugned provision is not to inhibit the celebration of human sexuality. However, it cannot be ignored that the realities of the pornography industry are far from the picture which the British Columbia Civil Liberties Association would have us paint. Shannon J., in *R. v. Wagner* (1985), described the materials more accurately when he observed:

> Women, particularly, are deprived of unique human character or identity and are depicted as sexual playthings, hysterically and instantly responsive to male sexual demands. They worship male genitals and their own value depends upon the quality of their genitals and breasts.

In my view, the kind of expression which is sought to be advanced does not stand on equal footing with other kinds of expression which directly engage the "core" of the freedom of expression values.

This conclusion is further buttressed by the fact that the targeted material is expression which is motivated, in the overwhelming majority of cases, by economic profit. This court held in *Rocket v. Royal College of Dental Surgeons of Ontario* (1990), that an economic motive for expression means that restrictions on the expression might "be easier to justify than other infringements".

I will now turn to an examination of the three basic aspects of the proportionality test.

(ii) Rational Connection

The message of obscenity which degrades and dehumanizes is analogous to that of hate propaganda. As the Attorney General of Ontario has argued in its factum, obscenity wields the power to wreak social damage in that a significant portion of the population is humiliated by its gross misrepresentations.

Accordingly, the rational link between s. 163 and the objective of Parliament relates to the actual causal relationship between obscenity and the risk of harm to society at large. On this point, it is clear that the literature of the social sciences remains subject to controversy....

The recent conclusions of the Fraser Report [*Pornography and Prostitution in Canada: Report of the Special Committee on Pornography and Prostitution*] (1985), could not postulate any causal relationship between pornography and the commission of violent crimes, the sexual abuse of children, or the disintegration of communities and society. This is in contrast to the findings of the MacGuigan Report (1978).

While a direct link between obscenity and harm to society may be difficult, if not impossible, to establish, it is reasonable to presume that exposure to images bears a causal relationship to changes in attitudes and beliefs....

In the face of inconclusive social science evidence, the approach adopted by our court in *Irwin Toy Ltd. v. Quebec (A.G.)* (1989) is instructive. In that case, the basis for the legislation was that television advertising directed at young children is *per se* manipulative. The court made it clear that in choosing its mode of intervention, it is sufficient that Parliament had a *reasonable basis....*

Similarly, in *R. v. Keegstra* (1990), the absence of proof of a causative link between hate propaganda and hatred of an identifiable group was discounted as a determinative factor in assessing the constitutionality of the hate literature provisions of the *Criminal Code....*

I am in agreement with Twaddle J.A. who expressed the view that Parliament was entitled to have a "reasoned apprehension of harm" resulting from the desensitization of individuals exposed to materials which depict violence, cruelty, and dehumanization in sexual relations.

Accordingly, I am of the view that there is a sufficiently rational link between the criminal sanction, which demonstrates our community's disapproval of the dissemination of materials which potentially victimize women and which restricts the negative influence which such materials have on changes in attitudes and behaviour, and the objective.

Finally, I wish to distinguish this case from *Keegstra*, in which the minority adopted the view that there was no rational connection between the criminalization of hate propaganda and its suppression. As McLachlin J. noted, prosecutions under the *Criminal Code* for racist expression have attracted extensive media coverage. The criminal process confers on the accused publicity for his or her causes and succeeds even in generating sympathy. The same cannot be said of the kinds of expression sought to be suppressed in the present case. The general availability of the subject materials and the rampant pornography industry are such that, in the words of Dickson C.J.C. in *Keegstra*, "pornography is not dignified by its suppression". In contrast to the hatemonger who may succeed, by the sudden media attention, in gaining an audience, the prohibition of obscene materials does nothing to promote the pornographer's cause.

(iii) Minimal Impairment

There are several factors which contribute to the finding that the provision minimally impairs the freedom which is infringed.

First, the impugned provision does not proscribe sexually explicit erotica without violence that is not degrading or dehumanizing. It is designed to catch material that creates a risk of harm to society. It might be suggested that proof of actual harm should be required. It is apparent from what I have said above that it is sufficient in this regard for Parliament to have a reasonable basis for concluding that harm will result and this requirement does not demand actual proof of harm.

Second, materials which have scientific, artistic or literary merit are not captured by the provision. As discussed above, the court must be generous in its application of the "artistic defence". For example, in certain cases, materials such as photographs, prints, books and films which may undoubtedly be produced with some motive for economic profit, may nonetheless claim the protection of the *Charter* insofar as their defining characteristic is that of aesthetic expression, and thus represent the artist's attempt at individual fulfilment. The existence of an accompanying economic motive does not, of itself, deprive a work of significance as an example of individual artistic or self-fulfilment.

Third, in considering whether the provision minimally impairs the freedom in question, it is legitimate for the court to take into account Parliament's past abortive attempts to replace the definition with one that is more explicit....The attempt to provide exhaustive instances of obscenity has been shown to be destined to fail. It seems that the only practicable alternative is to strive towards a more abstract definition of obscenity which is contextually sensitive and responsive to progress in the knowledge and understanding of the phenomenon to which the legislation is directed. In my view, the standard of "undue exploitation" is therefore appropriate. The intractable nature of the problem and the impossibility of precisely defining a notion which is inherently elusive makes the possibility of a more explicit provision remote. In this light, it is appropriate to question whether, and at what cost, greater legislative precision can be demanded....

Finally, I wish to address the arguments of the interveners, Canadian Civil Liberties Association and Manitoba Association for Rights and Liberties, that the objectives of this kind of legislation may be met by alternative, less intrusive measures. First, it is submitted that reasonable time, manner and place restrictions would be preferable to outright prohibition. I am of the view that this argument should be rejected. Once it has been established that the objective is the avoidance of harm caused by the degradation which many women feel as "victims" of the message of obscenity, and of the negative impact exposure to such material has on perceptions and attitudes towards women, it is untenable to argue that these harms could be avoided by placing restrictions on access to such material. Making the materials more difficult to obtain by increasing their cost and reducing their availability does not achieve the same objective. Once Parliament has reasonably concluded that certain acts are harmful to certain groups in society and to society in general, it would be inconsistent, if not hypocritical, to argue that such acts could be committed in more restrictive conditions. The harm sought to be avoided would remain the same in either case.

It is also submitted that there are more effective techniques to promote the objectives of Parliament. For example, if pornography is seen as encouraging violence against women, there are certain activities which discourage it – counselling rape victims to charge their assailants, provision of shelter and assistance for battered women, campaigns for laws against discrimination on the grounds of sex, education to increase the sensitivity of law enforcement agencies and other governmental authorities. In addition, it is submitted that education is an under-used response.

It is noteworthy that many of the above suggested alternatives are in the form of *response* to the harm engendered by negative attitudes against women. The role of the impugned provision is to control the dissemination of the very images that contribute to such attitudes. Moreover, it is true that there are additional measures which could alleviate the problem of violence against women. However, given the gravity of the harm, and the threat to the values at stake, I do not believe that the measure chosen by Parliament is equalled by the alternatives which have been suggested. Education, too, may offer a means of combating negative attitudes to women, just as it is currently used as a means of addressing other problems dealt with in the *Criminal Code*. However, there is no reason to rely on education alone. It should be emphasized that this is in no way intended to deny the value of other educational and counselling measures to deal with the roots and effects of negative attitudes. Rather, it is only to stress the arbitrariness and unacceptability of the claim that such measures represent the sole legitimate means of addressing the phenomenon. Serious social problems such as violence against women require multi-pronged approaches by government. Education and legislation are not alternatives but complements in addressing such problems. There is nothing in the *Charter* which requires Parliament to choose between such complementary measures.

(iv) Balance Between Effects of Limiting Measures and Legislative Objective

The final question to be answered in the proportionality test is whether the effects of the law so severely trench on a protected right that the legislative objective is outweighed by the infringement. The infringement on freedom of expression is confined to a measure designed to prohibit the distribution of sexually explicit material accompanied by violence, and those without violence that are degrading or dehumanizing. As I have already concluded, this kind of expression lies far from the core of the guarantee of freedom of expression. It appeals only to the most base aspect of individual fulfilment, and it is primarily economically motivated.

The objective of the legislation, on the other hand, is of fundamental importance in a free and democratic society. It is aimed at avoiding harm, which Parliament has reasonably concluded will be caused directly or indirectly, to individuals, groups such as women and children, and consequently to society as a whole, by the distribution of these materials. It thus seeks to enhance respect for all members of society, and non-violence and equality in their relations with each other.

I therefore conclude that the restriction on freedom of expression does not outweigh the importance of the legislative objective.

I conclude that while s. 163(8) infringes s. 2(b) of the *Charter* – freedom of expression – it constitutes a reasonable limit and is saved by virtue of the provisions of s. 1.

RJR-MACDONALD INC. V.
ATTORNEY-GENERAL OF CANADA

Supreme Court of Canada

[1995] 3 S.C.R. 199

This case involves tobacco companies and their freedom to engage in "commercial speech", that is, advertising. The *Tobacco Products Control Act* passed in 1996 put severe restrictions on tobacco advertising and promotion. When RJR-MacDonald and Imperial challenged provisions of the Act it conceded that there were health risks associated with tobacco use and that the government's objective of protecting Canadians was legitimate. For its part, the government conceded that it had violated RJR-MacDonald freedom of expression. The tobacco companies argued, however, that in the absence of scientific proof that advertising causes tobacco addiction, the manner in which the government sought to achieve its objective was not proportional to the degree of infringement of the companies' freedom of expression. The tobacco companies were successful and the legislation was sent back for modification.

In the interchange between Mr. Justice La Forest in dissent and Madame Justice McLachlin reproduced here we can see a split between two different approaches to freedom of expression. La Forest prefers to put the freedom "in context", and in effect to rank the importance of the expression that is being protected. The lower in significance, the less protection the form of expression deserves, and the more deference to Parliament and its aims is due. McLachlin, by contrast, not only disagrees that "commercial speech" ranks with pornography and hate literature, but insists that Parliament should not be let off the hook when it limits anyone's freedom of expression.

* * * *

Mr. Justice La Forest, Madame Justice L'Heureux-Dubé, and Mr. Justice Gonthier (dissenting):

The Attorney-General conceded that the prohibition on advertising and promotion under the [*Tobacco Products Control*] Act constitutes an infringement of the appellants' right to freedom of expression under s. 2(b) of the *Charter*, and directed his submissions solely to justifying the infringement under s. 1 of the *Charter*. In my view, the Attorney General was correct in making this concession. This court has, on a number of occasions, held that prohibitions against engaging in commercial expression by advertising infringe upon the freedom of expression....

[Evidence of harm and deference to Parliament]

The appellants [RJR-MacDonald and Imperial] have conceded that the objective of protecting Canadians from the health risks associated with tobacco use, and informing them about these risks, is pressing and substantial. Rather than focusing upon the objective, the appellants submit that the measures employed under the Act are not proportional to the objective...[They submit] that the facts respecting the harmful effect of tobacco are irrelevant to the application of the proportionality analysis....

With respect, I disagree. In my view, the nature and scope of the health problems raised by tobacco consumption are highly relevant to the s. 1 analysis, both in determining the appropriate standard of justification and in weighing the relevant evidence. In this respect, it is essential to keep in mind that tobacco addiction is a unique, and somewhat perplexing, phenomenon. Despite the growing recognition of the detrimental health effects of tobacco use, close to a third of the population continues to use tobacco products on a regular basis. At this point, there is no definitive scientific explanation for tobacco addiction, nor is there a clearly understood causal connection between advertising, or any other environmental factor, and tobacco consumption. This is not surprising. One cannot understand the causal connection between advertising and consumption, or between tobacco and addiction, without probing deeply into the mysteries of human psychology....

It appears, then, that there is a significant gap between our understanding of the health *effects* of tobacco consumption and of the root *causes* of tobacco consumption. In my view, this gap raises a fundamental institutional problem that must be taken into account in undertaking the s. 1 balancing. Simply put, a strict application of the proportionality analysis in cases of this nature would place an impossible onus on Parliament by requiring it to produce definitive social scientific evidence respecting the root causes of a pressing area of social concern every time it wishes to address its effects. This could have the effect of virtually paralyzing the operation of government in the socio-economic sphere. As I noted in *McKinney*, predictions respecting the ramifications of legal rules upon the social and economic order are not matters capable of precise measurement, and are often "the product of a mix of conjecture, fragmentary knowledge, general experience and knowledge of the needs, aspirations and resources of society, and other components". To require Parliament to wait for definitive social science conclusions every time it wishes to make social policy would impose an unjustifiable limit on legislative power by attributing a degree of scientific accuracy to the art of government which, in my view, is simply not consonant with reality....

In enacting this legislation, Parliament was facing a difficult policy dilemma. On the one hand, Parliament is aware of the detrimental health effects of tobacco use, and has a legitimate interest in protecting Canadians from, and in informing them about, the dangers of tobacco use. Health underlies many of our most cherished rights and values, and the protection of public health is one of the fundamental responsibilities of Parliament. On the other hand, however, it is clear that a prohibition on the manufacture, sale or use of tobacco products is unrealistic. Nearly seven million Canadians use tobacco products, which are highly addictive. Undoubtedly, a prohibition of this nature would lead to an increase in illegal activity, smuggling and, quite possibly, civil disobedience. Well aware of these difficulties, Parliament choose a less drastic, and more incremental, response to the tobacco health problem. In prohibiting the advertising and promotion of tobacco products, as opposed to their manufacture or sale, Parliament has sought to achieve a compromise among the competing interests of smokers, non-smokers and manufacturers, with an eye to protecting vulnerable groups in society. Given the fact that advertising, by its very nature, is intended to influence consumers and create demand, this was a reasonable policy decision....

Seen in this way, it is clear that the Act is the very type of legislation to which this court has generally accorded a high degree of deference. In drafting this legislation, which is directed toward a laudable social goal and is designed to protect vulnerable groups, Parliament was required to compile and assess complex social science evidence and to mediate between competing social interests. Decisions such as these are properly assigned to our elected representatives, who have at their disposal the necessary resources to undertake them, and who are ultimately accountable to the electorate....

[The nature of the right that is infringed]

In my view, the harm engendered by tobacco, and the profit motive underlying its promotion, place this form of expression as far from the "core" of freedom of expression values as prostitution, hate-mongering, or pornography, and thus entitle[s] it to a very lower degree of protection under s. 1. It must be kept in mind that tobacco advertising serves no political, scientific or artistic ends; nor does it promote participation in the political process. Rather, its sole purpose is to inform consumers about, and promote the use of, a product that is harmful, and often fatal, to the consumers who use it. The main, if not sole, motivation for this advertising is, of course, profit. The sale of tobacco products in Canada generates enormous profits for the three companies who dominate the market....In 1992, for example, earnings from Imperial's operations alone reached $432,000,000....

The appellants, both of whom are large multinational corporations, spend millions of dollars every year to promote their products (in 1987 alone, RJR and Imperial spent over $75 million dollars on advertising and promotion). The large sums these companies spend on advertising allow them to employ the most advanced advertising and social psychology techniques to convince potential buyers to buy their products. The sophistication of the advertising campaigns employed by these corporations, in my view, undermines their claim to freedom of expression protection because it creates an enormous power differential between these companies and tobacco consumers in the "marketplace of ideas"....

Minimal impairment

The next step in the proportionality analysis is to determine whether the legislative means chosen impair the right or freedom in question as little as possible. The appellants submit that Parliament has unjustifiably imposed a complete prohibition on tobacco advertising and promotion when it could have imposed a partial prohibition with equal effectiveness. They suggest that Parliament could have instituted a partial prohibition by forbidding "lifestyle" advertising (which seeks to promote an image by associating the consumption of the product with a particular lifestyle) or advertising directed at children, without at the same time prohibiting "brand preference" advertising (which seeks to promote one brand over another based on the colour and design of the package) or "informational" advertising (which seeks to inform the consumer about product content, taste and strength and the availability of different or new brands). According to the appellants, there is no need to prohibit brand preference or informal advertising because both are targeted solely at smokers, and serve a beneficial function by promoting consumer choice.

In my view, the appellants' argument fails for the same reasons that I have discussed throughout my s. 1 analysis. The relevance of context cannot be understated in s. 1 balancing, particularly at the minimal impairment stage. This court has on many occasions stated that the degree of required fit between means and ends will vary depending upon both the nature of the right and the nature of the legislation....Thus, the minimal impairment requirement does not impose an obligation on the government to employ the least intrusive measures available. Rather, it only requires it to demonstrate that the measures employed were the least intrusive, *in light of both the legislative objective and the infringed right*....

Taking into account the legislative context, it is my view that the measures adopted under the Act satisfy the *Oakes* minimal-impairment requirement. It must be kept in mind that the infringed right at issue in these cases is the right of tobacco corporations to advertise the only legal product sold in Canada which, when used precisely as directed, harms and often kills those who use it.

Madame Justice McLachlin:

[Deference to Parliament]

...care must be taken not to extend the notion of deference too far. Deference must not be carried to the point of relieving the government of the burden which the *Charter* places upon it of demonstrating that the limits it has imposed on guaranteed rights are reasonable and justifiable. Parliament has its role: to choose the appropriate response to social problems within the limiting framework of the Constitution. But the courts also have a role: to determine, objectively and impartially, whether Parliament's choice falls within the limiting framework of the Constitution. The courts are no more permitted to abdicate their responsibility than is Parliament. To carry judicial deference to the point of accepting Parliament's view simply on the basis that the problem is serious and the solution difficult, would be to diminish the role of the courts in the constitutional process and to weaken the structure of rights upon which our Constitution and our nation is founded.

[The right infringed]

La Forest J. supports his conclusion that Parliament should be permitted to choose such measures as it sees fit by contrasting the importance of Parliament's objective with the low value of the expression at issue. This way of answering the minimal impairment requirement raises a number of concerns. First, to argue that the importance of the legislative objective justifies more deference to the government at the stage of evaluating minimal impairment, is to engage in the balancing between objective and deleterious effect contemplated by the third stage of the proportionality analysis in *Oakes*. While it may not be of great significance where this balancing takes place, care must be taken not to devalue the need for demonstration of minimum impairment by arguing the legislation is important and the infringement of no great moment.

Second, just as care must be taken not to overvalue the legislative objective beyond its actual parameters, so care must be taken not to undervalue the expression at issue. Commercial speech, while arguably less important than some forms of speech, nevertheless should not be lightly dismissed....Tobacco consumption has not been banned in Canada. Yet the advertising ban deprives those who lawfully choose to smoke of information relating to price, quality and even health risks associated with different brands....

Third, in finding that the commercial speech here at issue is entitled "to a very low degree of protection under s. 1" and that "an attenuated level of s. 1 justification is appropriate in these cases", La Forest J. places a great deal of reliance on the fact that the appellants are motivated by profit. I note that the same may be said for many business persons or corporations that challenge a law as contrary to freedom of expression. While this court has stated that restrictions on commercial speech may be easier to justify than other infringements, no link between the claimant's motivation and the degree of protection has been recognized. Book sellers, newspaper owners, toy sellers – all are linked by their shareholders' desire to profit from the corporation's business activity, whether the expression sought to be protected is closely linked to the core values of freedom of expression or not. In my view, motivation to profit is irrelevant to the determination of whether the government has established that the law is reasonable or justified as an infringement of freedom of expression.

Minimal impairment

As the second step in the proportionality analysis, the government must show that the measures at issue impair the right of free expression as little as reasonably possible in order to achieve the legislative objective. The impairment must be "minimal", that is, the law must be carefully tailored so that rights are impaired no more than necessary. The tailoring process seldom admits of perfection and the courts must accord some leeway to the legislator. If the law falls within a range of reasonable alternatives, the courts will not find it over-broad merely because they can conceive of an alternative which might better tailor objective to infringement....On the other hand, if the government fails to explain why a significantly less intrusive and equally effective measure was not chosen, then the law may fail....

I turn first to the prohibition on advertising contained in s. 4 of the law. It is, as has been observed, complete. It bans all forms of advertising of Canadian tobacco products while explicitly exempting all foreign advertising of non-Canadian products which are sold in Canada. It extends to advertising which arguably produces benefits to the consumer while having little or no conceivable impact on consumption. Purely informational advertising, simple reminders of package appearance, advertising for new brands and advertising showing relative tar content of different brands – all these are included in the ban. Smoking is a legal activity yet consumers are deprived of an important means of learning about product availability to suit their preferences and to compare brand content with an aim to reducing the risk to their health.

As noted...while one may conclude as a matter of reason and logic that lifestyle advertising is designed to increase consumption, there is no indication that purely informational or brand preference advertising would have this effect. The government had before it a variety of less intrusive measures when it enacted the total ban on advertising, including, a partial ban which would allow information and brand preference advertising; a ban on lifestyle advertising only; measures such as those in Quebec's *Consumer Protection Act* to prohibit advertising aimed at children and adolescents; and labelling requirements only (which Health and Welfare believed would be preferable to an advertising ban)....In my view, any of these alternatives would be a reasonable impairment of the right to free expression, given the important objective and the legislative context.

These considerations suggest that the advertising ban imposed by s. 4 of the Act may be more intrusive of freedom of expression than is necessary to accomplish its goals. Indeed, Health and Welfare proposed less-intrusive regulation instead of a complete prohibition on advertising. Why then, did the government adopt such a broad ban? The record provides no answer to this question. The government presented no evidence in defence of the total ban, no evidence comparing its effects to less invasive bans....

Having found [that] the requirement of minimum impairment is not satisfied...it is unnecessary to proceed to the final stage of the proportionality analysis under s. 1 – balancing the negative effects of the infringement of rights against the positive benefits associated with the legislative goal. A finding that the law impairs the right more than required contradicts the assertion that the infringement is proportionate. Neither the fact that commercial expression may be entitled to a lesser degree of protection than certain other forms of expression, nor the importance of reducing tobacco consumption, even to a small extent, negate this proposition. Freedom of expression, even commercial expression, is an important and fundamental tenet of a free and democratic society. If Parliament wishes to infringe this freedom, it must be prepared to offer good and sufficient justification for the infringement and its ambit. This it has not done.

NATIVE WOMEN'S ASSOCIATION OF CANADA V. CANADA

Supreme Court of Canada

(1995) 199 N.R. 1

In September 1991, the Canadian Government set up the Beaudoin-Dobbie Committee to look into proposals for constitutional reform. One of these proposals involved a right to aboriginal self-government, and in order to ensure participation by aboriginal groups across Canada, the Government provided funding to four national aboriginal organizations and invited representatives to participate in the Committee's discussions. The Native Women's Association of Canada was not one of those groups, and its leadership was concerned that the other groups were male-dominated and were not supportive of the Charter and its explicit gender-equality process, section 28. The N.W.A.C. brought this *Charter* case to order the Government to stop funding the four organizations until it was provided with equal funding and the right to participate.

At issue here is an important feature of the classical liberal understanding of freedom of expression. Traditionally, this freedom is understood to be "negative", in the sense that it prohibits the Government from interfering with expression. There is also, however, a "positive" reading of the freedom, one which requires the Government to facilitate expression, by providing resources and "a platform" for expression. Although the Court was unanimous in turning down N.W.A.C.'s request, Mr. Justice Sopinka and Madame Justice L'Heureux-Dubé, disagreed about the status in law of the positive version of freedom of expression.

* * * *

Mr. Justice Sopinka, Chief Justice Lamer, and Justices La Forest, Gonthier, Cory, Iacobucci and Major:

This case raises the issue of the extent to which the freedom of expression and equality provisions of the *Charter* require that government funding be provided to various groups in order to promote the representation of certain interests at constitutional reform discussions. Specifically, where the Government of Canada provides funding to certain Aboriginal groups, alleged to be male-dominated, does s. 2(b) in combination with s. 28 o the *Charter* oblige the Government of Canada to provide equal funding to an association claiming to represent the interests of female Aboriginal persons so that they may also express their views at the constitutional discussions?...

The respondents argued that the four Aboriginal groups were given something extra from which N.W.A.C. was excluded. While it is conceded that s. 2(b) does not include the right to any particular means of expression, the respondents contend that if the government chooses to fund and to offer a voice to anti-*Charter*, male-led Aboriginal organization, it is under a constitutional duty to do so equitably and in accordance with the *Charter*. Therefore, the government must also fund and invite participation by N.W.A.C. It is submitted that such a result is mandated by the decision of this court in *Haig v. Canada* (1993),...as well as by s. 28 of the *Charter* which guarantees the rights and freedoms of the *Charter* equally to male and female persons....

It is beyond dispute that freedom of expression is a guaranteed right and a value of fundamental importance in our society....Traditionally, the cases involving s. 2(b) of the *Charter* have dealt with situations whereby the government has attempted, in some way, to limit or interfere with one's freedom of expression. In the present situation, the respondents are requesting the court to consider whether there may be a positive duty on governments to facilitate expression in certain circumstances.

Whether freedom of expression includes a positive right to be provided with specific means of expression was recently considered for the first time by this court in *Haig*. That case involved a somewhat similar fact situation in that the issue arose in the context of a referendum held by the federal government in all the provinces and territories, except Quebec, concerning proposed amendments to the Canadian Constitution. At the same time, Quebec held its own referendum. Due to a change in residence, Mr. Haig did not meet the requirements to be eligible to vote in either referendum. Mr. Haig contended that the order-in-council establishing the referendum...infringed his rights under s.2(b) of the *Charter*. It was not disputed that the casting of a ballot in the referendum was a form of expression. However, Mr. Haig argued that s. 2(b) required not only protection from interference, but an affirmative role on the part of the state in providing the specific means of expression.

Writing for the majority, L'Heureux-Dubé, J. noted that the "case law and doctrinal writings have generally conceptualized freedom of expression in terms of negative rather than positive entitlements":

It has not yet been decided that, in circumstances such as the present ones, a government has a constitutional obligation under s. 2(b) of the *Charter* to provide *a particular platform* to facilitate the exercise of freedom of expression. The traditional view, in colloquial terms, is that the freedom of expression contained in s. 2(b) prohibits gags, but does not compel the distribution of megaphones.

Although the traditional conceptualization of freedom of expression has been concerned with governmental action that interferes with one's ability to convey meaning, L'Heureux-Dubé, J. recognized the possibility that in some situations mere governmental complacency is not enough. That is, "true freedom of expression must be broader than simply the right to be free from interference":

> ...a situation might arise in which, in order to make a fundamental freedom meaningful, a posture of restraint would not be enough, and positive governmental action might be required. This might, for example, take the form of legislative intervention aimed at preventing certain conditions which muzzle expression, or ensuring public access to certain kinds of information.

However, it was concluded that no positive governmental action was required in order to provide Mr. Haig with a right to vote in the referendum. The *Charter* does not guarantee Canadians a right to vote in a referendum. Furthermore, the referendum actually presented a forum for and encouraged expression. Thus, it could not be said that Mr. Haig's s.2(b) *Charter* rights were violated....

Therefore, *Haig* establishes the principle that generally the government is under no obligation to fund or provide a specific platform of expression to an individual or a group. However, the decision in *Haig* leaves open the possibility that, in certain circumstances, positive governmental action may be required in order to make the freedom of expression meaningful. Furthermore, in some circumstances where the government does provide such a platform, it must not do so in a discriminatory fashion contrary to the *Charter*. It is this last proposition which the respondents rely in conjunction with s. 28 of the *Charter*....

At this point, I should add that it cannot be said that every time the Government of Canada chooses to fund or consult a certain group, thereby providing a platform upon which to convey certain views, that the government is also required to fund a group purporting to represent the opposite point of view. Otherwise, the implications of this proposition would be untenable. For example, if the government chooses to fund a women's organization to study the issue of abortion to assist in drafting proposed legislation, can it be argued that the government is bound by the Constitution to provide equal funding to a group purporting to represent the rights of fathers? If this was the intended scope of s. 2(b) of the *Charter*, the ramifications on government spending would be far-reaching indeed....

Therefore, while it may be true that the government cannot provide a particular means of expression that has the effect of discriminating against a group, it cannot be said that merely by consulting an organization, or organizations, purportedly representing a male or female point of view, the government must automatically consult groups representing the opposite perspective. It will be rare indeed that the provision of a platform or funding to one or several organizations will have the effect of suppressing another's freedom of speech....

There is no question here of the Government of Canada attempting to suppress N.W.A.C.'s expression of its point of view with respect to the Constitution. The s. 2(b) argument advanced is dependent on a finding that the funding of and participation by N.W.A.C. were essential to provide an equal voice for the rights of women. A corollary to this submission is that the funded groups are not representative of native women because they advocate a male-dominated aboriginal self-government. This is the submission that was accepted by the Court of Appeal and is the foundation of its judgment. A review of the factual record reveals that there is no evidence to support the contention that the funded groups were less representative of the viewpoint of women with respect to the Constitution. Nor was there any evidence with respect to the level of support of N.W.A.C. by women as compared to the funded groups. As well, the evidence does not support the contention that the funded groups advocate a male-dominated form of self-government....

Although I would hope that it is evident from these reasons, I wish to stress that nothing stated in them is intended to detract in any way from any contention by or on behalf of Aboriginal women that they face racial and sexual discrimination which impose serious hurdles to their equality.

Madam Justice L'Heureux-Dubé, (concurring):

Although I am in general agreement with my colleague Sopinka J.'s reasons as well as with the result he reaches, I feel that since he relies in great part on *Haig v. Canada*, his interpretation of this case mandates some comments on my part.

...I cannot agree with my colleague when he states that *Haig* "establishes the principle that generally the government is under no obligation to fund or provide a specific platform of expression to an individual or a group". In my view, *Haig* rather stands for the proposition that the government *in that particular case* was under no constitutional obligation to provide for the right to a referendum under s. 2(b) of the *Charter*, but that if and when the government does decide to provide a specific platform of expression, it must do so in a manner consistent with the *Charter*.

This court has always fostered a broad approach to the interpretation of s. 2(b) of the *Charter*, freedom of expression being an important aspect of the healthy functioning of the democratic process....*Haig* is consistent with this approach in that it underlines the possible consequences of disparate financing of viewpoints and the importance of promoting a variety of views. It is also recognized in *Haig* "that a philosophy of non-interference may not *in all circumstances* guarantee the optimal functioning of the marketplace of ideas".

The approach in *Haig* is one that in fact affords significant relevance to circumstances, and this is why I am of the view that in certain ones, funding or consultation may be mandated by the Constitution by virtue of the fact that when the government does decide to facilitate the expression of views, it must do so in a manner that is mindful of the *Charter*. In this respect, one must note that the circumstances in which the government may be held to a positive obligation in terms of providing a specific platform of expression invariably depend on the nature of the evidence presented by the parties.

III EQUALITY RIGHTS

Of all the rights contained in the *Charter*, the equality rights guaranteed by section 15 have the greatest potential for shaping Canada's social policy in the future. Equality is as fundamental a political value as any mentioned in the *Charter*, but it is also the most open to competing interpretations, legal and philosophical. Section 15 speaks of four kinds of equality, although it remains unclear how they differ. At the same time, federal and provincial human rights codes contain provisions that also attempt to secure equality, but with respect to the more concrete concerns of employment, housing and other everyday, private matters.

Legal and philosophical debates over the scope of equality have spawned several competing accounts of what a political commitment to equality entails. These range from formal guarantees of the equal application of the law to prohibitions against discrimination and guarantees of equality of opportunity to, finally, affirmative commitments to equality of condition with substantial redistributive consequences. The cases in this Part set out some of these background debates. They also indicate, however roughly, the direction in which our equality jurisdiction may be moving.

ATTORNEY-GENERAL OF CANADA V. LAVELL

Supreme Court of Canada

[1974] S.C.R. 1349

This is a famous pre-*Charter* equality rights case involving a provision of the Federal *Indian Act* that denied Indian status to
Indian women who married non-Indian men but did not deny
Indian status to Indian men when they married non-Indian
women. Mrs. Lavell challenged this gender-based discrimination by appealing to sections 1 and 2 of the *Canadian Bill of
Rights* (1960). The fact that a majority of the court, led by Mr.
Justice Ritchie, rejected her argument is often cited as proof
that the purely statutory and non-constitutional *Bill of Rights*
did not adequately protect equality rights. Doubtless, the
Lavell case would be decided differently under the *Charter.*
Nonetheless, this case demonstrates that there is another, minimal interpretation of legal equality that implicitly resides in
our law and will be recognized by courts. Philosophically speaking, this conception of legal equality is equivalent to the rule of
law.

* * * *

*Mr. Justice Ritchie, Chief Justice Fauteux and Justices Martland and Jud-
son:*

[Canadian Bill of Rights]

1. It is hereby recognized and declared that in Canada there have
existed and shall continue to exist without discrimination by reason of race, national origin, colour, religion or sex, the following
human rights and fundamental freedoms, namely,

(b) the right of the individual to equality before the law and the
protection of the law;...

In my opinion, the question to be determined in these appeals is
confined to deciding whether the Parliament of Canada in defining
the prerequisites of Indian status so as not to include women of Indian birth who have chosen to marry non- Indians, enacted a law which
cannot be sensibly construed and applied without abrogating,

abridging or infringing the rights of such women to equality before the law.

In my view the meaning to be given to the language employed in the *Bill of Rights* is the meaning which it bore in Canada at the time when the Bill was enacted, and it follows that the phrase "equality before the law" is to be construed in light of the law existing in Canada at that time.

In considering the meaning to be attached to "equality before the law" as those words occur in s. 1(b) of the Bill, I think it important to point out that in my opinion this phrase is not effective to invoke the egalitarian concept exemplified by the 14th Amendment of the U.S. Constitution as interpreted by the Courts of that country. I think rather that, having regard to the language employed in the second paragraph of the preamble to the *Bill of Rights*, the phrase "equality before the law" as used in s. 1 is to be read in its context as a part of "the rule of law" to which overriding authority is accorded by the terms of that paragraph.

In this connection I refer to *Stephen's Commentaries on the Laws of England*, 21st ed., vol. III (1950), where it is said in Vol. III at p. 337:

Now the great constitutional lawyer Dicey, writing in 1885 was so deeply impressed by the absence of arbitrary governments present and past, that he coined the phrase "the rule of law" to express the regime under which Englishmen lived; and he tried to give precision to it in the following words which have exercised a profound influence on all subsequent thought and conduct.

"That the 'rule of law,' which forms a fundamental principle of the constitution has three meanings, or may be regarded from three different points of view...."

The second meaning proposed by Dicey is the one with which we are here concerned and it was stated in the following terms:

It means again equality before the law or the equal subjection of all classes to the ordinary law of the land administered by the ordinary courts; the "rule of law" in this sense excludes the idea of any exemption of officials or others from the duty of obedience to the law which governs other citizens or from the jurisdiction of the ordinary courts.

"Equality before the law" in this sense is frequently invoked to demonstrate that the same law applies to the highest official of Government as to any other ordinary citizen, and in this regard Professor F. R. Scott, in delivering the Plaunt Memorial Lectures on *Civil Liberties and Canadian Federalism* (1959), speaking of the case of *Roncarelli v. Duplessis,* had occasion to say:

> It is always a triumph for the law to show that it is applied equally to all without fear or favour. This is what we mean when we say that all are equal before the law.

The relevance of these quotations to the present circumstances is that "equality before the law" as recognized by Dicey as a segment of the rule of law, carries the meaning of equal subjection of all classes to the ordinary law of the land *as administered by the ordinary Courts,* and in my opinion the phrase "equality before the law" as employed in s. 1(b) of the administration or application of the law by the law enforcement authorities and the ordinary Courts of the land....

RE ONTARIO HUMAN RIGHTS COMMISSION ET AL
AND SIMPSON-SEARS LTD.

Supreme Court of Canada

[1985] 2 S.C.R. 536

Mrs. O'Malley, as a full-time sale clerk for Simpsons-Sears, was
required to work Friday evenings on a rotating basis and on two
Saturdays out of three. After a couple of years of employment
she became a member of the Seventh-Day Adventist Church, a
tenet of which is that the Sabbath, on Saturday, must be strictly
kept. Unable to work Saturdays, she was discharged from her
full-time position. Mrs. O'Malley brought a complaint to
Ontario's Human Rights Commission alleging discrimination
and a violation of s. 4(1)(g) of the *Ontario Human Rights Code*.
When the case came before it, the Supreme Court of Canada
considered what a commitment to equality demands when
there has been a case of discrimination that is not only not
intentional, but also seems justifiable on business grounds. This
case helped to bring into our equality jurisprudence the notion
of a "duty to accommodate".

* * * *

Mr. Justice McIntyre:

The complaint, alleging discrimination in a condition of employment, based on her creed, came before Professor Edward J. Ratushny, appointed under the *Ontario Human Rights Code* as a board of
inquiry to hear and determine the complaint. After outlining the
facts, he succinctly stated the questions in issue in these terms:

Assuming (as in this case) that a general employment condition is
established without a discriminatory motive and for legitimate
business reasons, can there be discrimination under the *Ontario
Human Rights Code* where that condition applies equally to all
employees but has the practical consequence of discriminating
against one or more of those employees on a prohibited ground
such as creed?

If so, and if the general employment condition has such a practical consequence, how far must an employer go in accommodating

the religious beliefs of such an employee in order to avoid a contravention of the Code?...

The discrimination complained of in this case is said to be discrimination on the basis of the creed of the complainant, which is forbidden b. s. 4 (1)(g) of the *Ontario Human Rights Code* as it then stood. The relevant portions of s. 4 are set out hereunder:

s. 4. (1) No person shall...(g) discriminate against any employee with regard to any term or condition of employment, because of race, creed, colour, age, sex, marital status, nationality, ancestry or place of origin of such person or employee.

It is asserted that the requirement to work on Saturdays, while itself an employment rule imposed for business reasons upon all employees, discriminates against the complainant because compliance with it requires her to act contrary to her religious beliefs and does not so affect other members of the employed group. The Board of Inquiry accepted this proposition, but it was firmly rejected in the judgment of the majority of the Divisional Court and in the Court of Appeal. It is the principal ground upon which this appeal is taken.

It will be seen at once that the problem confronting the court involves consideration of unintentional discrimination on the part of the employer and as well the concept of adverse effect discrimination. To begin with, we must consider the nature and purpose of human rights legislation....

...The Code aims at the removal of discrimination. This is to state the obvious. Its main approach, however, is not to punish the discriminator, but rather to provide relief for the victim of discrimination. It is the result or the effect of the action complained of which is significant. If it does, in fact, cause discrimination; if its effect is to impose on one person or group of persons obligations, penalties, or restrictive conditions not imposed on other members of the community, it is discriminatory.

Without express statutory support in Ontario, inquiry board chairmen and judges have recognized the principle that an intention to discriminate is not a necessary element of the discrimination generally forbidden in Canadian human rights legislation....

I do not consider that to adopt such an approach does any violence to the *Ontario Human Rights Code*, nor would it be impractical in its application. To take the narrower view and hold that intent is a required element of discrimination under the Code would seem to me to place a virtually insuperable barrier in the way of a complainant seeking a remedy. It would be extremely difficult in most circumstances to prove motive, and motive would be easy to cloak in the formation of rules which, though imposing equal standards, could create injustice and discrimination by the equal treatment of those who are unequal. Furthermore, as I have endeavoured to show, we are dealing here with consequences of conduct rather than with punishment for misbehaviour. In other words, we are considering what are essentially civil remedies. The proof of intent, a necessary requirement in our approach to criminal and punitive legislation, should not be a governing factor in construing human rights legislation aimed at the elimination of discrimination. It is my view that the courts below were in error in finding an intent to discriminate to be a necessary element of proof....

Where discrimination in connection with employment on grounds of a person's creed is found, is that person automatically entitled to remedies provided in the *Ontario Human Rights Code*? One of the arguments advanced in this court and in the courts below was based on the fact that the Code, while prohibiting discrimination on the basis of creed, contains no saving or justifying clause for the protection of the employer. Such a saving provision is found in s. 4(6) for cases concerning discrimination on the basis of age, sex, and marital status – the *bona fide* occupational qualification defence. This omission was said to create a vacuum in the Code and was relied on for the proposition that only intentional discrimination was prohibited because without some such protection the innocent discriminator would be defenceless. While I reject that argument as support for a limitation of the Code to intentional discrimination, I do not on the other hand accept the proposition that on a showing of adverse effect discrimination on the basis of religion the right to a remedy is automatic.

No question arises in a case involving direct discrimination. Where a working rule or condition of employment is found to be discriminatory on a prohibited ground and fails to meet any statutory justification test, it is simply struck down. In the case of discrimination on the basis of creed resulting from the effect of a condition or rule rationally related to the performance of the job and not on its face discriminatory, a different result follows. The working rule or condition is not struck down, but its effect on the complainant must be considered, and if the purpose of the *Ontario Human Rights Code* is to be given effect some accommodation must be required from the employer for the benefit of the complainant. The Code must be construed and flexibly applied to protect the right of the employee who is subject to discrimination and also to protect the right of the employer to proceed with the lawful conduct of his business. The Code was not intended to accord rights to one to the exclusion of the rights of the other. American courts have met this problem with what has been described as a "duty to accommodate", short of undue hardship, on the part of the employers....In Canada, boards of inquiry under human rights legislation have adopted this concept and it was formulated by the board of inquiry in this case by Professor Ratushny as:

> ...the very general standard of whether the employer acted reasonably in attempting to accommodate the employee in all of the circumstances of the case as well as in the context of the general scope and objects of the Code.

The reasonable standard, referred to by Professor Ratushny, and the duty to accommodate, referred to in the American cases, provide that where it is shown that a working rule has caused discrimination it is incumbent upon the employer to make a reasonable effort to accommodate the religious needs of the employee, short of undue hardship to the employer in the conduct of his business. There is no express statutory base for such a proposition in the Code. Hence, the vacuum in the Code and the question: Should such a doctrine be imported to fill it?

The question is not free from difficulty. No problem is found with the proposition that a person should be free to adopt any religion he or she may choose and to observe the tenets of that faith. This general concept of freedom of religion has been well-established in our society and was a recognized and protected right long before the human rights codes of recent appearance were enacted. Difficulty arises when the question is posed of how far the person is entitled to go in the exercise of his religious freedom. At what point in the profession of his faith and the observance of its rules does he go beyond the mere exercise of his rights and seek to enforce upon others conformance with his beliefs? To what extent, if any, in the exercise of his religion is a person entitled to impose a liability upon another to do some act or accept some obligation he would not otherwise have done or accepted?...To put the question in the individual context of this case: in the honest desire to exercise her religious practices, how far can an employee compel her employer in the conduct of his business to conform with, or to accommodate, such practices? How far, it may be asked, may the same requirement be made of fellow employees and, for that matter, of the general public?

These questions raise difficult problems. It is not, in my view, either wise or possible to venture an answer that would apply generally. We are, however, faced with the necessity of finding an answer at least for this case and, therefore, in the nature of the judicial process an answer for similar cases. In my view, for this case the answer lies in the *Ontario Human Rights Code*, its purpose, and its general provisions. The Code accords the right to be free from discrimination in employment. While no right can be regarded as absolute, a natural corollary to the recognition of a right must be the social acceptance of a general duty to respect and to act within reason to protect it. In any society the rights of one will inevitably come into conflict with the rights of others. It is obvious then that all rights must be limited in the interest of preserving a social structure in which each right may receive protection without undue interference with others. This will be especially important where special relationships exist, in the case at bar the relationship of employer and employee. In this case, consistent with the provisions and intent of the *Ontario Human Rights Code*, the employee's right requires reasonable steps towards an accommodation by the employer.

Accepting the proposition that there is a duty to accommodate imposed on the employer, it becomes necessary to put some realistic limit on it. The duty in a case of adverse effect discrimination on the basis of religion or creed is to take reasonable steps to accommodate the complainant, short of undue hardship: in other words, to take such steps as may be reasonable to accommodate without undue interference in the operation of the employer's business and without undue expense to the employer. Cases such as this raise a very different issue from those which rest on direct discrimination. Where direct discrimination is shown the employer must justify the rule, if such a step is possible under the enactment in question, or it is struck down. Where there is adverse effect discrimination on account of creed the offending order or rule will not necessarily be struck down. It will survive in most cases because its discriminatory effect is limited to one person or to one group, and it is the effect upon them rather than upon the general work force which must be considered. In such case there is no question of justification raised because the rule, if rationally connected to the employment, needs no justification; what is required is some measure of accommodation. The employer must take reasonable steps towards that end which may or may not result in full accommodation. Where such reasonable steps, however, do not fully reach the desired end, the complainant, in the absence of some accommodating steps on his own part such as an acceptance in this case of part-time work, must either sacrifice his religious principles or his employment.

...I would therefore allow the appeal with costs and direct that the respondent pay to the complainant as compensation the difference between the sum of her earnings while engaged as a part-time employee of the respondent from October 23, 1978 to July 6, 1979, and the amount she would have earned as a full- time employee during that period.

LAW SOCIETY OF BRITISH COLUMBIA ET AL V.
ANDREWS ET AL

Supreme Court of Canada

[1989] 1 S.C.R. 143

Although the discrimination at issue in this case may not be a
major social problem (Andrews challenged the rule that he be
a Canadian citizen before becoming a member of the B.C. bar),
it gave the Supreme Court the opportunity to examine section
15 of the *Charter* more thoroughly than it had done before. The
case has had a profound effect on the legal conception of
equality in this country. Among the issues addressed here are:
the so-called "similarly situated" or "formal" analysis of equality;
the nature of, and test for, discriminatory laws; the relationship
between the *Charter* and Human Rights Codes; and the relation
between the equality provisions in section 15 and the "reasonable limitation" provision in section 1 of the *Charter*. (Although
the judgment given below was in dissent, Mr. Justice McIntyre
wrote the judgment for a unanimous court on the crucial issue
of the interpretation of section 15.)

* * * *

Mr. Justice McIntyre (dissenting):

The Concept of Equality

Section 15(1) of the *Charter* provides for every individual a guarantee
of equality before and under the law, as well as the equal protection
and equal benefit of the law without discrimination. This is not a general guarantee of equality; it does not provide for equality between
individuals or groups within society in a general or abstract sense,
nor does it impose on individuals or groups an obligation to accord
equal treatment to others. It is concerned with the application of the
law. No problem regarding the scope of the word "law", as employed
in s. 15(1), can arise in this case because it is an Act of the Legislature which is under attack. Whether other governmental or *quasi-*
governmental regulations, rules or requirements may be termed laws
under s. 15(1) should be left for cases in which the issue arises.

   The concept of equality has long been a feature of Western

thought. As embodied in s. 15(1) of the *Charter*, it is an elusive concept and, more than any of the other rights and freedoms guaranteed in the *Charter*, it lacks precise definition....

It is a comparative concept, the condition of which may only be attained or discerned by comparison with the conditions of others in the social and political setting in which the question arises. It must be recognized at once, however, that every difference in treatment between individuals under the law will not necessarily result in inequality and, as well, that identical treatment may frequently produce serious inequality. This proposition has found frequent expression in the literature on the subject but, as I have noted on a previous occasion, nowhere more aptly than in the well-known words of Frankfurter J. in *Dennis v. United States* (1950)...:

> It is a wise man who said that there is no greater inequality than the equal treatment of unequals.

The same thought has been expressed in this court in the context of s. 2(b) of the *Charter* in *R. v. Big M Drug Mart Ltd.* (1985) where Dickson C.J.C. said:

> The equality necessary to support religious freedom does not require identical treatment of all religions. In fact, the interests of true equality may well require differentiation in treatment.

In simple terms, then, it may be said that a law which treats all identically and which provides equality of treatment between "A" and "B" might well cause inequality for "C", depending on differences in personal characteristics and situations. To approach the ideal of full equality before and under the law – and in human affairs an approach is all that can be expected – the main consideration must be the impact of the law on the individual or the group concerned. Recognizing that there will always be an infinite variety of personal characteristics, capacities, entitlements and merits among those subject to a law, there must be accorded, as nearly as may be possible, an equality of benefit and protection and no more of the restrictions, penalties or burdens imposed upon one than another. In other words, the admittedly unattainable ideal should be that a law expressed to bind all should not because of irrelevant personal differences have a more burdensome or less beneficial impact on one than another.

McLachlin J.A. in the Court of Appeal expressed the view that:

...the essential meaning of the constitutional requirement of equal protection and equal benefit is that persons who are "similarly situated be similarly treated" and conversely, that persons who are "differently situated be differently treated"...

In this, she was adopting and applying as a test a proposition which seems to have been widely accepted with some modifications in both trial and appeal court decisions throughout the country on s. 15(1) of the *Charter*....The reliance on this concept appears to have derived, at least in recent times, from J.T. Tussman and J. tenBroek, "The Equal Protection of Laws" (1949), 37 *Calif. L. Rev.* 341. The similarly situated test is a restatement of the Aristotelian principle of formal equality – that "things that are alike should be treated alike, while things that are unalike should be treated unalike in proportion to their unalikeness".

The test as stated, however, is seriously deficient in that it excludes any consideration of the nature of the law. If it were to be applied literally, it could be used to justify the Nuremberg laws of Adolf Hitler. Similar treatment was contemplated for all Jews. The similarly situated test would have justified the formalistic separate but equal doctrine of *Plessy v. Ferguson* (1896)....

...[M]ere equality of application to similarly situated groups or individuals does not afford a realistic test for violation of equality rights. For, as has been said, a bad law will not be saved merely because it operates equally upon those to whom it has application. Nor will a law necessarily be bad because it makes distinctions.

A similarly situated test focusing on the equal application of the law to those to whom it has application could lead to results akin to those in *Bliss v. A.-G. Can.* (1978). In *Bliss*, a pregnant woman was denied unemployment benefits to which she would have been entitled had she not been pregnant. She claimed that the *Unemployment Insurance Act* violated the equality guarantees of the *Canadian Bill of Rights* because it discriminated against her on the basis of her sex. Her claim was dismissed by this court on the grounds that there was no discrimination on the basis of sex, since the class into which she fell under the Act was that of pregnant persons, and within that class, all persons were treated equally. This case, of course, was decided before the advent of the *Charter*.

I would also agree with the following criticism of the similarly situated test made by Kerans J. A. in *Mahe v. Alta. (Gov't)* (1987):

...the test accepts an idea of equality which is almost mechanical, with no scope for considering the reason for the distinction. In consequence, subtleties are found to justify a finding of dissimilarity which reduce the test to a categorization game. Moreover, the test is not helpful. After all, most laws are enacted for the specific purpose of offering a benefit or imposing a burden on some persons and not on others. The test catches every conceivable difference in legal treatment.

For the reasons outlined above, the test cannot be accepted as a fixed rule or formula for the resolution of equality questions arising under the *Charter*. Consideration must be given to the content of the law, to its purpose, and its impact upon those to whom it applies, and also upon those whom it excludes from its application. The issues which will arise from case to case are such that it would be wrong to attempt to confine these considerations within such a fixed and limited formula.

It is not every distinction or differentiation in treatment at law which will transgress the equality guarantees of s. 15 of the *Charter*. It is, of course, obvious that legislatures may – and to govern effectively must – treat different individuals and groups in different ways. Indeed, such distinctions are one of the main preoccupations of legislatures. The classifying of individuals and groups, the making of different provisions respecting such groups, the application of different rules, regulations, requirements and qualifications to different persons is necessary for the governance of modern society. As noted above, for the accommodation of differences, which is the essence of true equality, it will frequently be necessary to make distinctions....

The principle of equality before the law has long been recognized as a feature of our constitutional tradition and it found statutory recognition in the *Canadian Bill of Rights*. However, unlike the *Canadian Bill of Rights*, which spoke only of equality before the law, s. 15(1) of the *Charter* provides a much broader protection. Section 15 spells out four basic rights: (1) the right to equality before the law; (2) the right to equality under the law; (3) the right to equal protection of the law; and (4) the right to equal benefit of the law. The inclusion of these last three additional rights in s. 15 of the *Charter* was an attempt to remedy some of the shortcomings of the right to equality in the *Canadian Bill of Rights*. It also reflected the expanded concept of discrimination being developed under the various Human Rights Codes since the enactment of the *Canadian Bill of Rights*. The shortcomings of the *Canadian Bill of Rights* as far as the right to equality is concerned are well known....It is readily apparent that the language of s. 15 was deliberately chosen in order to remedy some of the perceived defects under the *Canadian Bill of Rights*. The antecedent statute is part of the "linguistic, philosophic and historical context" of s. 15 of the *Charter*.

It is clear that the purpose of s. 15 is to ensure equality in the formulation and application of the law. The promotion of equality entails the promotion of a society in which all are secure in the knowledge that they are recognized at law as human beings equally deserving of concern, respect and consideration. It has a large remedial component....It must be recognized, however, as well that the promotion of equality under s. 15 has a much more specific goal than the mere elimination of distinctions. If the *Charter* was intended to eliminate all distinctions, then there would be no place for sections such as s. 27 (multicultural heritage); s. 2(a) (freedom of conscience and religion); s. 25 (aboriginal rights and freedoms); and other such provisions designed to safeguard certain distinctions. Moreover, the fact that identical treatment may frequently produce serious inequality is recognized in s. 15(2), which states that the equality rights in s. 15(1) do "not preclude any law, program or activity that has as its object the amelioration of conditions of disadvantaged individuals or groups"....

Discrimination

The right to equality before and under the law, and the rights to the equal protection and benefit of the law contained in s. 15, are granted with the direction contained in s. 15 itself that they be without discrimination. Discrimination is unacceptable in a democratic society because it epitomizes the worst effects of the denial of equality, and discrimination reinforced by law is particularly repugnant. The worst oppression will result from discriminatory measures having the force of law. It is against this evil that s. 15 provides a guarantee.

Discrimination as referred to in s. 15 of the *Charter* must be understood in the context of pre-*Charter* history. Prior to the enactment of s. 15(1), the legislatures of the various provinces and the federal Parliament had passed during the previous fifty years what may be generally referred to as Human Rights Acts. With the steady increase in population from the earliest days of European emigration into Canada and with the consequential growth of industry, agriculture and commerce and the vast increase in national wealth which followed, many social problems developed. The contact of the European immigrant with the indigenous population, the steady increase in immigration bringing those of neither French nor British background, and in more recent years the greatly expanded role of women in all forms of industrial, commercial and professional activity led to much inequality and many forms of discrimination. In great part these developments, in the absence of any significant legislative protection for the victims of discrimination, called into being the Human Rights Acts. In 1944, the *Racial Discrimination Act, 1944* was passed, to be followed in 1947 by the *Saskatchewan Bill of Rights Act, 1947* and in 1960 by the *Canadian Bill of Rights.* Since then every jurisdiction in Canada has enacted broad-ranging Human Rights Acts which have attacked most of the more common forms of discrimination found in society....

What does discrimination mean? The question has arisen most commonly in a consideration of the Human Rights Acts and the general concept of discrimination under those enactments has been fairly well settled. There is little difficulty, drawing upon the cases in this court, in isolating an acceptable definition....

...I would say then that discrimination may be described as a distinction, whether intentional or not but based on grounds relating to personal characteristics of the individual or group, which has the effect of imposing burdens, obligations, or disadvantages on such individual or group not imposed upon others, or which withholds or limits access to opportunities, benefits, and advantages available to other members of society. Distinctions based on personal characteristics attributed to an individual solely on the basis of association with a group will rarely escape the charge of discrimination, while those based on an individual's merits and capacities will rarely be so classed.

The court in the case at bar must address the issue of discrimination as the term is used in s. 15(1) of the *Charter.* In general, it may be said that the principles which have been applied under the Human Rights Acts are equally applicable in considering questions of discrimination under s. 15(1). Certain differences arising from the difference between the *Charter* and the Human Rights Acts must, however, be considered. To begin with, discrimination in s. 15(1) is limited to discrimination caused by the application or operation of law, whereas the Human Rights Acts apply also to private activities. Furthermore, and this is a distinction of more importance, all the Human Rights Acts passed in Canada specifically designate a certain limited number of grounds upon which discrimination is forbidden. Section 15(1) of the *Charter* is not so limited. The enumerated grounds in s. 15(1) are not exclusive and the limits, if any, on grounds for discrimination which may be established in future cases await definition. The enumerated grounds do, however, reflect the most common and probably the most socially destructive and historically practised bases of discrimination and must, in the words of s. 15(1), receive particular attention. Both the enumerated grounds themselves and other possible grounds in discrimination recognized under s. 15(1) must be interpreted in a broad and generous manner, reflecting the fact that they are constitutional provisions not easily repealed or amended but intended to provide a "continuing framework for the legitimate exercise of governmental power" and, at the same time, for "the unremitting protection" of equality rights.

It should be noted as well that when the Human Rights Acts create exemptions or defences, such as a *bona fide* occupational requirement, an exemption for religious and political organizations, or definitional limits on age discrimination, these generally have the effect of completely removing the conduct complained of from the reach of the Act....Where discrimination is forbidden in the Human Rights Acts, it is done in absolute terms, and where a defence or exception is allowed, it, too, speaks in absolute terms and the discrimination is excused. There is, in this sense, no middle ground. In the *Charter*, however, while s. 15(1), subject always to subs.(2), expresses its prohibition of discrimination in absolute terms, s. 1 makes allowance for a reasonable limit upon the operation of s. 15(1). A different approach under s. 15(1) is therefore required. While discrimination under s. 15(1) will be of the same nature and in descriptive terms will fit the concept of discrimination developed under the Human Rights Acts, a further step will be required in order to decide whether discriminatory laws can be justified under s. 1. The onus will be on the state to establish this. This is a distinct step called for under the *Charter* which is not found in most Human Rights Acts, because in those Acts justification for or defence to discrimination is generally found in specific exceptions to the substantive rights.

Relationship Between s. 15(1) and s. 1 of the Charter

In determining the extent of the guarantee of equality in s. 15(1) of the *Charter*, special consideration must be given to the relationship between subs. 15(1) and s. 1. It is indeed the presence of s. 1 in the *Charter* and the interaction between these sections which has led to the differing approaches to a definition of the s. 15(1) right, and which has made necessary a judicial approach differing from that employed under the *Canadian Bill of Rights*. Under the *Canadian Bill of Rights*, a test was developed to distinguish between justified and unjustified legislative distinctions within the concept of equality before the law itself in the absence of anything equivalent to the s. 1 limit....It may be noted as well that the 14th Amendment to the American Constitution, which provides that no state shall deny to any person within its jurisdiction the "equal protection of the laws", contains no limiting provisions similar to s. 1 of the *Charter*. As a result, judicial consideration has led to the development of varying standards of scrutiny of alleged violations of the equal protection provision which restrict or limit the equality guarantee within the concept of equal protection itself. Again, article 14 of the *European Convention of Human Rights*, which secures the rights guaranteed therein without discrimination, lacks a s. 1 or its equivalent and has also developed a limit within the concept itself....The distinguishing feature of the *Charter*, unlike the other enactments, is that consideration of such limiting factors is made under s. 1. This court has described the analytical approach to the *Charter* in *R. v. Oakes* (1986) the essential feature of which is that the right guaranteeing sections be kept analytically separate from s. 1. In other words, when confronted with a problem under the *Charter*, the first question which must be answered will be whether or not an infringement of a guaranteed right has occurred. Any justification of an infringement which is found to have occurred must be made, if at all, under the broad provisions of s. 1. It must be admitted at once that the relationship between these two sections may well be difficult to determine on a wholly satisfactory basis. It is, however, important to keep them analytically distinct if for no other reason than the different attribution of the burden of proof. It is for the citizen to establish that his or her *Charter* right has been infringed and for the state to justify the infringement.

Approaches to s. 15(1)

Three main approaches have been adopted in determining the role of s. 15(1), the meaning of discrimination set out in that section, and the relationship between s. 15(1) and s. 1. The first one, which was advanced by Professor Peter Hogg in *Constitutional Law of Canada* (2nd ed. 1985), would treat every distinction drawn by law as discrimination under s. 15(1). There would then follow a consideration of the distinction under the provisions of s. 1 of the *Charter*....[Peter Hogg] reached this conclusion on the basis that, where the *Charter* right is expressed in unqualified terms, s. 1 supplies the standard of justification for any abridgment of the right. He argued that the word "discrimination" in s. 15(1) could be read as introducing a qualification in the section itself, but he preferred to read the word in a neutral sense because this reading would immediately send the matter to s. 1, which was included in the *Charter* for this purpose.

The second approach put forward by McLachlin J.A. in the Court of Appeal [hearing this case] involved a consideration of the reasonableness and fairness of the impugned legislation under s. 15(1). She stated...:

> The ultimate question is whether a fair-minded person, weighing the purposes of legislation against its effects on the individuals adversely affected, and giving due weight to the right of the Legislature to pass laws for the good of all, would conclude that the legislative means adopted are reasonable or unfair.

She assigned a very minor role to s. 1 which would, it appears, be limited to allowing in times of emergency, war, or other crises the passage of discriminatory legislation which would normally be impermissible.

A third approach, sometimes described as an "enumerated or analogous grounds" approach, adopts the concept that discrimination is generally expressed by the enumerated grounds. Section 15(1) is designed to prevent discrimination based on these and analogous grounds. The approach is similar to that found in human rights and civil rights statutes which have been enacted throughout Canada in recent times. The following excerpts from the judgment of Hugessen J. in *Smith, Kline & French Laboratories Ltd. v. A.-G. Can.* (1986), illustrate this approach....

The answer, in my view, is that the text of the section itself contains its own limitations. It only proscribes discrimination amongst the members of categories which are themselves similar. Thus the issue, for each case, will be to know which categories are permissible in determining similarity of situation and which are not. It is only in those cases where the categories themselves are not permissible, where equals are not treated equally, that there will be a breach of equality rights.

As far as the text of s. 15 itself is concerned, one may look to whether or not there is "discrimination", in the pejorative sense of that word, and as to whether the categories are based upon the grounds enumerated or grounds analogous to them. The inquiry, in effect, concentrates upon the personal characteristics of those who claim to have been unequally treated. Questions of stereotyping, of historical disadvantagement, in a word, of prejudice, are the focus and there may even be a recognition that for some people equality has a different meaning than for others.

The analysis of discrimination in this approach must take place within the context of the enumerated grounds and those analogous to them. The words "without discrimination" require more than a mere finding of distinction between the treatment of groups or individuals. Those words are a form of qualifier built into s. 15 itself and limit those distinctions which are forbidden by the section to those which involve prejudice or disadvantage.

I would accept the criticisms of the first approach made by McLachlin J.A. in the Court of Appeal. She noted that the labelling of every legislative distinction as an infringement of s. 15(1) trivializes the fundamental rights guaranteed by the *Charter* and, secondly, that to interpret "without discrimination" as "without distinction" deprives the notion of discrimination of content....In rejecting the Hogg approach, I would say that it draws a straight line from the finding of a distinction to a determination of its validity under s. 1, but my objection would be that it virtually denies any role for s. 15(1).

I would reject, as well, the approach adopted by McLachlin J.A. She seeks to define discrimination under s. 15(1) as an unjustifiable or unreasonable distinction. In so doing she avoids the mere distinction test but also makes a radical departure from the analytical approach to the *Charter* which has been approved by this Court. In the result, the determination would be made under s. 15(1) and virtually no role would be left for s. 1.

The third or "enumerated and analogous grounds" approach most closely accords with the purposes of s. 15 and the definition of discrimination outlined above and leaves questions of justification to s. 1. However, in assessing whether a complainant's rights have been infringed under s. 15(1), it is not enough to focus only on the alleged ground of discrimination and decide whether or not it is an enumerated or analogous ground. The effect of the impugned distinction or classification on the complainant must be considered. Once it is accepted that not all distinctions and differentiations created by law are discriminatory, then a role must be assigned to s. 15(1) which goes beyond the mere recognition of a legal distinction. A complainant under s. 15(1) must show not only that he or she is not receiving equal treatment before and under the law or that the law has a differential impact on him or her in the protection or benefit accorded by law but, in addition, must show that the legislative impact of the law is discriminatory.

Where discrimination is found, a breach of s. 15(1) has occurred and – where s. 15(2) is not applicable – any justification, any consideration of the reasonableness of the enactment, indeed, any consideration of factors which could justify the discrimination and support the constitutionality of the impugned enactment would take place under s. 1. This approach would conform with the directions of this court in earlier decisions concerning the application of s. 1 and at the same time would allow for the screening out of the obviously trivial and vexatious claim. In this, it would provide a workable approach to the problem.

EGAN V. THE QUEEN IN RIGHT OF CANADA

Supreme Court of Canada

[1995] 2 S.C.R. 513

This case, which concerns the denial of spousal allowance under the *Old Age Security Act* to a homosexual partner, displays a range of judicial opinion on the nature and application of section 15 of the *Charter*. The appellants James Egan and John Norris Nesbit lost by the slimmest of margins (5-4), and though the official majority opinion is that there was no legally-recognized discrimination, there are two persuasive dissents given. La Forest, for the majority, uses a somewhat formalistic approach to section 15 and commits himself to the claim that the purpose of the Act is not that of alleviating poverty among cohabiting elderly spouses, but of supporting heterosexual couples because only they can bring forth and care for children. Justices Cory and Iacobucci take him task for this and other aspects of his judgement. Madame Justice L'Heureux-Dubé, uses her dissent to go back to basics and argue that since respect for human dignity is at the heart of equality, any legislation that has the effect of promoting or perpetuating the view that some people are less worthy than others is discriminatory.

Despite the controversy and disagreement, all nine Justices did agree that sexual orientation is "analogous to the enumerated grounds" of section 15 – which is to say that, with respect to section 15 protections against discrimination, sexual orientation is on par with race, national or ethnic origin, colour, sex, age, and mental and physical disability.

* * * *

Mr. Justice La Forest, Chief Justice Lamer and Justices Gonthier and Major:

There is no discrimination

This appeal concerns the constitutionality of ss. 2 and 19(1) of the *Old Age Security Act* which accord to spouses of pensioners under the Act whose income falls below a stipulated amount, an allowance when they reach the age of 60, payable until they themselves become pensioners at age 65. The appellants maintain these provisions violate s. 15 of the *Charter* as discriminating against persons living in a homosexual relationship because the effect of the definition of "spouse" in s. 2 is to restrict the allowances to spouses in a hetero-sexual union, i.e., those who are legally married or who live in a common law relationship....

While I ordinarily have reservations about concessions of consti-tutional issues, I have no difficulty accepting the appellants' con-tention that whether or not sexual orientation is based on biological or physiological factors, which may be a matter of some controversy, it is a deeply personal characteristic that is either unchangeable or changeable only at unacceptable person costs, and so falls within the ambit of s. 15 protection as being analogous to the enumerated grounds....

What then is discrimination? There are several comments in the course of McIntyre J.'s remarks in *Andrews* that go a long way towards clarifying the concept:

I would say then that discrimination may be described as a dis-tinction, whether intentional or not but based on grounds relating to personal characteristics of the individual or group, which has the effect of imposing burdens, obligations, or disadvantages on such individual or group not imposed upon others, or which with-holds or limits access to opportunities, benefits, and advantages available to other members of society.

As Gonthier J. has noted in *Miron v. Trudel*, [finding discrimina-tion] this involves a three-step analysis:

The first step looks to whether the law has drawn a distinction between the claimant and others. The second step then questions whether the distinction results in disadvantage, and examines whether the impugned law imposes a burden, obligation or disad-vantage on a group of persons to which the claimant belongs which is not imposed on others, or does not provide them with a benefit which it grants others....The third step assesses whether the distinction is based on an irrelevant personal characteristic which is either enumerated in s. 15(1) or one analogous thereto.

There is no question that the first step is satisfied in this case. Par-liament has clearly made a distinction between the claimant and oth-ers. This, of course, does not carry one very far....The second step will also, in general at least, not be of great assistance. Ordinarily deci-sions do result in advantages or disadvantages to individuals and groups, sometimes intentionally, sometimes unintentionally. Parliament, as I mentioned, is in the business of making choices, and this inevitably involves the distribution of benefits and burdens in our society....

I turn then to the third step of the analysis....Since it has already been accepted that "sexual orientation" is an analogous ground under s. 15(1), all that remains to be considered under this step is whether the distinction made by Parliament is relevant...[Gonthier J.] notes that in assessing relevancy for this purpose one must look at "the nature of the personal characteristic and its relevancy to the functional values underlying the law". At this stage, he adds, one must necessarily undertake a form of comparative analysis to determine whether particular facts give rise to inequality....

In embarking upon this comparative analysis, I shall begin with an example of the statue with a view to determining "the functional values underlying the law". I shall then examine the personal characteristic here in issue to determine its relevancy to these functional values....

[Looking at the history of the *Old Age Security Act*] Parliament, in addition to providing greater benefits to the elderly in need, long ago took special account of married couples in need....The singling out of legally married and common law couples as the recipients of benefits necessarily excludes all sorts of other couples living together such as brothers and sisters or other relatives, regardless of sex, and others who are not related, whatever reasons these other couples may have for doing so and whatever their sexual orientation....

What reason or purpose, then, can be assigned to the distinction made by Parliament? It seems to me that it is both obvious and deeply rooted in our fundamental values and traditions....Simply stated, what Parliament clearly had in mind was to accord support to married couples who were aged and elderly, and this for the advancement of public policy central to society. Moreover, in recognition of changing social realities, s. 2 was amended so that whenever the term "spouse" was used in the Act it was to be construed to extend beyond legal married couples to couples in a common law marriage....Suffice it to say that marriage has from time immemorial been firmly grounded in our legal tradition, one that is itself a reflection of long-standing philosophical and religious traditions. But its ultimate *raison d'être* transcends all of these and is firmly anchored in the biological and social realities that heterosexual couples have the unique ability to procreate, that most children are the product of these relationships, and that they are generally cared for and nurtured by those who live in that relationship. In this sense, marriage is by nature heterosexual. It would be possible to legally define marriage to include homosexual couples, but this would not change the biological and social realities that underlie the traditional marriage....

In a word, the distinction made by Parliament is grounded in a social relationship, a social unit that is fundamental to society. That unit, as I have attempted to explain, is unique. It differs from all other couples, including homosexual couples. Other excluded couples, it is true, do not have to be described by reference to sex or sexual preferences, but this is of no moment. The distinction adopted by Parliament is relevant, indeed essential, to describe the relationship in the way the statute does so as to differentiate the couples described in the statute from all couples that do not serve the social purposes for which the Legislature has made the distinction. Homosexual couples are not, therefore, discriminated against; they are simply included with these other couples.

Mr. Justice Sopinka:

There is discrimination, but it is saved by s. 1

I agree with the respondent the Attorney General of Canada that government must be accorded some flexibility in extending social benefits and does not have to be pro-active in recognizing new social relationships. It is not realistic for the court to assume that there are unlimited funds to address the needs of all. A judicial approach on this basis would tend to make a government reluctant to create any new social benefit schemes because their limits would depend on an accurate prediction of the outcome of court proceedings under s. 15(1) of the *Charter*....This court has recognized that it is legitimate for the government to make choices between disadvantaged groups and that it must be provided with some leeway to do so.

Mr. Justice Cory, Mr. Justice Iacobucci and Madame Justice McLachlin (dissenting):

There is discrimination...

Looking at the plain wording of the Act, as opposed to any proposed objective of the legislation, it is clear that, in circumstances where the combined income of the pensioner and the opposite-sex spouse falls below a certain level, the Act confers a spousal benefit upon the opposite-sex spouse who is between the ages of 60 and 64. It is not necessary that the spouses be married. The only two requirements for eligibility are that the spouses have lived together for one year and that their combined income falls below the fixed level....

It is argued that the appellants were not denied equal benefit of the law because the legislation was only intended to confer a benefit upon either heterosexual couples who have raised children or upon dependent female spouses. These submissions cannot be accepted.

The Act makes no reference to children. Further, the minimal requirements pertaining to common law couples make it apparent that it would apply to heterosexual couples who have never had children or those who have had children in relationships other than their present one....Similarly, it cannot be said that the Act was designed to benefit only women. A concern about dependent female spouses may have motivated the creation of the spousal allowance. However, from its inception, the spousal allowance has been available equally to male and female spouses....

...[L]ooking at the Act from the perspective of the appellants, it can be seen that the legislation denies homosexual couples equal benefit of the law. The Act does this not on the basis of merit or need, but solely on the basis of sexual orientation. The definition of "spouse" as someone of the opposite sex reinforces the stereotype that homosexuals cannot and do not form lasting, caring, mutually supportive relationships with economic interdependence in the same manner as heterosexual couples. The appellants' relationship vividly demonstrates the error of that approach. The discriminatory impact can hardly be deemed to be trivial when the legislation reinforces prejudicial attitudes based on such faulty stereotypes. The effect of the impugned provision is clearly contrary to s. 15's aim of protecting human dignity, and therefore the distinction amounts to discrimination on the basis of sexual orientation....

...not saved by s. 1

I conclude that the underinclusiveness of the Act is not a reasonable limit. Although the purpose of the legislation is laudable, it has been implemented in a discriminatory manner in that an equally deserving group meeting the criteria by the law is denied benefits based on an irrelevant personal characteristic....

If the goal of the legislation is the alleviation of poverty among cohabiting elderly "spouses", then how can this be but incompletely attained by denying otherwise eligible households the spousal allowance merely because of discrimination based on sexual orientation? The exclusion of same-sex partners is simply not rationally connected to the goal of alleviating poverty among elderly couples. If there is an intention to ameliorate the position of a group, it cannot be considered entirely rational to assist only a portion of that group. A more rationally connected means to the end would be to assist the entire group, as that is the very objective which is sought.

Madame Justice L'Heureux-Dubé, (dissenting):

This court has recognized that inherent human dignity is at the heart of individual rights in a free and democratic society. More than any other right in the *Charter*, s. 15 gives effect to this notion. Building upon this foundation, I believe that the essence of "discrimination" was captured by McIntyre J. ... in *Andrews*:

> It is clear that the purpose of s. 15 is to ensure equality in the for-mulation and application of the law. *The promotion of equality entails the promotion of a society in which all are secure in the knowledge that they are recognized at law as human beings equally deserving of concern, respect and consideration.*

Equality, as that concept is enshrined as a fundamental human right within s. 15 of the *Charter*, means nothing if it does not represent a commitment to recognizing each person's equal worth as a human being, regardless of individual differences. Equality means that our society cannot tolerate legislative distinctions that treat certain peo-ple as second-class citizens, that demean them, that treat them as less capable for no good reason, or that otherwise offend fundamental human dignity....

We can further inform our understanding of the purpose of s. 15 by recognizing what it is *not*. The *Charter* is a document of civil, political and legal rights. It is not a charter of economic rights. This is not to say, however, that economic prejudices or benefits are irrel-evant to determinations under s. 15 of the *Charter*. Quite the con-trary. Economic benefits or prejudices are relevant to s.15, but are more accurately regarded as symptomatic of the types of distinctions that are at the heart of s. 15: those that offend inherent human dignity.

Finally, we must bear in mind that it has been recognized by this court that an important, though not necessarily exclusive, purpose of s. 15 is the prevention or reduction of distinctions that may worsen the circumstances of those who have already suffered marginaliza-tion or historical disadvantage in our society.

To summarize, at the heart of s. 15 is the promotion of a society in which all are secure in the knowledge that they are recognized at law as equal human beings, equally capable, and equally deserving. A person or group of persons has been discriminated against within the meaning of s. 1 of the *Charter* when members of that group have been made to feel, by virtue of the impugned legislative distinction, that they are less capable, or less worthy of recognition or value as human beings or as members of Canadian society, equally deserving of concern, respect and consideration. These are the core elements of a definition of "discrimination" – a definition that focuses on *impact* (i.e., discriminatory effect) rather than on *constituent elements* (i.e., the grounds of the distinction)....

In my view, for an individual to make out a violation of their rights under s. 15(1) of the *Charter*, he or she must demonstrate the following three things:

(1) that there is a legislative distinction;

(2) that this distinction results in a denial of one of the four equality rights on the basis of the rights claimant's membership in an identifiable group;

(3) that this distinction is "discriminatory" within the meaning of s. 15.

...A distinction is discriminatory within the meaning of s. 15 where it is capable of either promoting or perpetuating the view that the individual adversely affected by this distinction is less capable, or less worthy of recognition or value as a human being or as a member of Canadian society, equally deserving of concern, respect and consideration. This examination should be undertaken from a subjective-objective perspective: i.e., from the point of view of the reasonable person, dispassionate and fully apprised of the circumstances, possessed of similar attributes to, and under similar circumstances as, the group of which the rights claimant is a member.

The means by which courts may give principled expression to this notion is perhaps best illustrated by a simple analogy. If a projectile were thrown against a soft surface, then it would leave a larger scar than if it were thrown against a resilient surface. In fact, the depth of the scar inflicted will generally be a function of both the nature of the affected surface and the nature of the projectile used. In my view, assessing discriminatory impact is, in principle, no different. In order for a court to determine from a subjective-objective perspective whether the impugned distinction will leave a non-trivial discriminatory "scar" on the group affected, it is instructive to consider two categories of factors: (1) the nature of the group adversely affected by the distinction and (2) the nature of the interest adversely affected by the distinction. In my view, neither is completely meaningful without the other.

[Madame Justice L'Heureux-Dubé, then goes on to agree with Mr. Justices Cory and Iacobucci]

EATON V. BRANT COUNTY BOARD OF EDUCATION

Supreme Court of Canada

[1997] 1 S.C.R. 241

What does equality demand? In this case a 12-year old child with cerebral palsy who is unable to speak or use sign language was moved out of the regular classroom, where she had been for three years, and into a special education class. Her parents refused to consent to this arguing that placement in a special class, even if motivated by a desire to meet her needs, amounts to "exclusion, segregation, and isolation from the mainstream", which is a denial of equal benefit of the law. The Identification, Placement and Review Committee argued that the placement was in Emily Eaton's best interests and indeed, given Emily's communication difficulties, leaving her in the regular class would only have the counter-productive effect of isolating and segregating her from her peers. In terms of section 15, the question before the court was: was Emily Eaton denied an advantage or benefit other children received, or subjected to a disadvantage or burden other children were spared? When does "special treatment" result in inequality?

* * * *

Mr. Justice Sopinka, and Mr. Justices Cory, Gonthier, Iacobucci, La Forest, Major and Madame Justices L'Heureux-Dubé, and McLachlin:

The issue in this case is whether a decision of the Ontario Special Education Tribunal (the "tribunal") confirming the placement of a disabled child in a special education class contrary to the wishes of her parents contravenes the equality provisions of s. 15(1) of the *Charter.*

The placement of children in special education programs and services is carried out pursuant to the provisions of ... the *Education Act.* Prior to 1980, there was no mandatory requirement that school boards provide such programs and a disabled person could be denied status as a resident pupil at elementary school if that person was "unable by reason of mental or physical handicap to profit by instruction in an elementary school."

A change in attitude with respect to disabled persons was initiated by [a report by Ontario's Department of Health in 1971]. With it

came the recognition of the desirability of integration and deinstitu-
tionalization. The change in attitude was reflected in changes in the
Education Act.

The current legal framework for the education of exceptional
pupils was adopted [in the 1980 *Education Amendment Act*]. The Act
and regulations made it mandatory for all school boards to provide
special education programs and services for exceptional pupils. The
policy of the Ministry of Education is that "[e]very exceptional child
has the right to be part of the mainstream of education to the extent
to which it is profitable."

While there has not been unanimity in the judgments of the court
with respect to all the principles relating to the application of s. 15 of
the *Charter*, I believe that the issue in this case can be resolved on the
basis of principles in respect of which there is no disagreement.
There is general agreement that before a violation of s. 15 can be
found, the claimant must establish that the impugned provision creates a distinction on a prohibited or analogous ground which with-
holds an advantage or benefit from, or imposes a disadvantage or
burden on, the claimant.

The principles that not every distinction on a prohibited ground
will constitute discrimination and that, in general, distinctions based
on presumed rather than actual characteristics are the hallmarks of
discrimination have particular significance when applied to physical
and mental disability. Avoidance of discrimination on this ground
will frequently require distinctions to be made taking into account
the actual personal characteristics of disabled persons. In *Andrews*,
McIntrye J. stated that the "accommodation of differences...is the
true essence of equality". This emphasizes the purposes of s. 15(1) of
the *Charter* is not only to prevent discrimination by the attribution of
stereotypical characteristics to individuals, but also to ameliorate the
position of groups within Canadian society who have suffered disadvantage by exclusion from mainstream society as has been the case
with disabled persons.

The principle object of certain of the prohibited grounds is the
elimination of discrimination by the attribution of untrue characteristics based on stereotypical attitudes relating to immutable conditions such as race or sex. In the case of disability, this is one of the
objectives. The other equally important objective seeks to take into
account the true characteristics of this group which act as headwinds
to the enjoyment of society's benefits and to accommodate them.
Exclusion from the mainstream of society results from the construction of a society based solely on "mainstream" attributes to which disabled persons will never be able to gain access. Whether it is the

impossibility of success at a written test for a blind person, or the need for ramp access to a library, the discrimination does not lie in the attribution of untrue characteristics to the disabled individual. The blind person cannot see and the person in a wheelchair needs a ramp. Rather, it is the failure to make reasonable accommodation, to fine-tune society so that its structures and assumptions do not result in the relegation and banishment of disabled persons from participation, which results in discrimination against them. The discrimination inquiry which uses "the attribution of stereotypical characteristics" reasoning as commonly understood is simply inappropriate here. It may be seen rather as a case of reverse stereotyping which, by not allowing for the condition of a disabled individual, ignores his or her disability and forces the individual to sink or swim within the mainstream environment. It is recognition of the actual characteristics and reasonable accommodation of these characteristics which is the central purpose of s. 15(1) in relation to disability.

The interplay of these objectives relating to disability is illustrated by the evolution of special education in Ontario. The earlier policy of exclusion to which I referred was influenced in large part by a stereotypical attitude to disabled persons that they could not function in a system designed for the general population. No account was taken of the true characteristics of individual members of the disabled population, nor was any attempt made to accommodate these characteristics. With the change in attitude influenced by the Williston report and other developments, the policy shifted to one which assessed the true characteristics of disabled persons with a view to accommodating them. Integration was the preferred accommodation but if the pupil could not benefit from integration a special program was designed to enable disabled pupils to receive the benefits of education which were available to others.

It follows that disability, as a prohibited ground, differs from other enumerated grounds such as race or sex because there is no individual variation with respect to these grounds. However, with respect to disability, this ground means vastly different things depending upon the individual and the context. This produces, among other things, the "difference dilemma" referred to by the interveners whereby segregation can be both protective of equality and violative of equality depending upon the person and the state of disability. In some cases, special education is a necessary adaptation of the mainstream world which enables some disabled pupils access to the learning environment they need in order to have an equal opportunity in education. While integration should be recognized as the norm of general application because of the benefits it generally provides, a presumption in favour of integrated schooling would work to the disadvantage of pupils who require special education in order to achieve equality. Schools focused on the needs of the blind or deaf, and special education for students with learning disabilities indicate the positive aspects of segregated education placement. Integration can be either a benefit or a burden depending on whether the individual can profit from the advantages that integration provides.

These are the basic principles in respect of which the tribunal's decision should be tested in order to determine whether that decision complies with s. 15(1).

It is quite clear that a distinction is being made under the Act between "exceptional" children and others. Other children are placed in the integrated classes. Exceptional children, in some cases, face an inquiry into their placement in the integrated or special classes. It is clear that the distinction between "exceptional" and other children is based on the disability of the individual child.

In its thorough and careful consideration of this matter, the tribunal sought to determine the placement that would be in the best interests of Emily from the standpoint of receiving the benefits that an education provides. In arriving at the conclusion, the tribunal considered Emily's special needs and strove to fashion a placement that would accommodate those special needs and enable her to benefit from the services that an educational program offers. The tribunal took into account the great psychological benefit that integration offers but found, based on the three years' experience in a regular class, that integration had had "the counter-productive effect of isolating her, of segregating her in the theoretically integrated setting."

The tribunal, therefore, balanced the various educational interests of Emily Eaton, taking into account her special needs, and concluded that the best possible placement was in the special class....Finally, the tribunal stated:

> ...our decision in favour of a special class placement does not relieve the school board and the parents of the obligation to collaborate creatively in a continuing effort to meet her present and future needs. Emily's is so unusual a case that unusual responses may well be necessary for her. Such achievements can only be realized through cooperation, and most important, compromise.

It seems incongruous that a decision reached after such an approach could be considered a burden or a disadvantage imposed on a child.

The Court of Appeal was of the view that the tribunal's reasoning infringed s. 15(1) because the *Charter* mandates a presumption in favour of integration. This presumption is displaced if the parents consent to a segregated placement. This is reflected in the remedy that the Court of Appeal found to be appropriate. Section 8 of the [*Education Amendment Act*, 1980] was to be read to include a direction that, unless the parents of a disabled child consent to the placement of the child in a segregated environment, the presumption applies.

In my view, the application of a test designed to secure what is in the best interests of the child will best achieve that objective if the test is unencumbered by a presumption. The operation of a presumption tends to render proceedings more technical and adversarial. Moreover, there is a risk that in some circumstances, the decision may be made by default rather than on the merits as to what is in the best interests of the child. I would also question the view that a presumption as to the best interests of a child is a constitutional imperative when the presumption can be automatically displaced by the decision of the child's parents. Such a result runs counter to decisions of this court that the parents' view of their child's best interests is not dispositive of the question.

I conclude that the placement of Emily which was confirmed by the tribunal did not constitute the imposition of a burden or disadvantage nor did it constitute the withholding of a benefit or advantage from the child. Neither the tribunal's order nor its reasoning can be construed as a violation of s. 15.

In the result, the appeal is allowed.

IV AUTONOMY AND SELF-DETERMINATION

In recent years, courts have been called upon to protect an entitlement that is arguably more fundamental than the rights and freedoms so far considered – human dignity and personal autonomy. In her dissent in the *Egan* case (see Part III), Madam Justice L'Heureux-Dubé argues that human dignity is at the heart of all of the rights in the *Charter*, and especially section 15 equality rights. Everyone is equal before the law because everyone deserves concern, respect and consideration. In practice, the law has sought to respect human dignity by preserving personal autonomy, or each individual's sovereignty over decisions that are theirs alone to make. The law has recognized that as social life becomes more complicated, more and more occasions arise when our privacy is invaded by "experts" who, in our "best interests", presume to make decisions about our lives.

It should not be surprising that much of the law in this area has arisen from the medical arena. Physicians and other health professionals are perhaps the clearest examples of experts who make decisions in our best interests. In this area of law, respect for autonomy takes the form of the doctrine of informed consent, which is outlined in the first case in this Part. By analogy, the abortion debate has been characterized in terms of a woman's right to be sovereign over her own body, as have cases of voluntary euthanasia and suicide. In Canada we have had several dramatic legal cases in this area, some of which are presented in this Part.

Conceptually, to argue that people have the right to make decisions for themselves – however foolish or unreasonable these decisions may seem to others – is to argue that no one should have this power over others. But there is an important exception to this rule, namely, the presumed right that parents have to make decisions for their children. Two recent cases in which parents insisted on the right to determine their children's fate are included in this Part to suggest how Canadian courts deal with this difficult issue.

MALETTE V. SHULMAN

Ontario Court of Appeal

(1990) 72 O.R. (2d) 417

After a car accident in which her husband was killed, Mrs. Georgette Malette was rushed, unconscious, to the closest hospital. The attending physician, Dr. Shulman, found her to be suffering from incipient shock because of blood loss and decided that a blood transfusion was necessary to preserve her life. Before he did, however, a nurse found in Mrs. Malette's purse a card that said that, as a Jehovah's Witness, she requested that no blood be administered to her under any circumstances. In part, the card read, "I fully realize the implications of this position, but I have resolutely decided to obey the Bible command...." After getting a second opinion and accepting full responsibility, Dr. Shulman administered the transfusions. Mrs. Malette recovered from her injuries, and a few months later sued Dr. Shulman for assault and battery. At trial, she won and was awarded damages of $20,000. Dr. Shulman appealed the ruling.

* * * *

Mr. Justice Robins:

I should perhaps underscore the fact that Dr. Shulman was not found liable for any negligence in his treatment of Mrs. Malette. The judge [in the original trial] held that he had acted "promptly, professionally and was well-motivated throughout" and that his management of the case had been "carried out in a competent, careful and conscientious manner" in accordance with the requisite standard of care. His decision to administer blood in the circumstances confronting him was found to be an honest exercise of his professional judgment which did not delay Mrs. Malette's recovery, endanger her life or cause her any bodily harm. Indeed, the judge concluded that the doctor's treatment of Mrs. Malette "may well have been responsible for saving her life"....

What then is the legal effect, if any, of the Jehovah's Witness card carried by Mrs. Malette? Was the doctor bound to honour the instructions of his unconscious patient or, given the emergency and his inability to obtain conscious instructions from his patient, was he entitled to disregard the card and act according to his best medical judgment?

To answer these questions and determine the effect to be given to the Jehovah's Witness card, it is first necessary to ascertain what rights a competent patient has to accept or reject medical treatment and to appreciate the nature and extent of those rights.

The right of a person to control his or her own body is a concept that has long been recognized at common law. The tort of battery has traditionally protected the interest in bodily security from unwanted physical interference. Basically, any intentional nonconsensual touching which is harmful or offensive to a person's reasonable sense of dignity is actionable. Of course, a person may choose to waive this protection and consent to the intentional invasion of this interest, in which case an action for battery will not be maintainable. No special exceptions are made for medical care, other than in emergency situations, and the general rules governing actions for battery are applicable to the doctor-patient relationship. Thus, as a matter of common law, a medical intervention in which a doctor touches the body of a patient would constitute a battery if the patient did not consent to the intervention. Patients have the decisive role in the medical decision-making process. Their right of self-determination is recognized and protected by the law. As Justice Cardozo proclaimed in his classic statement: "Every human being of adult years and sound mind has a right to determine what shall be done with his own body; and a surgeon who performs an operation without his patient's consent commits an assault, for which he is liable in damages": *Schloendoff v. Society of New York Hospital* (1914).

The doctrine of informed consent has developed in the law as the primary means of protecting a patient's right to control his or her medical treatment. Under the doctrine, no medical procedure may be undertaken without the patient's consent obtained after the patient has been provided with sufficient information to evaluate the risks and benefits of the proposed treatment and other available options. The doctrine presupposes the patient's capacity to make a subjective treatment decision based on her understanding of the necessary medical facts provided by the doctor and on her assessment of her own personal circumstances. A doctor who performs a medical procedure without having first furnished the patient with the information needed to obtain an informed consent will have infringed the patient's right to control the course of her medical care, and will be liable in battery even though the procedure was performed with a high degree of skill and actually benefited the patient.

The right of self-determination which underlies the doctrine of informed consent also obviously encompasses the right to refuse medical treatment. A competent adult is generally entitled to reject a specific treatment or all treatment, or to select an alternate form of treatment, even if the decision may entail risks as serious as death and may appear mistaken in the eyes of the medical profession or of the community. Regardless of the doctor's opinion, it is the patient who has the final say on whether to undergo the treatment. The patient is free to decide, for instance, not to be operated on or not to undergo therapy or, by the same token, not to have a blood transfusion. If a doctor were to proceed in the face of a decision to reject the treatment, he would be civilly liable for his unauthorized conduct notwithstanding his justifiable belief that what he did was necessary to preserve the patient's life or health. The doctrine of informed consent is plainly intended to ensure the freedom of individuals to make choices concerning their medical care. For this freedom to be meaningful, people must have the right to make choices that accord with their own values regardless of how unwise or foolish those choices may appear to others.

The emergency situation is an exception to the general rule requiring a patient's prior consent. When immediate medical treatment is necessary to save the life or preserve the health of a person who, by reason of unconsciousness or extreme illness, is incapable of either giving or withholding consent, the doctor may proceed without the patient's consent. The delivery of medical services is rendered lawful in such circumstances either on the rationale that the doctor has implied consent from the patient to give emergency aid or, more accurately in my view, on the rationale that the doctor is privileged by reason of necessity in giving the aid and is not to be held liable for so doing. On either basis, in an emergency the law sets aside the requirement of consent on the assumption that the patient, as a reasonable person, would want emergency aid to be rendered if she were capable of giving instructions....

On the facts of the present case, Dr. Shulman was clearly faced with an emergency. He had an unconscious, critically ill patient on his hands who, in his opinion, needed blood transfusions to save her life or preserve her health. If there were no Jehovah's Witness card he undoubtedly would have been entitled to administer blood transfusions as part of the emergency treatment and could not have been held liable for so doing. In those circumstances he would have had no indication that the transfusions would have been refused had the patient then been able to make her wishes known and, accordingly, no reason to expect that, as a reasonable person, she would not consent to the transfusions.

However, to change the facts, if Mrs. Malette, before passing into unconsciousness, had expressly instructed Dr. Shulman, in terms comparable to those set forth on the card, that her religious convictions as a Jehovah's Witness were such that she was not to be given a blood transfusion under any circumstances and that she fully realized the implications of this position, the doctor would have been confronted with an obviously different situation. Here, the patient, anticipating an emergency in which she might be unable to make decisions about her health care contemporaneous with the emergency, has given explicit instructions that blood transfusions constitute an unacceptable medical intervention and are not to be administered to her. Once the emergency arises, is the doctor none the less entitled to administer transfusions on the basis of his honest belief that they are needed to save his patient's life?

The answer, in my opinion, is clearly no. A doctor is not free to disregard a patient's advance instructions given at the time of the emergency. The law does not prohibit a patient from withholding consent to emergency medical treatment, nor does the law prohibit a doctor from following his patient's instructions. While the law may disregard the absence of consent in limited emergency circumstances, it otherwise supports the right of competent adults to make decisions concerning their own health care by imposing civil liability on those who perform medical treatment without consent.

The patient's decision to refuse blood in the situation I have posed was made prior to and in anticipation of the emergency. While the doctor would have had the opportunity to dissuade her on the basis of his medical advice, her refusal to accept his advice or her unwillingness to discuss or consider the subject would not relieve him of his obligation to follow her instructions. The principles of self-determination and individual autonomy compel the conclusion that the patient may reject blood transfusions even if harmful consequences may result and even if the decision is generally regarded as foolhardy. Her decision in this instance would be operative after she lapsed into unconsciousness, and the doctor's conduct would be unauthorized. To transfuse a Jehovah's Witness in the face of her explicit instructions to the contrary would, in my opinion, violate her right own body and show disrespect for the religious values by which she has chosen to live her life.

The distinguishing feature of the present case – and the one that makes this a case of first impression – is, of course, the Jehovah's Witness card on the person of the unconscious patient. What then is the effect of the Jehovah's Witness card?...

Accepting for the moment that there is no reason to doubt that the card validly expressed Mrs. Malette's desire to withhold consent to blood transfusions, why should her wishes not be respected? Why should she be transfused against her will? The appellant's [Dr. Shulman's] answer, in essence, is that the card cannot be effective when the doctor is unable to provide the patient with the information she would need before making a decision to withhold consent in this specific emergency situation. In the absence of an informed refusal, the appellant submits that Mrs. Malette's right to protection against unwanted infringements of her bodily integrity must give way to countervailing societal interests which limit a person's right to refuse medical treatment. The appellant identifies two such interests as applicable to the unconscious patient in the present situation: first, the interest of the state in preserving life and, second, the interest of the state in safeguarding the integrity of the medical profession.

The state undoubtedly has a strong interest in protecting and preserving the lives and health of its citizens. There clearly are circumstances where this interest may override the individual's right to self-determination. For example, the state may in certain cases require that citizens submit to medical procedures in order to eliminate a health threat to the community or it may prohibit citizens from engaging in activities which are inherently dangerous to their lives. But this interest does not prevent a competent adult from refusing life-preserving medical treatment in general or blood transfusions in particular.

The state's interest in preserving the life or health of a competent patient must generally give way to the patient's stronger interest in directing the course of her own life. As indicated earlier, there is no law prohibiting a patient from declining necessary treatment or prohibiting a doctor from honouring the patient's decision. To the extent that the law reflects the state's interest, it supports the right of individuals to make their own decisions. By imposing civil liability on those who perform medical treatment without consent even though the treatment may be beneficial, the law serves to maximize individual freedom of choice. Recognition of the right to reject medical treatment cannot, in my opinion, be said to depreciate the interest of the state in life or in the sanctity of life. Individual free choice and self-determination are themselves fundamental constituents of life. To deny individuals freedom of choice with respect to their health care can only lessen, and not enhance, the value of life. This state interest, in my opinion, cannot properly be invoked to prohibit Mrs. Malette from choosing for herself whether or not to undergo blood transfusions.

Safeguarding the integrity of the medical profession is patently a legitimate state interest worthy of protection. However, I do not agree that this interest can serve to limit a patient's right to refuse blood transfusions. I recognize, of course, that the choice between violating a patient's private convictions and accepting her decision is hardly an easy one for members of a profession dedicated to aiding the injured and preserving life. The patient's right to determine her own medical treatment is, however, paramount to what might otherwise be the doctor's obligation to provide needed medical care. The doctor is bound in law by the patient's choice even though that choice may be contrary to the mandates of his own conscience and professional judgment. If patient choice were subservient to conscientious medical judgment, the right of the patient to determine her own treatment, and the doctrine of informed consent, would be rendered meaningless. Recognition of a Jehovah's Witness' right to refuse blood transfusions cannot, in my opinion, be seen as threatening the integrity of the medical profession or the state's interest in protecting the same.

In sum, it is my view that the principal interest asserted by Mrs. Malette in this case – the interest in the freedom to reject, or refuse to consent to, intrusions of her bodily integrity – outweighs the interest of the state in the preservation of life and health and the protection of the integrity of the medical profession. While the right to decline medical treatment is not absolute or unqualified, those state interests are not in themselves sufficiently compelling to justify forcing a patient to submit to nonconsensual invasions of her person. The interest of the state in protecting innocent third parties and preventing suicide are, I might note, not applicable to the present circumstances....

At issue here is the freedom of the patient as an individual to exercise her right to refuse treatment and accept the consequences of her own decision. Competent adults, as I have sought to demonstrate, are generally at liberty to refuse medical treatment even at the risk of death. The right to determine what shall be done with one's own body is a fundamental right in our society. The concepts inherent in this right are the bedrock upon which the principles of self-determination and individual autonomy are based. Free individual choice in matters affecting this right should, in my opinion, be accorded very high priority. I view the issues in this case from that perspective....

One further point should be mentioned. The appellant argues that to uphold the trial decision places a doctor on the horns of a dilemma, in that, on the one hand, if the doctor administers blood in this situation and saves the patient's life, the patient may hold him liable in battery while, on the other hand, if the doctor follows the patient's instructions and, as a consequence, the patient dies, the doctor may face an action by dependants alleging that, notwithstanding the card, the deceased would, if conscious, have accepted blood in the face of imminent death and the doctor was negligent in failing to administer the transfusions. In my view, that result cannot conceivably follow. The doctor cannot be held to have violated either his legal duty or professional responsibility towards the patient or the patient's dependants when he honours the Jehovah's Witness card and respects the patient's right to control her own body in accordance with the dictates of her conscience. The onus is clearly on the patient. When members of the Jehovah's Witness faith choose to carry cards intended to notify doctors and other providers of health care that they reject blood transfusions in an emergency, they must accept the consequences of their decision. Neither they nor their dependants can later be heard to say that the card did not reflect their true wishes. If harmful consequences ensue, the responsibility for those consequences is entirely theirs and not the doctor's....

In the result, for these reasons, I would dismiss the appeal and the cross-appeal, both with costs.

R. V. MORGENTALER

Supreme Court of Canada

[1988] 1 S.C.R. 30

In this landmark case, a majority of the Supreme Court found Canada's abortion law to be unconstitutional. Section 251 of the *Criminal Code* made it a criminal offence to "procure a miscarriage of a female person" and then outlined a procedure which, if followed, would afford a complete defence to the charge. So, if a pregnant woman's request for an abortion was accepted by a therapeutic abortion committee of an accredited or approved hospital, on the grounds that the continuation of the pregnancy would endanger her health, and if the abortion was performed by a qualified medical practitioner, neither the practitioner nor the woman would be guilty of an indictable offence. Some members of the court felt that this complex procedure, and the unavailability of abortion in parts of the country, violated a woman's right to fair treatment. Madam Justice Wilson, however, in a concurring judgment, took the stronger stand and founded her judgment directly on the value of autonomy.

* * * *

Madam Justice Wilson:

At the heart of this appeal is the question whether a pregnant woman can, as a constitutional matter, be compelled by law to carry the foetus to term. The legislature has proceeded on the basis that she can be so compelled and, indeed, has made it a criminal offence punishable by imprisonment under s. 251 of the *Criminal Code* for her or her physician to terminate the pregnancy unless the procedural requirements of the section are complied with.

My colleagues, the Chief Justice and Justice Beetz, have attacked those requirements in reasons which I have had the privilege of reading. They have found that the requirements do not comport with the principles of fundamental justice in the procedural sense and have concluded that, since they cannot be severed from the provisions creating the substantive offence, the whole of s. 251 must fall.

With all due respect, I think that the court must tackle the primary issue first. A consideration as to whether or not the procedural requirements for obtaining or performing an abortion comport with fundamental justice is purely academic if such requirements cannot as a constitutional matter be imposed at all. If a pregnant woman cannot, as a constitutional matter, be compelled by law to carry the foetus to term against her will, a review of the procedural requirements by which she may be compelled to do so seems pointless. Moreover, it would, in my opinion, be an exercise in futility for the legislature to expend its time and energy in attempting to remedy the defects in the procedural requirements unless it has some assurance that this process will, at the end of the day, result in the creation of a valid criminal offence. I turn, therefore, to what I believe is the central issue that must be addressed....

In order to ascertain the content of the right to liberty we must, as Dickson C.J. stated in R. v. *Big M Drug Mart Ltd. (1985)*, commence with an analysis of the purpose of that right....We are invited, therefore, to consider the purpose of the *Charter* in general and of the right to liberty in particular.

The *Charter is* predicated on a particular conception of the place of the individual in society. An individual is not a totally independent entity disconnected from the society in which he or she lives. Neither, however, is the individual a mere cog in an impersonal machine in which his or her values, goals and aspirations are subordinated to those of the collectivity. The individual is a bit of both. The *Charter* reflects this reality by leaving a wide range of activities and decisions open to legitimate government control while at the same time placing limits on the proper scope of that control. Thus, the rights guaranteed in the *Charter* erect around each individual, metaphorically speaking, an invisible fence over which the state will not be allowed to trespass. The role of the courts is to map out, piece by piece, the parameters of the fence.

The *Charter* and the right to individual liberty guaranteed under it are inextricably tied to the concept of human dignity. Professor Neil MacCormick, *Legal Right and Social Democracy: Essays in Legal and Political Philosophy* (1982), speaks of liberty as "a condition of human self-respect and of that contentment which resides in the ability to pursue one's own conception of a full and rewarding life". He says at p. 41:

To be able to decide what to do and how to do it, to carry out one's own decisions and accept their consequences, seems to me essential to one's self-respect as a human being, and essential to the possibility of that contentment. Such self-respect and contentment are in my judgment fundamental goods for human beings, the worth of life itself being on condition of having or striving for them. If a person were deliberately denied the opportunity of self-respect and that contentment, he would suffer deprivation of his essential humanity....

The idea of human dignity finds expression in almost every right and freedom guaranteed in the *Charter*. Individuals are afforded the right to choose their own religion and their own philosophy of life, the right to choose with whom they will associate and how they will express themselves, the right to choose where they will live and what occupation they will pursue. These are all examples of the basic theory underlying the *Charter*, namely, that the state will respect choices made by individuals and, to the greatest extent possible, will avoid subordinating these choices to any one conception of the good life.

Thus, an aspect of the respect for human dignity on which the *Charter* is founded is the right to make fundamental personal decisions without interference from the state. This right is a crucial component of the right to liberty. Liberty is a phrase capable of a broad range of meaning. In my view, this right, properly construed, grants the individual a degree of autonomy in making decisions of fundamental personal importance.

This view is consistent with the position I took in the case of *Jones v. The Queen* (1986). One issue raised in that case was whether the right to liberty in s. 7 of the *Charter* included a parent's right to bring up his children in accordance with his conscientious beliefs. In concluding that it did I stated at pp. 318-19:

> I believe that the framers of the Constitution in guaranteeing "liberty" as a fundamental value in a free and democratic society had in mind the freedom of the individual to develop and realize his potential to the full, to plan his own life to suit his own character, to make his own choices for good or ill, to be non-conformist, idiosyncratic and even eccentric – to be, in today's parlance, "his own person" and accountable as such. John Stuart Mill described it as "pursuing our own good in our own way". This, he believed, we should be free to do "so long as we do not attempt to deprive others of theirs or impede their efforts to obtain it".

He added:

> "Each is the proper guardian of his own health, whether bodily *or* mental and spiritual. Mankind are greater gainers by suffering each other to live as seems good to themselves than by compelling each to live as seems good to the rest."

Liberty in a free and democratic society does not require the state to approve the personal decisions made by its citizens; it does, however, require the state to respect them....

In my opinion, the respect for individual decision-making in matters of fundamental personal importance reflected in the American jurisprudence also informs the Canadian *Charter*. Indeed, as the Chief Justice pointed out in *R. v. Big M Drug Mart Ltd.* (1985), beliefs about human worth and dignity "are the *sine qua non* of the political tradition underlying the *Charter*". I would conclude, therefore, that the right to liberty contained in s. 7 guarantees to every individual a degree of personal autonomy over important decisions intimately affecting their private lives.

The question then becomes whether the decision of a woman to terminate her pregnancy falls within this class of protected decisions. I have no doubt that it does. This decision is one that will have profound psychological, economic and social consequences for the pregnant woman. The circumstances giving rise to it can be complex and varied and there may be, and usually are, powerful considerations militating in opposite directions. It is a decision that deeply reflects the way the woman thinks about herself and her relationship to others and to society at large. It is not just a medical decision; it is a profound social and ethical one as well. Her response to it will be the response of the whole person.

It is probably impossible for a man to respond, even imaginatively, to such a dilemma not just because it is outside the realm of his personal experience (although this is, of course, the case) but because he can relate to it only by objectifying it, thereby eliminating the subjective elements of the female psyche which are at the heart of the dilemma. As Noreen Burrows, lecturer in European Law at the University of Glasgow, has pointed out in her essay on "International Law and Human Rights: the Case of Women's Rights", in *Human Rights: From Rhetoric to Reality* (1986), the history of the struggle for human rights from the eighteenth century on has been the history of men struggling to assert their dignity and common humanity against an overbearing state apparatus. The more recent struggle for women's rights has been a struggle to eliminate discrimination, to achieve a place for women in a man's world, to develop a set of legislative reforms in order to place women in the same position as men. It has *not* been a struggle to define the rights of women in relation to their special place in the societal structure and in relation to the biological distinction between the two sexes. Thus, women's needs and aspirations are only now being translated into protected rights. The right to reproduce or not to reproduce which is in issue in this case is one such right and is properly perceived as an integral part of modern woman's struggle to assert *her* dignity and worth as a human being.

Given then that the right to liberty guaranteed by s. 7 of the *Charter* gives a woman the right to decide for herself whether or not to terminate her pregnancy, does s. 251 of the *Criminal Code* violate this right? Clearly it does. The purpose of the section is to take the decision away from the woman and give it to a committee. Furthermore, as the Chief Justice correctly points out, the committee bases its decision on "criteria entirely unrelated to [the pregnant woman's] priorities and aspirations". The fact that the decision whether a woman will be allowed to terminate her pregnancy is in the hands of a committee is just as great a violation of the woman's right to personal autonomy in decisions of an intimate and private nature as it would be if a committee were established to decide whether a woman should be allowed to continue her pregnancy. Both these arrangements violate the woman's right to liberty by deciding for her something that she has the right to decide for herself....

I agree with the Chief Justice and with Beetz J. that the right to "security of the person" under s. 7 of the *Charter* protects both the physical and psychological integrity of the individual. State enforced medical or surgical treatment comes readily to mind as an obvious invasion of physical integrity. Lamer J. held in *Mills v. The Queen* (1986), that the right to security of the person entitled a person to be protected against psychological trauma as well – in that case the psychological trauma resulting from delays in the trial process under s. 11(b) of the *Charter*. He found that psychological trauma could take the form of "stigmatization of the accused, loss of privacy, stress and anxiety resulting from a multitude of factors, including possible disruption of family, social life and work, legal costs, uncertainty as to outcome and sanction". I agree with my colleague and I think that his comments are very germane to the instant case because, as the Chief Justice and Beetz J. point out, the present legislative scheme for the obtaining of an abortion clearly subjects pregnant women to considerable emotional stress as well as to unnecessary physical risk. I believe, however, that the flaw in the present legislative scheme goes much deeper than that. In essence, what it does is assert that the woman's capacity to reproduce is not to be subject to her own control. It is to be subject to the control of the state. She may not choose whether to exercise her existing capacity or not to exercise it. This is not, in my view, just a matter of interfering with her right to liberty in the sense (already discussed) of her right to personal autonomy in decision making, it is a direct interference with her physical "person" as well. She is truly being treated as a means – a means to an end which she does not desire but over which she has no control. She is the passive recipient of a decision made by others as to whether her body is to be used to nurture a new life. Can there be anything that comports less with human dignity and self-respect? How can a woman in this position have any sense of security with respect to her person? I believe that s. 251 of the *Criminal Code* deprives the pregnant woman of her right to security of the person as well as her right to liberty.

ATTORNEY-GENERAL OF B.C. V. ASTAFOROFF

British Columbia Supreme Court

[1983] 6 W.W.R. 322

Mary Astaforoff was an elderly Doukhobor woman serving time in a provincial prison for arson. Although granted parole, she chose to stay and, in an attempt to free two other Doukhobor prisoners, decided to go on a hunger strike, something she had done several times before as a form of religious protest. The Attorney-General of British Columbia, at the request of the Attorney-General of Canada, asked the Supreme Court whether it had the authority to force-feed Astaforoff in order to preserve her life. In effect, the Court was asked whether the state had the authority, or the obligation, to prevent a suicide.

* * * *

Mr. Justice Bouck:

Before discussing the law, I think I must relate how the grisly business of force-feeding actually occurs. It was related to me in this way. First of all, it is necessary to get a plastic tube of sufficient length to reach through the nose into the stomach. Two different problems then present themselves. The patient can be sedated or left conscious. If barbiturates are administered, the gagging reflex is lost almost entirely and there is a danger that the tube may be inserted into the lungs rather than the stomach. Should that occur and feeding is commenced, the patient can drown.

Alternatively, if the patient remains conscious, force may be used to insert the tube into the nose and push it down into the stomach. Again, it is still possible that the tube may take the wrong path and end up in the lungs. Instances have occurred in the past where people have died from the consequences of force-feeding.

Even when the correct procedure is followed, there is nothing to stop the patient from either removing the tube or vomiting up the nutrients forced into his or her stomach, unless perhaps restraint is applied 24 hours a day.

If force-feeding is ordered, it is likely that she will remain conscious during the process. She is a frail and weak human being whose body will be subjected to the indignity of this procedure. How long it will last nobody really knows. It might be for a period of weeks or months, at least until her mandatory supervision release date on 28th November 1983. In her age and condition there is a possibility that she might even die from the results of the turmoil caused by the force-feeding itself.

The provincial medical practitioners employed by the prison officials object to participating in the affair because they say their code of ethics restricts them from invading the body of a patient in this way when it is against her will.

I now turn to the law. The legal duty of the Attorney General for British Columbia is described in s. 197 of the *Criminal Code of Canada*. The relevant provisions read:

197.(1) Every one is under a legal duty...

(c) to provide necessaries of life to a person under his charge if that person
(i) is unable, by reason of detention, age, illness, insanity or other cause, to withdraw himself from that charge, and
(ii) is unable to provide himself with necessaries of life.

According to the province, it made available to the prisoner the necessaries of life but she chooses not to accept them. In reply, the respondents contend that the law should be interpreted to read that the province must forcibly provide her with these necessaries. I do not think the *Criminal Code* should be defined to mean that provincial jail officials and others having someone under their care and control must force the necessaries of life upon that person. This sort of conduct could lead to all kinds of abuse. Therefore, I reject this portion of the respondent's argument....

What Mary Astaforoff is trying to do is commit suicide. The law does not countenance suicide. While it is not a crime, because it is obvious that there can be no punishment, the *Criminal Code* says it is an offence to counsel or procure a person to commit suicide, or aid or abet a person in the commission of suicide: s. 224. But idly standing by without encouraging a person to commit suicide is no crime. A mere spectator to a suicide cannot be convicted of any criminal offence.

Nonetheless, it is the duty of every person to use reasonable care in preventing a person from committing suicide. What is reasonable depends upon the facts. For example, if a jail guard sees a prisoner trying to hang himself in his cell, then it seems reasonable that he should take steps to prevent the inmate from taking his own life. On the other hand, if a person climbs to the top of a bridge and threatens to jump, the law does not impose a legal duty on anyone to risk his own life by climbing the bridge in attempting to get the person down. In that situation, it is reasonable if steps are taken to encourage the jumper by shouts or other methods of communication not to jump.

As I see it, my responsibility is to decide whether, under the particular circumstances of this case, there is a legal duty cast upon the province to force-feed the respondent against her will in order to prevent her from committing suicide. If there is this duty, then should I make the order compelling the prison officials to carry it out.

I am aware of the responsibility of the court to preserve the sanctity of life. It is a moral as well as a legal duty. However, in the circumstances of this case the facts are against the motion of the Attorney General for Canada. The prisoner has a long history of fasting. Her health is very poor. There is the danger that she might die by the applying of the procedure necessary to get nutrients into the stomach. She is free to leave the prison, but chooses to remain there and starve herself to death. Given these facts, I cannot find that it is reasonable that the Attorney General for British Columbia and the prison authorities under his direction should force-feed her in order to prevent her suicide .

If she becomes unconscious or incapable of making a rational decision, that is another matter. Then she will be unable to make a free choice. But while she is lucid no law compels the provincial officers to apply force to her against her will.

It follows that the motion of the Attorney General for Canada must be dismissed.

RODRIGUEZ V. ATTORNEY-GENERAL OF B.C.

British Columbia Court of Appeal

[1992] 4 W.W.R. 109

Sue Rodriguez suffered from an incurable and degenerative disease of the motor neurons of the brain and spinal cord called Lou Gehrig's disease. She decided that, before the disease progressed to the point of complete paralysis and a slow and painful death, she would ensure that, when she felt the time was right, she could kill herself. Since she would be physically unable to fulfill that wish, she would require the assistance of a physician. Section 241 of the *Criminal Code*, however, prohibits anyone from aiding or abetting another person to commit suicide. Does this provision undermine her autonomy by overruling her decisions about her own death; or does it protect the sanctity of human life and prevent a social harm?

When the matter reached the Supreme Court of Canada, a majority held that section 241 reflected a legitimate state interest in protecting the vulnerable and was fully consistent with a social consensus that human life must be respected and that care must be taken not to undermine the institutions that protect it. The dissent raised other issues. Earlier, however, in the British Columbia Court of Appeal decision, Chief Justice McEachern directly addressed the issue of autonomy and argued that s. 241 unjustifiably violated Sue Rodriguez's right of self-determination.

* * * *

Chief Justice McEachern (dissenting):

To put the case in proper context, it is important to mention certain historical matters of interest and importance. At common law, it was an offence for a person to attempt to commit suicide, or to counsel, aid or abet another person to do so.

Canada's first *Criminal Code,* enacted in 1892, codified the common law as just stated. The common law prohibitions were continued through successive revisions of the *Code.* In 1972 the offence of attempting suicide was deleted from the *Code.* The sparse debates in the House of Commons suggest this was done because suicide was

considered to be a social or health problem. The offence of counselling, aiding and abetting suicide, however, was not deleted and the
present *Code* s. 241 has remained in force in the following terms since
1972:

241. Every one who

(a) counsels a person to commit suicide, or
(b) aids or abets a person to commit suicide, whether suicide
ensues or not, is guilty of an indicatable offence and liable to
imprisonment for a term not exceeding fourteen years.

Prior to 1972 there were usually around 300 to 400 convictions under
the predecessor sections to s. 241. Since 1972, there have been prac-
tically no prosecutions for counselling or aiding suicide under s. 241.
More than one-half of the American States have legislation similar to
s. 241.

The Law Reform Commission of Canada gave careful consideration to the question of physician assisted suicide. In its 1982 Working
Paper No. 28, the Commission stopped just short of recommending
the "decriminalization" of assisted suicide because of concern about
abuse but then stated:

At the same time, in order to acknowledge more fully the undeniable element of altruism and compassion involved in some cases
of assistance provided to a terminally ill loved one, and because we
are not convinced that the imposition of a criminal sentence is
appropriate in such a case, the Commission proposes the addition
to section [241] of the present Criminal Code of a second subsection as follows:

241. (2) No person shall be persecuted for an offence under the
present section without the personal written authorization of the
Attorney-General.

In my judgment, the intention of the above was that assisted suicide
of terminally ill persons would be effectively decriminalized because
it was expected that the Attorney-General would not give authorization to prosecute in such cases.

At the same time, the Working Paper recognized that a "...[physi-
cian's] decision to terminate or not to initiate useless treatment is
sound medical practice and should be legally recognized as such",
and recommended that this "already recognized common law prin-

ciple" should be clearly expressed in the Criminal Code. The Working Paper also proposed that:

> ...criminal law should formally recognize in the Criminal Code the principle that a competent person has the right to refuse treatment or to demand that it be stopped.

Discussion on the Working Paper disclosed widespread disagreement on the recommendations requiring the authority of the Attorney-General for assisted suicide prosecutions. In its 1983 Report to the Minister of Justice, the Commission accordingly withdrew that recommendation giving three reasons:

> First, it was thought that the decision of an Attorney-General to authorize or not to authorize a prosecution would be perceived to be based upon political grounds; secondly, that the law might [be] applied differently in the various provinces, suggesting that life did not have the same value in different parts of Canada; and thirdly, the Commission considered that "...since this offence is almost never prosecuted, requiring an additional procedure would amount to its *de facto* abolition.

At the same time, the Commission continued to recommend that the *Criminal Code* should be amended to provide that its homicide provisions should not be interpreted as requiring a physician to undertake medical treatment against the wishes of a patient, or to continue medical treatment when such treatment "has become therapeutically useless", or from preventing a physician to "cease administering appropriate palliative care intended to eliminate or to relieve the suffering of a person, for the sole reason that such care or measures are likely to shorten the life expectancy of this person."

I take it that the Commission was sympathetic to the decriminalization of assisted suicide, but was not able to develop adequate safeguards against abuse. No action has been taken on any of these recommendations of the Law Reform Commission....

The current view of the British Columbia College of Physicians and Surgeons is disclosed in a Statement made by the College dated November 21, 1991, in connection with a physician who was found to have ordered "...frequent repeated doses of medication to patients exceeding what was sufficient to produce and maintain freedom from pain and suffering in patients believed to be close to inevitable death."

The doctor in that case took the position that he was involved in terminal palliative care, and, with family agreement, he was merely withholding active treatment and assuring relief from further suffering.

The College decided not to pursue disciplinary action and the Crown decided after investigation not to lay charges against the doctor, but the College took the opportunity to say:

> "Active euthanasia", or "mercy killing" – whether requested by a mentally competent patient or by the patient's legal representative when the patient is mentally incompetent – is illegal under existing Canadian law.

Notwithstanding this history, physicians and terminally ill patients have some limited options. First, those who are mentally competent can instruct their physicians that they are not to be given life-support treatment to continue their lives unduly. Physicians instructed not to treat patients are liable in damages if they disregard such instructions: *Malette v. Shulman* (1990). Such patients eventually die either from starvation or from the untreated consequences of their condition.

Patients undergoing life-support treatment are entitled to direct such treatment be discontinued, in which event, they too, inevitably die: *Nancy B. v. Hotel-Dieu de Quebec* (1992).

It is believed that unofficial euthanasia has been practised in Holland on a very large scale for some time. In 1990 a Committee was established to look into such question and it reported upwards of 25,000 cases a year. There were unofficial rules of careful conduct which the committee found were rarely followed. The most serious breaches of the rules consisted of inadequate reporting....

On February 4 of this year, the highest Court in the United Kingdom, the House of Lords, authorized the termination of life-support systems for a brain-dead patient whose parents gave their consent as surrogates, and that patient died on March 3, 1993....

Apart from these high profile cases, there have always been many cases in this and other countries where physicians, in the best interest of their patients, have furnished "palliative" care where unusually heavy doses of pain relieving drugs are administered with or without the consent of the patient or surrogates, and with full knowledge that such medication may accelerate the death of the patient. As already mentioned, the various governing bodies of the medical professions recognize and approve this. The distinction, which seems to give comfort to the medical profession, is said to be that medication must be given with the primary intention of relieving pain and mental suffering so as to permit the patient to die without excessive pain rather than to accelerate death.

No records or statistics for this kind of palliative care are kept but it is obvious that, assuming a patient is terminally ill and approaching inevitable death, there is only a conceptual line which lacks practical reality between physician assisted suicide and palliative care. In the former, however, the competent patient has a say about when she or he will end a hopeless life which is no longer bearable. In the latter, the patient's death is mercifully accelerated, but she or he must await the failure of body processes from starvation, choking or pneumonia, hopefully under sufficient sedation so that physical pain will be min-imized. During palliative care, the quality of psychological pain for mentally competent patients (and their families), must be enor-mously greater if their medication permits them lucid intervals....

Considering the nature of the rights protected by the *Charter* in other cases, I have no doubt that a terminally ill person facing what the Appellant faces, qualifies under the value system upon which the *Charter is* based to protection under the rubric of either liberty or security of her person. This would include at least the lawful right of a terminally ill person to terminate her own life, and, in my view, to assistance under proper circumstances .

It would be wrong, in my view, to judge this case as a contest between life and death. The *Charter is* not concerned only with the fact of life, but also with the quality and dignity of life. In my view, death and the way we die is a part of life itself. I shall now endeavour to explain the basis upon which I have reached this conclusion....

...[Section 7 of the *Charter*] was enacted for the purpose of ensur-ing human dignity and individual control, so long as it harms no one else. When one considers the nobility of such purpose, it must follow as a matter of logic as much as of law, that any provision which impos-es an indeterminate period of senseless physical and psychological suffering upon someone who is shortly to die anyway cannot conform with any principle of fundamental justice. Such a provision, by any measure, must clearly be characterized as the opposite of fundamen-tal justice....

I would accordingly declare that the operation of *Code* s. 241 vio-lates the Appellant's liberty and security of the person which are rights guaranteed to her by s. 7 of the *Canadian Charter of Rights and Freedoms,* and that, upon compliance with the conditions hereafter stated, neither the Appellant nor any physician assisting her to attempt to commit, or to commit suicide, will by that means commit any offence against the law of Canada. The said conditions are as fol-lows.

First, the Appellant must be mentally competent to make a decision to end her own life, such competence to be certified in writing by a treating physician and by an independent psychiatrist who has examined her not more than 24 hours before arrangements are put in place which will permit the Appellant to actually terminate her life and such arrangements must only be operative while one of such physicians is actually present with the Appellant.

Such certificate must include the professional opinion of the physicians not just that she is competent, but also that, in the opinion of such physicians, she truly desires to end her life and that, in their opinion, she has reached such decision of her own free will without pressure or influence from any source other than her circumstances....

Secondly, in addition to being mentally competent, the physicians must certify that, in their opinion, (1) the Appellant is terminally ill and near death, and that there is no hope of her recovering; (2) that she is, or but for medication would be, suffering unbearable physical pain or severe psychological distress; (3) that they have informed her, and that she understands, that she has a continuing right to change her mind about terminating her life; and, (4) when, in their opinion, the Appellant would likely die (a) if palliative care is being or would be administered to her, and (b) if palliative care should not be administered to her.

Thirdly, not less than three clear days before any psychiatrist examines the Appellant for the purposes of preparing a certificate for the purposes aforesaid, notice must be given to the Regional Coroner for the area or district where the Appellant is to be examined, and the Regional Coroner or his nominee, who must be a physician, may be present at the examination of the Appellant by a psychiatrist in order to be satisfied that the Appellant does indeed have mental competence to decide, and does in fact decide, to terminate her life.

Fourthly, one of the physicians giving any certificate as aforesaid must re-examine the Appellant each day after the above-mentioned arrangements are put in place to ensure she does not evidence any change in her intention to end her life. If she commits suicide, such physician must furnish a further certificate to the Coroner confirming that, in his or her opinion, the Appellant did not change her mind.

Fifthly, no one may assist the Appellant to attempt to commit suicide or to commit suicide after the expiration of thirty-one days from the date of the first mentioned certificate, and, upon the expiration of that period, any arrangement made to assist the Appellant to end her life must immediately be made inoperative and discontinued. I include this condition to ensure, to the extent it can be ensured, that the Appellant has not changed her mind since the time she was examined by a psychiatrist.

This limitation troubles me greatly as I would prefer that the Appellant be permitted a free choice about the time when she wishes to end her life. I am, however, unwilling to leave it open for a longer period because of the concern I have that the Appellant might change her mind. She is able to proceed at her preferred pace by delaying the time for her psychiatric examination until the time she thinks she is close to the time when she wishes to end her ordeal. If she delays causing her death for more than thirty-one days after such examination then there is a risk either that she had not finally made up her mind, or that, as is everyone's right, she has changed it, or possibly that she is no longer competent to make such a decision.

Lastly, the act actually causing the death of the Appellant must be the unassisted act of the Appellant herself, and not of anyone else.

These conditions have been prepared in some haste because of the urgency of the Appellant's circumstances, and I would not wish judges in subsequent applications to regard them other than as guidelines....

I only wish to add that...I must admit to having profound misgivings about almost every aspect of this case. I can only hope that Parliament in its wisdom will make it unnecessary for further cases of this kind to be decided by judges. I accede to this application only because I believe it is a salutary principle that every person who has a right, must also have a remedy.

B. (R.) V. CHILDREN'S AID SOCIETY OF TORONTO

Supreme Court of Canada

[1995] 1 S.C.R. 315

Sheena B. was a very sick infant who had reached a stage where her physicians believed that she might require a blood transfusion to treat a potentially fatal congestive heart failure. Her parents, who are Jehovah's Witnesses, objected on religious grounds to the blood transfusion. Following a emergency hearing of the Provincial Court, the Children's Aid Society was granted a temporary wardship of Sheena for the purpose of consenting to a blood transfusion, if it should prove medically necessary. Sheena eventually received the transfusion and the wardship order was terminated. Nonetheless, the parents sought to have the Provincial Court's decision overturned on the ground that it constituted an interference with their rights as parents to determine their child's medical treatment. The case made its way to the Supreme Court of Canada, where the issue was broadened, and restated in terms of a general "right of parents to rear their children without undue interference by the state", or parental liberty.

Although the court was unanimous that the Provincial Court was correct to issue the wardship order, on the question of the scope of parental liberty the court dramatically split. Mr. Justice La Forest argued that the law must recognize the right of parents to make decisions for their children and interfere only in the rarest case. By contrast, Mr. Justice Iacobucci made it clear that parents have no right to risk the life of their child, for whatever reason: although each of us can refuse any medical procedure for ourselves, "it is quite another matter to speak for another separate individual, especially when that individual cannot speak for herself".

* * * *

Mr. Justice La Forest, and Mr. Justice Gonthier and Madame Justice McLachlin:

This appeal raises the constitutionality of state interference with child-rearing decisions. The appellants are parents who argue that the Ontario *Child Welfare Act* infringes their right to choose medical treatment for their infant in accordance with the tenets of their faith. They claim that this right is protected under both ss. 7 and 2(a) of the *Canadian Charter of Rights and Freedoms....*

Although I am of the view that the principles of fundamental justice have been complied with in the present case, I nonetheless propose to comment on the scope of the protection afforded by the *Charter* as it relates to the right of parents to choose medical treatment for their infant....An examination of the scope of the liberty interest appears warranted, since its formulation may affect the determination of the principles of fundamental justice. I also note that while this case can be disposed of solely on the issue of the right of parents to choose medical treatment for their infant, it is not without consequence for child protection as a whole. Intervention may well be compelling here, but this appeal raises the more general question of the right of parents to rear their children without undue interference by the state.

The appellants claim that parents have the right to choose medical treatment for their infant, relying for this contention on s. 7 of the *Charter*, and more precisely on the liberty interest. They assert that the right enures in the family as an entity, basing this argument on statements made by American courts in the definition of liberty under their Constitution. While, as I will indicate, American experience may be useful in defining the scope of the liberty interest protected under our Constitution, I agree that s. 7 of the *Charter* does not afford protection to the integrity of the family unit as such. The Canadian *Charter*, and s. 7 in particular, protects individuals. It is the individual's right to liberty under the *Charter* with which we are here concerned. The concept of the integrity of the family unit is itself premised, at least in part, on that of parental liberty....

The term "liberty" has yet to be authoritatively defined in this court, although comments have been made on both ends of the spectrum....In *R. v. Jones*, speaking alone in dissent, Wilson J. gave a broad formulation of the concept of liberty. She stated:

> I believe that the framers of the Constitution in guaranteeing "liberty" as a fundamental value in a free and democratic society had in mind the freedom of the individual to develop and realize his potential to the full, to plan his own life to suit his own character, to make his own choices for good or ill, to be non-conformist, idiosyncratic and even eccentric – to be, in to-day's parlance, "his own person" and accountable as such. John Stuart Mill described it as "pursuing our own good in our own way". This, he believed, we

should be free to do "so long as we do not attempt to deprive others of theirs or impede their efforts to obtain it".

While she was of the view that s. 7 protected the right of parents to bring up and educate their children according to their conscientious beliefs, Wilson J. acknowledged that this freedom was not "untrammelled". Some limits could be placed on the interest, as "liberty" did not imply the right to bring up and educate one's children "as one sees fit".

On the other hand, Lamer J. speaking for himself alone in *Reference re ss. 193 and 195.1(1)(c) of the Criminal Code* rejected the line of American cases pertaining to contractual liberty, noting that such an extension of the liberty interest had also been subject to criticism in the United States. The text of the Canadian *Charter* – which does not mention "property" – and the context of its adoption were sufficiently different to mandate a distinct interpretation. According to him, s. 7, which appears in the *Charter* under the heading "Legal Rights", had to be construed in light of the rights enunciated in ss. 8 to 14, which set out traditional criminal law guarantees. Further, the term "liberty" had to be read in conjunction with its modifier, the principles of fundamental justice. Thus, a restriction on liberty had to occur as a result of an interaction with the justice system....He summarized his position as follows:

> Put shortly, I am of the view that s. 7 is implicated when the state, by resorting to the justice system, restricts an individual's physical liberty *in any circumstances.* Section 7 is also implicated when the state restricts individuals' security of the person by interfering with, or removing from them, control over their physical or mental integrity. Finally, s. 7 is implicated when the state, either directly or through its agents, restricts certain privileges or liberties by using the threat of punishment in cases of non-compliance.

Lamer J. added, however, that "This is not to say that 'liberty' as a value underlying the *Charter* does not permeate the document in a broader, more general sense, especially as it relates to the maintenance of Canada as a 'free and democratic society'"....

The above-cited cases give us an important indication of the meaning of the concept of liberty. On the one hand, liberty does not mean unconstrained freedom. Freedom of the individual to do what he or she wishes must, in any organized society, be subjected to numerous constraints for the common good. The state undoubtedly has the right to impose many types of restraints on individual behaviour, and not all limitations will attract *Charter* scrutiny. On the other hand, liberty does not mean mere freedom from physical restraint. In a free and democratic society, the individual must be left room for personal autonomy to live his or her own life and to make decisions that are of fundamental personal importance....

The United States Supreme Court has given a liberal interpretation to the concept of liberty, as it relates to family matters. It has elevated both the notion of the integrity of the family unit and that of parental rights to the status of constitutional values, through its interpretation of the Fifth and Fourteenth Amendments....Despite the lack of unanimity on the formulation of liberty and the role of the courts in reviewing legislation, the dicta on liberty, insofar as family matters are concerned, have been consistently broad. In *Prince v. Massachusetts* (1944), although the court upheld a statute prohibiting child labour, Rutledge J. stated, for the court:

> It is cardinal with us that the custody, care and nurture of the child reside first in the parents, whose primary function and freedom include preparation for obligations the state can neither supply nor hinder.

Where to draw the line between interests and regulatory powers falling within the accepted ambit of state authority will often raise difficulty. But much on either side of the line is clear enough. On that basis, I would have thought it plain that the right to nurture a child, to care for its development, and to make decisions for it in fundamental matters such as medical care, are part of the liberty interest of a parent. The common law has long recognized that parents are in the best position to take care of their children and make all the decisions necessary to ensure their well-being....Although the philosophy underlying state intervention has changed over time, most contemporary statutes dealing with child protection matters, and in particular the Ontario Act, while focusing on the best interest of the child, favour minimal intervention. In recent years, courts have expressed some reluctance to interfere with parental rights, and state intervention has been tolerated only when necessity was demonstrated. This only serves to confirm that the parental interest in bringing up, nurturing and caring for a child, including medical care and moral upbringing, is an individual interest of fundamental importance to our society.

The respondents have argued that the "parental liberty" asserted by the appellants is an obligation owed to the child which does not fall within the scope of s. 7 of the *Charter*. Some decisions seem to give credit to this thesis. In *Re L.(C.P.)* (1988), for example, a case similar to the present one, Riche J. observed:

> The parents have individual rights which they hold as members of society. With respect to their children, they have obligations or responsibilities. The parents have a right to custody of their children while they are children and for as long as they discharge their obligations to those children. The parents maintain a right to attempt to raise their children in the same religious faith as theirs. As between the parents and the children, the parents have few rights and many obligations.

While acknowledging that parents bear responsibilities towards their children, it seems to me that they must enjoy correlative rights to exercise them. The contrary view would not recognize the fundamental importance of choice and personal autonomy in our society. As already stated, the common law has always, in the absence of demonstrated neglect or unsuitability, presumed that parents should make all significant choices affecting their children, and has afforded them a general liberty to do as they choose. This liberty interest is not a parental right tantamount to a right of property in children. (Fortunately, we have distanced ourselves from the ancient juridical conception of children as chattels of their parents). The state is now actively involved in a number of areas traditionally conceived of as properly belonging to the private sphere. Nonetheless, our society is far from having repudiated the privileged role parents exercise in the upbringing of their children. This role translates into a protected sphere of parental decision-making which is rooted in the presumption that parents should make important decisions affecting their children both because parents are more likely to appreciate the best interests of their children and because the state is ill equipped to make such decisions itself. Moreover, individuals have a deep personal interest as parents in fostering the growth of their own children. This is not to say that the state cannot intervene when it considers it necessary to safeguard the child's autonomy or health. But such intervention must be justified. In other words, parental decision-making must receive the protection of the *Charter* in order for state interference to be properly monitored by the courts, and be permitted only when it conforms to the values underlying the *Charter*.

The respondents also argued that the infant's rights were paramount to those of the appellants and, on that basis alone, state intervention was justified....Children undeniably benefit from the *Charter*, most notably in its protection of their rights to life and to the security of their person. As children are unable to assert these, our society presumes that parents will exercise their freedom of choice in a manner that does not offend the rights of their children. If one considers the multitude of decisions parents make daily, it is clear that in practice, state interference in order to balance the rights of parents and children will arise only in exceptional cases. In fact, we must accept that parents can, at times, make decisions contrary to their children's wishes – and rights – as long as they do not exceed the threshold dictated by public policy, in its broad conception. For instance, it would be difficult to deny that a parent can dictate to his or her child the place where he or she will live, or which school he or she will attend. However, the state can properly intervene in situations where parental conduct falls below the socially acceptable threshold. But in doing so, the state is limiting the constitutional rights of parents rather than vindicating the constitutional rights of children....

Once it is decided that the parents have a liberty interest, further balancing of parents' and children's rights should be done in the course of determining whether state interference conforms to the principles of fundamental justice, rather than when defining the scope of the liberty interest. Even assuming that the rights of children can qualify the liberty interest of their parents, that interest exists nonetheless. In the case at bar, the application of the Act deprived the appellants of their right to decide which medical treatment should be administered to their infant. In so doing, the Act has infringed upon the parental "liberty" protected in s. 7 of the *Charter*. I now propose to determine whether this deprivation was made in accordance with the principles of fundamental justice....

An examination of the application of the impugned provisions to the facts of this case amply demonstrates that the legislative scheme, which deprives parents of their right to choose medical treatment for their infant under certain circumstances, is in accordance with the principles of fundamental justice.

Mr Justice Iacobucci, and Justices Major and Cory (concurring):

We have read the reasons of Mr. Justice La Forest, and we agree with the result that there has been no unconstitutional violation of the appellants' rights....However, we respectfully disagree with La Forest J.'s reliance on s. 1 of the *Charter* and the principles of fundamental justice in s. 7 in order to establish the constitutionality of the repealed *Child Welfare Act*. Instead, we conclude that the class of parents caught by [the *Child Welfare Act*] simply cannot benefit from the protection of the liberty interest in s. 7....

We find that the right to liberty embedded in s. 7 does not include a parent's right to deny a child medical treatment that has been adjudged necessary by a medical professional. Although the scope of "liberty" as understood by s. 7 is expansive, it is certainly not all-encompassing....Not all individual activity should immediately qualify as an exercise of "liberty" and hence be *prima facie* entitled to constitutional protection, subject only to the limits consonant with fundamental justice or s. 1....

This is clearly a case where Sheena's right to liberty, security of the person, and potentially even to life is deprived. It is important to note that the abridgment of Sheena's s. 7 rights operates independently from the question whether the parents honestly believe that their refusal to consent to the transfusion is in the best interests of the child, since such a refusal shall, according to the appellants, prevent her from being "defiled in the eyes of God". Whether or not her parents' motivations are well-intentioned, the physical effects upon Sheena of the refusal to transfuse blood are equally deleterious.

We note that La Forest J. holds that "liberty" encompasses the right of parents to have input into the education of their child. In fact, "liberty" may very well permit parents to choose among *equally effective* types of medical treatment for their children, but we do not find it necessary to determine this question in the instant case. We say this because, assuming without deciding that "liberty" has such a reach, it certainly does not extend to protect the appellants in the case at bar. There is simply no room within s. 7 for parents to override the child's right to life and security of the person.

In any event, there is an immense difference between sanctioning some input into a child's education and protecting a parent's right to refuse their children medical treatment that a professional adjudges to be necessary and for which there is no legitimate alternative. The child's right to life must not be so completely subsumed to the parental liberty to make decisions regarding that child. In our view, the best way to ensure this outcome is to view an exercise of parental liberty which seriously endangers the survival of the child as falling outside s. 7.

Our colleague's reasons open the door to the possibility that a violation of a guardian's s. 7 rights will be found should the state deny a guardians his or her right to refuse a child in his or her charge medical treatment *and* should that denial fail to conform with fundamental justice. In the case at bar, Sheena's condition, although believed to be serious, was not sufficiently urgent to prevent the Children's Aid Society from seeking a court-ordered wardship, thereby complying with procedural fundamental justice. But what if Sheena were injured in a car accident and required an immediate blood transfusion to save her life? Even if her parents would have been in agreement that the transfusion was necessary and urgently required, their personal convictions would still likely have compelled them to refuse their daughter the treatment. To this end, this exercise of parental liberty can engender the death of an infant.

We find it counter-intuitive that "parental liberty" would permit a parent to deny a child medical treatment felt to be necessary until some element of procedural fundamental justice is complied with. Although an individual may refuse any medical procedures upon his own person, it is quite another matter to speak for another separate individual, especially when that individual cannot speak for herself and, in Sheena's case, has never spoken for herself. The rights enumerated in the *Charter* are individual rights to which children are clearly entitled in their relationships with the state and all persons – regardless of their status as strangers, friends, relatives, guardians or parents....

The exercise of parental beliefs that grossly invades the "best interests" of the child is not activity protected by the right to "liberty" in s. 7. To hold otherwise would be to risk undermining the ability of the state to exercise its legitimate *parens patriae* jurisdiction and jeopardize the *Charter*'s goal of protecting the most vulnerable members of society. As society becomes increasingly cognizant of the fact that the family is often a very dangerous place for children, the *parens patriae* jurisdiction assumes greater importance. Although there are times when the family should be shielded from the intrusions of the state, Sheena's situation is one in which the state should be readily able to intervene not only to protect the public interest, but also to preserve the security of infants who cannot yet speak for themselves.

R. V. LATIMER

Saskatchewan Court of Appeal

(1995) 128 S.R. 19

At various times, there has been a call to reform Canada's homicide laws to acknowledge that "mercy killing" is morally different from other forms of intentional killing and should not be subjected to the same level of punishment. If a father intentionally kills his young daughter because he wants to spare her a lifetime of unremitting pain, then it might seem outrageous to punish him like any other first degree murderer. But that is how Mr. Latimer described what he did on October 24, 1993.

Mr. Latimer was convicted of first degree murder, based in part on his confession. He then argued before Saskatchewan's Court of Appeal that the mandatory sentence of life imprisonment without eligibility for parole for ten years was "greater than is warranted or necessary, considering the facts of the case and the accused's background". The jury at trial were unanimous in their recommendation that the Court impose a minimum sentence, with parole as soon as possible. Latimer's lawyer asked for a constitutional exemption from the mandatory sentence. Justices Tallis and Bayda came to opposite conclusions, leaving the issue to eventually be decided by the Supreme Court of Canada.

* * * *

Mr. Justice Tallis:

On November 16, 1994, following a jury trial for first degree murder, the appellant Robert Latimer was convicted of second degree murder for the killing of Tracy, his 12 year old daughter. The presiding judge imposed the mandatory sentence of life imprisonment without eligibility for parole for ten years....

In October 1993, Tracy, who was 12 years old, suffered from severe cerebral palsy – a permanent condition caused by brain damage at birth. She was quadriplegic. Her physical handicaps of palsy and quadriplegia were such that she was bedridden for most of the time. Except for some slight head and facial movements she was immobile. She was physically helpless and unable to care for herself. She was in continual pain....

In February 1990, Tracy underwent surgery for the purpose of balancing the muscles around her pelvis. In August 1992 she underwent further surgery to reduce the abnormal curvature in her back. This surgery was successful but problems then developed in her right hip which became dislocated. This caused considerable pain....

Speaking generally, the Latimer family provided constant care for their daughter Tracy. During the period July to October 1993 she was placed in a group home in North Battleford to provide respite for the family particularly while Mrs. Latimer was pregnant.

After Tracy returned home, Kathleen Johnson, a Social Service worker, learned that an application for permanent placement at the group home had been received from the Latimer family. On October 12, 1993 she spoke to the appellant by phone to ascertain more details of the family's application and wishes. During this discussion the appellant advised her that it was not an urgent matter. If there was any immediate opening at the home he was not sure if they wanted a placement.

While in the appellant's care on Sunday, October 24, 1993 Tracy passed away at her family farm home near Wilkie....In this statement, the appellant describes how he removed Tracy from her bed and placed her in the cab of a pickup truck in a shed. He then hooked the hose to the exhaust and placed the other end through the back window of the cab. After he left Tracy exposed to carbon monoxide in the cab for a significant period of time, he determined that she was dead and then placed her back in her bed at the house...the appellant was formally charged with first degree murder....

We think that it is self-evident that the interests involved in the instant case are more substantial, both on an individual and societal level, than those generally involved in the crime of murder.

Section 7 of the *Charter* was enacted for the protection and benefit of all citizens – whether healthy or handicapped. This approach comports with the state's interest in the protection and preservation of human life. Speaking generally, all civilized nations demonstrate their commitment to life by treating homicide as a serious crime. Moreover, many countries including Canada have laws imposing criminal penalties on one who assists another to commit suicide.

But in the context presented here, society has more particular interests at stake. Tracy was not in a position to make an informed and voluntary choice to exercise a hypothetical right to refuse treatment or any other right. Furthermore, this case does not involve medical decisions concerning continuation or termination of life sustaining treatment. Accordingly such bioethical issues are not before the Court for consideration.

We observe that the choice between life and death is a deeply personal decision of obvious and overwhelming finality. Since Tracy was handicapped there is accordingly no evidence of any desire to terminate her own life by withdrawal of hydration or nutrition.

But this case is not about withdrawal of hydration and nutrition to bring about termination of life. The appellant assumed the role of a surrogate decision-maker and in that role he decided to actively terminate Tracy's life. He first considered shooting her and then successfully pursued the alternative path of carbon monoxide poisoning. In so doing, he decided that her quality of life was of such diminished value that she should not live. In our opinion the learned trial judge was correct in concluding that "[l]ife was not kind to Tracy but it was a life that was hers to make of what she could."

In this situation it is a fair inference that such a decision would never have been suggested or considered if Tracy were not handicapped and in extreme pain. This difference in approach between handicapped and non-handicapped children directly reflects a sense that the life of a handicapped child is of significantly less value than the life of a non-handicapped child in extreme pain. A pivotal question to be considered is, "If the child were not permanently disabled, but in extreme pain, would there be any question about making heroic efforts to sustain and maintain life?" If the answer is no, then the decision would appear to be clearly predicated upon the diminished value assigned to the life of a handicapped child. One would not be so inspired by love and compassion to take the life of the non-handicapped child.

Our law does not authorize such surrogate decision-making based on the assessments of the personal worth or social utility of another's life or the value of that life to the individual involved or to others. Our society, through its criminal law, may properly decline to make judgments about the quality of life that a particular individual may enjoy, and simply assert an unqualified interest in the preservation of human life. Surrogate decision-makers are not entitled to arrogate to themselves the life and death decisions under review in this case....

This homicide involves a significant degree of premeditation. The appellant contemplated taking Tracy's life before performing the act that caused her death. It was "intentional" in every sense of the word. Although he did so to spare her further pain, this approach ignores many other relevant considerations. As a self-appointed surrogate decision-maker, he was not entitled to take the criminal law into his own hands and terminate her life. Furthermore, society, through the operation of the criminal law is entitled to guard against potential abuses in such situations. Accordingly statutory penalties are fashioned to meet the broad objectives and purposes of the criminal law.

In the circumstances of this case we reject the appellant's request for a constitutional exemption from the prescribed sentences for second degree murder. It is open to Parliament to modify the existing law by appropriate legislation that establishes sentencing criteria for "mercy" killing. In the meantime, it is not for the Court to pass on the wisdom of Parliament with respect to the range of penalties to be imposed on those found guilty of murder....We dismiss the appellant's application for a constitutional exemption and affirm the sentence imposed by the learned trial judge.

Chief Justice Bayda (dissenting):

The appellant is a typical, salt of the earth, 42 year-old prairie farmer, born and raised on a farm near Wilkie, Saskatchewan...[After their marriage] Mrs. Latimer joined the appellant in his farming operation and they lived their entire married lives on the farm. Four children were born to them: Tracy in 1980, a son in 1983, another daughter in 1985 and their youngest in 1993. The appellant is a devoted family man, devoted to his wife and his children. He is a loving, caring, nurturing person who actively participated in the daily care of the children and in particular the caring and nurturing of Tracy....

The appellant has no criminal record. He poses no risk to society and requires no rehabilitation. He enjoys a very healthy and wholesome reputation in the community.

The appellant did not commit an irrational, depraved, brutal, sordid killing having its genesis in and motivated by some base impulse or emotion such as hate, anger, greed, self-gratification, jealousy, selfishness or some combination of those vices, all of which are considered by people to be negative and destructive. On the contrary, the workings of the appellant's intellect and will reveal a mind conditioned day in and day out, week in and week out, month in and month out, year in and year out, for a period of 13 years by his disabled daughter's pain culminating in what appears to be at the very least a severe preoccupation or an obsession with that pain....

It is a fair inference and an important one to keep in mind that she was not put into her father's truck because she was disabled. She was put there because of her pain, something very different from her disability. She was put there because her father loved her too much to watch her suffer. While the killing was a purposeful one, it had its genesis in altruism and was motivated by love, mercy and compassion or a combination of those virtues, generally considered by people to be life-enhancing and affirmative.

As for the physical components of the act, they did not produce a violent, painful killing. The act showed no heinousness or abnormal or aberrant behaviour. Rather, the act was committed in a gentle, painless and compassionate way.

The actor himself was not a murderous thug, devoid of conscience, whose life has been one of violence, greed, contempt for the law and total disrespect for human beings. On the contrary, the actor was a nurturing, caring, giving, respectful, law-abiding responsible parent of the victim....

For the foregoing reasons, I find that the appropriate and just remedy for the violation of the appellant's s. 12 *Charter* right is a constitutional exemption from the mandatory minimum sentence requirement for second degree murder....In the result, I would allow the appeal from sentence, set aside the sentence imposed by the trial judge and direct the parties to appear before this Court at a time to be designated to make their submissions respecting the sentence that ought to be imposed without regard to the mandatory minimum sentence requirements.

V PROCEDURAL JUSTICE

Although political philosophers since Aristotle have recognized several kinds of justice, these cases look at the justice that everyone agrees is fundamental to the law – *procedural justice,* the justice of means, rather than ends. "The law must be fairly applied in each case". "Everyone has the right to be heard and to defend themselves". "Everyone has the right to unbiased treatment by courts and administrative agencies". These are some of the principles that Canadian lawyers have traditionally called the "rules of natural justice" ("due process" in the US).

Section 7 of the *Charter* guarantees that everyone has – in addition to the right to life, liberty and security of the person – "the right not to be deprived thereof except in accordance with the principles of fundamental justice". There is no dispute that, at least, the phrase "principles of fundamental justice" refers to natural justice; but as the cases below suggest, the phrase may refer to additional, and more powerful, principles.

RONCARELLI V. DUPLESSIS

Supreme Court of Canada

[1959] S.C.R. 121

In this very famous case, the Supreme Court of Canada was asked whether there are any implicit, legal limitations on the exercise of what appears to be the absolute discretion of an administrative official. In particular, if a statute gives an official the absolute power to grant, refuse or cancel liquor licences as he or she sees fit, and then proceeds to peremptorily cancel someone's licence on dubious grounds, does the victim of this treatment have any legal recourse? In arguing, for the majority, that discretion is never so absolute that it can be exercised arbitrarily, capriciously, or for purposes irrelevant to the nature of the legislation, Mr. Justice Rand helped to define the scope of procedural justice in Canadian law.

* * * *

Mr. Justice Rand and Justice Judson:

The material facts from which my conclusion is drawn are these. The appellant was the proprietor of a restaurant in a busy section of Montreal which in 1946 through its transmission to him from his father had been continuously licensed for the sale of liquor for approximately 34 years; he is of good education and repute and the restaurant was of a superior class. On December 4th of that year, while his application for annual renewal was before the Liquor Commission, the existing licence was cancelled and his application for renewal rejected, to which was added a declaration by the respondent [Mr. Maurice Duplessis, then Prime Minister and Attorney-General of Quebec] that no future licence would ever issue to him. These primary facts took place in the following circumstances.

For some years the appellant [Mr. Frank Roncarelli] had been an adherent of a rather militant Christian religious sect known as the Witnesses of Jehovah. Their ideology condemns the established church institutions and stresses the absolute and exclusive personal relation of the individual to the Deity without human intermediation or intervention.

The first impact of their proselytizing zeal upon the Roman Catholic church and community in Quebec, as might be expected, produced a violent reaction. Meetings were forcibly broken up, property damaged, individuals ordered out of communities, in one case out of the Province, and generally, within the cities and towns, bitter controversy aroused. The work of the Witnesses was carried on both by word of mouth and by the distribution of printed matter, the latter including two periodicals known as "The Watch Tower" and "Awake", sold at a small price.

In 1945 the provincial authorities began to take steps to bring an end to what was considered insulting and offensive to the religious beliefs and feelings of the Roman Catholic population. Large scale arrests were made of young men and women, by whom the publications mentioned were being held out for sale, under local by-laws requiring a licence for peddling any kind of wares. Altogether almost one thousand of such charges were laid. The penalty involved in Montreal, where most of the arrests took place, was a fine of $40, and as the Witnesses disputed liability, bail was in all cases resorted to.

The appellant, being a person of some means, was accepted by the Recorder's Court as bail without question, and up to November 12, 1946 he had gone security in about 380 cases, some of the accused being involved in repeated offences. Up to this time there had been no suggestion of impropriety: the security of the appellant was taken as so satisfactory that at times, to avoid delay when he was absent from the city, recognizances were signed by him in blank and kept ready for completion by the Court officials. The reason for the accumulation of charges was the doubt that they could be sustained in law. Apparently the legal officers of Montreal, acting in concert with those of the Province, had come to an agreement with the attorney for the Witnesses to have a test case proceeded with. Pending that, however, there was no stoppage of the sale of the tracts and this became the annoying circumstance that produced the volume of proceedings....

At no time did [Roncarelli] take any part in the distribution of the tracts: he was an adherent of the group but nothing more. It was shown that he had leased to another member premises in Sherbrooke which were used as a hall for carrying on religious meetings: but it is unnecessary to do more than mention that fact to reject it as having no bearing on the issues raised. Beyond the giving of bail and being an adherent, the appellant is free from any relation that could be tortured into a badge of character pertinent to his fitness or unfitness to hold a liquor licence.

The mounting resistance that stopped the surety bail sought other means of crushing the propagandist invasion and among the circumstances looked into was the situation of the appellant. Admittedly an adherent, he was enabling these protagonists to be at large to carry on their campaign of publishing what they believed to be the Christian truth as revealed by the Bible; he was also the holder of a liquor licence, a "privilege" granted by the Province, the profits from which, as it was seen by the authorities, he was using to promote the disturbance of settled beliefs and arouse community disaffection generally. Following discussions between the then Mr. Archambault, as the personality of the Liquor Commission, and the chief prosecuting officer in Montreal, the former, on or about November 21st, telephoned to the respondent, advised him of those facts, and queried what should be done. Mr. Duplessis answered that the matter was serious and that the identity of the person furnishing bail and the liquor licensee should be put beyond doubt. A few days later, that identity being established through a private investigator, Mr. Archambault again communicated with the respondent and, as a result of what passed between them, the licence, as of December 4, 1946, was revoked.

In the meantime, about November 25, 1946, a blasting answer had come from the Witnesses. In an issue of one of the periodicals, under the heading "Quebec's Burning Hate", was a searing denunciation of what was alleged to be the savage persecution of Christian believers. Immediately instructions were sent out from the department of the Attorney-General ordering the confiscation of the issue and proceedings were taken against one Boucher charging him with publication of a seditious libel.

It is then wholly as a private citizen, an adherent of a religious group, holding a liquor licence and furnishing bail to arrested persons for no other purpose than to enable them to be released from detention pending the determination of the charges against them, and with no other relevant considerations to be taken into account, that he is involved in the issues of this controversy.

The complementary state of things is equally free from doubt. From the evidence of Mr. Duplessis and Mr. Archambault alone, it appears that the action taken by the latter as the General Manager and sole member of the Commission was dictated by Mr. Duplessis as Attorney-General and Prime Minister of the Province; that that step was taken as a means of bringing to a halt the activities of the Witnesses, to punish the appellant for the part he had played not only by revoking the existing licence but in declaring him barred from one "forever", and to warn others that they similarly would be stripped of provincial "privileges" if they persisted in any activity directly or indirectly related to the Witnesses and to the objectionable campaign. The respondent felt that action to be his duty, something which his conscience demanded of him; and as representing the Provincial Government his decision became automatically that of Mr. Archambault and the Commission....

In these circumstances, when the *de facto* power of the Executive over its appointees at will to such a statutory public function is exercised deliberately and intentionally to destroy the vital business interests of a citizen, is there any legal redress by him against the person so acting?...

The field of licensed occupations and businesses of this nature is steadily becoming of greater concern to citizens generally. It is a matter of vital importance that a public administration that can refuse to allow a person to enter or continue a calling which, in the absence of regulation, would be free and legitimate, should be conducted with complete impartiality and integrity; and that the grounds for refusing or cancelling a permit should unquestionably be such and such only as are incompatible with the purposes envisaged by the statute: the duty of a Commission is to serve those purposes and those only. A decision to deny or cancel such a privilege lies within the "discretion" of the Commission; but that means that decision is to be based upon a weighing of considerations pertinent to the object of the administration.

In public regulation of this sort there is no such thing as absolute and untrammelled "discretion", that is that action can be taken on any ground or for any reason that can be suggested to the mind of the administrator; no legislative Act can, without express language, be taken to contemplate an unlimited arbitrary power, exercisable for any purpose, however capricious or irrelevant, regardless of the nature or purpose of the statute. Fraud and corruption in the Commission may not be mentioned in such statutes but they are always implied as exceptions. "Discretion" necessarily implies good faith in discharging public duty; there is always a perspective within which a statute is intended to operate; and any clear departure from its lines or objects is just as objectionable as fraud or corruption. Could an applicant be refused a permit because he had been born in another Province, or because of the colour of his hair? The ordinary language of the Legislature cannot be so distorted.

To deny or revoke a permit because a citizen exercises an unchallengeable right totally irrelevant to the sale of liquor in a restaurant is equally beyond the scope of the discretion conferred. There was here not only revocation of the existing permit but a declaration of a future, definitive disqualification of the appellant to obtain one: it was to be "forever". This purports to divest his citizenship status of its incident of membership in the class of those of the public to whom such a privilege could be extended. Under the statutory language here, that is not competent to the Commission and *a fortiori* to the Government or the respondent. There is here an administrative tribunal which, in certain respects, is to act in a judicial manner;...what could be more malicious than to punish this licensee for having done what he had an absolute right to do in a matter utterly irrelevant to the *Alcoholic Liquor Act?* Malice in the proper sense is simply acting for a reason and purpose knowingly foreign to the administration, to which was added here the element of intentional punishment by what was virtually vocation outlawry.

It may be difficult if not impossible in cases generally to demonstrate a breach of this public duty in the illegal purpose served; there may be no means, even if proceedings against the Commission were permitted by the Attorney-General, as here they were refused, of compelling the Commission to justify a refusal or revocation or to give reasons for its action; on these questions I make no observation; but in the case before us that difficulty is not present: the reasons are openly avowed.

The act of the respondent through the instrumentality of the Commission brought about a breach of an implied public statutory duty toward the appellant; it was a gross abuse of legal power expressly intended to punish him for an act wholly irrelevant to the statute, a punishment which inflicted on him, as it was intended to do, the destruction of his economic life as a restaurant keeper within the Province. Whatever maybe the immunity of the Commission or its member from an action for damages, there is none in the respondent. He was under no duty in relation to the appellant and his act was an intrusion upon the functions of a statutory body. The injury done by him was a fault engaging liability within the principles of the underlying public law of Quebec. That, in the presence of expanding administrative regulation of economic activities, such a step and its consequences are to be suffered by the victim without recourse or remedy, that an administration according to law is to be superseded by action dictated by and according to the arbitrary likes, dislikes and irrelevant purposes of public officers acting beyond their duty,would signalize the beginning of disintegration of the rule of law as a fundamental postulate of our constitutional structure. An administration of licences on the highest level of fair and impartial treatment to all may be forced to follow the practices of "first come, first served", which makes the strictest observance of equal responsibility to all of even greater importance; at this stage of developing government it would be a danger of high consequence to tolerate such a departure from good faith in executing the legislative purpose. It should be added, however, that principle is not, by this language, intended to be extended to ordinary governmental employment: with that we are not here concerned.

It was urged by Mr. Beaulieu that the respondent, as the incumbent of an office of state, so long as he was proceeding in "good faith", was free to act in a matter of this kind virtually as he pleased. The office of Attorney-General traditionally and by statute carries duties that relate to advising the Executive, including here, administrative bodies, enforcing the public law and directing the administration of justice. In any decision of the statutory body in this case, he had no part to play beyond giving advice on legal questions arising. In that role his action should have been limited to advice on the validity of a revocation for such a reason or purpose and what that advice should have been does not seem to me to admit of any doubt. To pass from this limited scope of action to that of bringing about a step by the Commission beyond the bounds prescribed by the Legislature for its exclusive action converted what was done into his personal act.

"Good faith" in this context, applicable both to the respondent and the General Manager, means carrying out the statute according to its intent and for its purpose; it means good faith in acting with a rational appreciation of that intent and purpose and not with an improper intent and for an alien purpose; it does not mean for the purposes of punishing a person for exercising an unchallengeable right; it does not mean arbitrarily and illegally attempting to divest a citizen of an incident of his civil status.

REFERENCE RE SECTION 94(2) OF THE MOTOR VEHICLE ACT

Supreme Court of Canada

[1985] 2 S.C.R. 486

British Columbia's *Motor Vehicle Act* made it an offence, punishable by fine or imprisonment, to drive when one's licence was suspended or when one was otherwise prohibited from driving. The problem was that this was an "absolute liability" offence, which meant that to prove guilt the Crown did not have to show that the driver actually knew of the suspension or prohibition (for more on these kinds of offences see *R. v. Sault Ste. Marie* in Part VI). Did such an offence offend the "principles of fundamental justice" guaranteed by section 7 of the *Charter?*

* * * *

Mr. Justice Lamer, Chief Justice Dickson and Justices Beetz, Chouinard and LeDain:

The term "principles of fundamental justice" is not a right, but a qualifier of the right not to be deprived of life, liberty and security of the person; its function is to set the parameters of that right.

Sections 8 to 14 address specific deprivations of the "right" to life, liberty and security of the person in breach of the principles of fundamental justice, and as such, violations of s. 7. They are therefore illustrative of the meaning, in criminal or penal law, of "principles of fundamental justice"; they represent principles which have been recognized by the common law, the international conventions and by the very fact of entrenchment in the *Charter,* as essential elements of a system for the administration of justice which is founded upon a belief in the dignity and worth of the human person and the rule of law.

Consequently, the principles of fundamental justice are to be found in the basic tenets and principles, not only of our judicial process, but also of the other components of our legal system.

We should not be surprised to find that many of the principles of fundamental justice are procedural in nature. Our common law has largely been a law of remedies and procedures and, as Frankfurter J. wrote in *McNabb v. U.S.* (1942), "the history of liberty has largely been the history of observance of procedural safeguards". This is not to say, however, that the principles of fundamental justice are limited solely to procedural guarantees. Rather, the proper approach to the determination of the principles of fundamental justice is quite simply one in which, as Professor L. Tremblay has written, "future growth will be based on historical roots".

Whether any given principle may be said to be a principle of fundamental justice within the meaning of s. 7 will rest upon an analysis of the nature, sources, *rationale* and essential role of that principle within the judicial process and in our legal system, as it evolves.

Consequently, those words cannot be given any exhaustive content or simple enumerative definition, but will take on concrete meaning as the courts address alleged violations of s. 7.

I now turn to such an analysis of the principle of *mens rea* and absolute liability offences in order to determine the question which has been put to the court in the present reference.

It has from time immemorial been part of our system of laws that the innocent not be punished. This principle has long been recognized as an essential element of a system for the administration of justice which is founded upon a belief in the dignity and worth of the human person and on the rule of law. It is so old that its first enunciation was in Latin *actus non facit reum nisi mens sit rea....*

In my view, it is because absolute liability offends the principles of fundamental justice that this Court created presumptions against legislatures having intended to enact offences of a regulatory nature falling within that category. This is not to say, however, and to that extent I am in agreement with the Court of Appeal, that, as a result, absolute liability *per se* offends s. 7 of the *Charter.*

A law enacting an absolute liability offence will violate s. 7 of the *Charter* only if and to the extent that it has the potential of depriving of life, liberty or security of the person.

Obviously, imprisonment (including probation orders) deprives persons of their liberty. An offence has the potential as of the moment it is open to the judge to impose imprisonment. There is no need that punishment, as in s. 94(2) [of the B.C. *Motor Vehicle Act]*, be made mandatory.

I am therefore of the view that the combination of imprisonment and of absolute liability violates s. 7 of the *Charter* and can only be salvaged if the authorities demonstrate under s. 1 that such a deprivation of liberty in breach of those principles of fundamental justice is, in a free and democratic society, under the circumstances, a justified reasonable limit to one's rights under s. 7.

[Mr. Justice Lamer went on to find that this violation of s. 7 was not saved by s. 1 of the *Charter.*]

Madame Justice Wilson: (concurring):

Unlike my colleague, I do not think that ss. 8 to 14 of the *Charter* shed much light on the interpretation of the phrase "in accordance with the principles of fundamental justice" as used in s. 7. I find them very helpful as illustrating facets of the right to life, liberty and security of the person. I am not ready at this point, however, to equate unreasonableness or arbitrariness or tardiness as used in some of these sections with a violation of the principles of fundamental justice as used in s. 7. Delay, for example, may be explained away or excused or justified on a number of grounds under s. 1. I prefer, therefore, to treat these sections as self-standing provisions, as indeed they are.

I approach the interpretive problem raised by the phrase "the principles of fundamental justice" on the assumption that the legislature was very familiar with the concepts of "natural justice" and "due process" and the way in which those phrases had been judicially construed and applied. Yet they chose neither. Instead, they chose the phrase "the principles of fundamental justice". What is "fundamental justice"? We know what "fundamental principles" are. They are the basic, bedrock principles that underpin a system. What would "fundamental principles of justice" mean? And would it mean something different from "principles of fundamental justice"? I am not entirely sure. We have been left by the legislature with a conundrum. I would conclude, however, that if the citizen is to be guaranteed his right to life, liberty and security of the person – surely one of the most basic rights in a free and democratic society – then he certainly should not be deprived of it by means of a violation of a fundamental tenet of our justice system.

It has been argued very forcefully that s. 7 is concerned only with procedural injustice but I have difficulty with that proposition. There is absolutely nothing in the section to support such a limited construction. Indeed, it is hard to see why one's life and liberty should be protected against procedural injustice and not against substantive injustice in a *Charter* that opens with the declaration:

Whereas Canada is founded upon principles that recognize the supremacy of God and the rule of law;

[and sets out the guarantee in broad and general terms as follows:]

1. The *Canadian Charter of Rights and Freedoms* guarantees the rights and freedoms set out in it subject only to such reasonable limits

prescribed by law as can be demonstrably justified in a free and democratic society.

I cannot think that the guaranteed right in s. 7 which is to be subject *only* to limits which are reasonable and justifiable in a free and democratic society can be taken away by the violation of a principle considered fundamental to our justice system. Certainly, the rule of law acknowledged in the preamble as one of the foundations on which our society is built is more than mere procedure. It will be for the courts to determine the principles which fall under the rubric "the principles of fundamental justice". Obviously, not all principles of law are covered by the phrase; only those which are basic to our system of justice.

I have grave doubts that the dichotomy between substance and procedure which may have served a useful purpose in other areas of the law such as administrative law and private international law should be imported into s. 7 of the *Charter*. In many instances the line between substance and procedure is a very narrow one. For example, the presumption of innocence protected by s. 11(d) of the *Charter* may be viewed as a substantive principle of fundamental justice but it clearly has both a substantive and a procedural aspect. Indeed, any rebuttable presumption of fact may be viewed as procedural, as going primarily to the allocation of the burden of proof. Nevertheless, there is also an interest of substance to be protected by the presumption, namely, the right of an accused to be treated as innocent until proved otherwise by the Crown. This right has both a societal and an individual aspect and is clearly fundamental to our justice system. I see no particular virtue in isolating its procedural from its substantive elements or *vice versa* for purposes of s.7.

RE SINGH AND MINISTER OF EMPLOYMENT AND IMMI-GRATION

Supreme Court of Canada

[1985] 1 S.C.R. 177

Sometimes, purely "procedural" rights are considered unimportant. The *Re Singh* case shows how significant and potentially powerful these rights really are. Mr. Singh and others challenged the procedural mechanisms in Canada's *Immigration Act, 1976* that were used to adjudicate applications for "convention refugee" status. If individuals claiming to be convention refugees are refused that status, then they have to convince the Immigration Appeal Board that they have a "well-founded fear of persecution for reasons of...political opinion." Singh and others objected that the procedures for this step in the process did not provide them with an adequate opportunity to state their case or to know the case against them. Agreeing that they had been unjustly treated on the basis of her interpretation of the rights included in s. 7, Madame Justice Wilson also discussed the issue of what rights *non-Canadians* have under Canadian law.

* * * *

Madame Justice Wilson, Chief Justice Dickson and Justice Lamer:

The Immigration Appeal Board's duties in considering an application for redetermination of a refugee status claim are set out in s. 71 which reads as follows:

71(1) Where the Board receives an application referred to in subsection 70(2), it shall forthwith consider the application and if, on the basis of such consideration, it is of the opinion that there are reasonable grounds to believe that a claim could, upon the hearing of the application, be established, it shall allow the application to proceed, and in any other case it shall refuse to allow the application to proceed and shall thereupon determine that the person is not a Convention refugee.

(2) Where pursuant to subsection (1) the Board allows an application to proceed, it shall notify the Minister of the time and place

where the application is to be heard and afford the Minister a reasonable opportunity to be heard.

(3) Where the Board has made its determination as to whether or not a person is a Convention refugee, it shall, in writing, inform the Minister and the applicant of its decision.

(4) The Board may, and at the request of the applicant or the Minister shall, give reasons for its determination.

If the board were to determine pursuant to s. 71(1) that the application should be allowed to proceed, the parties are all agreed that the hearing which would take place pursuant to s. 71(2) would be a *quasi*-judicial one to which full natural justice would apply. The board is not, however, empowered by the terms of the statute to allow a redetermination hearing to proceed in every case. It may only do so if "it is of the opinion that there are reasonable grounds to believe that a claim could, upon the hearing of the application, be established...." In *Re Kwiatkowsky and Minister of Employment & Immigration* (1982), this court interpreted those words as requiring the board to allow the claim to proceed only if it is of the view that "it is more likely than not" that the applicant will be able to establish his claim at the hearing....

The substance of the appellants' case, as I understand it, is that they did not have a fair opportunity to present their refugee status claims or to know the case they had to meet. I do not think there is any basis for suggesting that the procedures set out in the *Immigration Act, 1976* were not followed correctly in the adjudication of these individuals' claims. Nor do I believe that there is any basis for interpreting the relevant provisions of the *Immigration Act, 1976* in a way that provides a significantly greater degree of procedural fairness or natural justice than I have set out in the preceding discussion. The Act by its terms seems to preclude this. Accordingly, if the appellants are to succeed, I believe that it must be on the basis that the *Charter* requires the court to override Parliament's decision to exclude the kind of procedural fairness sought by the appellants.

(1) Are the Appellants Entitled to the Protection of s. 7 of the Charter?

Section 7 of the *Charter* states that "Everyone has the right to life, liberty and security of the person and the right not to be deprived thereof except in accordance with the principles of fundamental justice". Counsel for the appellants contrasts the use of the word "Everyone" in s. 7 with the language used in other sections, for example, "Every citizen of Canada" in s. 3, "Every citizen of Canada and every person who has the status of a permanent resident of Canada" in s. 6(2) and "Citizens of Canada" in s. 23. He concludes that "Everyone" in s. 7 is intended to encompass a broader class of persons than citizens and permanent residents. Counsel for the Minister concedes that "everyone" is sufficiently broad to include the appellants in its compass and I am prepared to accept that the term includes every human being who is physically present in Canada and by virtue of such presence amenable to Canadian law.

That premise being accepted, the question then becomes whether the rights the appellants seek to assert fall within the scope of s. 7. Counsel for the Minister does not concede this. He submits that the exclusion or removal of the appellants from Canada would not infringe "the right to life, liberty and security of the person"....

It seems to me that in attempting to decide whether the appellants have been deprived of the right to life, liberty and security of the person within the meaning of s. 7 of the *Charter*, we must begin by determining what rights the appellants have under the *Immigration Act, 1976.* As noted earlier, s. 5(1) of the Act excludes from persons other than those described in s. 4 the right to come into or remain in Canada. The appellants therefore do not have such a right. However, the Act does accord a Convention refugee certain rights which it does not provide to others, namely, the right to a determination from the Minister based on proper principles as to whether a permit should issue entitling him to enter and remain in Canada (ss. 4(2) and 37); the right not to be returned to a country where his life or freedom would be threatened (s. 55); and the right to appeal a removal order or a deportation order made against him (s. 72(2)(a), (b) and (3)).

We must therefore ask ourselves whether the deprivation of these rights constitutes a deprivation of the right to life, liberty and security of the person within the meaning of s. 7 of the *Charter.* Even if we accept the "single right" theory advanced by counsel for the Minister in interpreting s. 7, I think we must recognize that the "right" which is articulated in s. 7 has three elements: life, liberty and security of the person. As I understand the "single right" theory, it is not suggested that there must be a deprivation of all three of these elements before an individual is deprived of his "right" under s. 7. In other words, I believe that it is consistent with the "single right" theory advanced by counsel to suggest that a deprivation of the appellants' "security of the person", for example, would constitute a deprivation of their "right" under s. 7, whether or not it can also be said that they have been deprived of their lives or liberty. Rather, as I understand it, the "single right" theory is advanced in support of a narrow construction of the words "life", "liberty" and "security of the person" as different aspects of a single concept rather than as separate concepts each of which must be construed independently....

To return to the facts before the court, it will be recalled that a Convention refugee is by definition a person who has a well-founded fear of persecution in the country from which he is fleeing. In my view, to deprive him of the avenues open to him under the Act to escape from that fear of persecution must, at the least, *impair* his right to life, liberty and security of the person in the narrow sense advanced by counsel for the Minister. The question, however, is whether such an impairment constitutes a "deprivation" under s. 7.

It must be acknowledged, for example, that even if a Convention refugee's fear of persecution is a well-founded one, it does not automatically follow that he will be deprived of his life or his liberty if he is returned to his homeland. Can it be said that Canadian officials have deprived a Convention refugee of his right to life, liberty and security of the person if he is wrongfully returned to a country where death, imprisonment or another form of persecution *may* await him? There may be some merit in counsel's submission that closing off the avenues of escape provided by the Act does not *per se* deprive a Convention refugee of the right to life or to liberty. It may result in his being deprived of life or liberty by others, but it is not certain that this will happen.

I cannot, however, accept the submission of counsel for the Minister that the denial of the rights possessed by a Convention refugee under the Act does not constitute a deprivation of his security of the person. Like "liberty", the phrase "security of the person" is capable of a broad range of meaning. The phrase "security of the person" is found in s. 1(a) of the *Canadian Bill of Rights* and its interpretation in that context might have assisted us in its proper interpretation under the *Charter.* Unfortunately, no clear meaning of the words emerges from the case law....The Law Reform Commission, in its Working Paper No. 26, *Medical Treatment and Criminal Law* (1980) suggested at p. 6 that:

> "The right to security of the person means not only protection of one's physical integrity, but the provision of necessaries for its support".

The Commission went on to describe the provision of necessaries in terms of art. 25, para. 1 of the *Universal Declaration of Human Rights* (1948) which reads:

Every one has the right to a standard of living adequate for the health and well-being of himself and of his family, including food, clothing, housing and medical care and necessary social services, and the right to security in the event of unemployment, sickness, disability, widowhood, old age, or other lack of livelihood in circumstances beyond his control.

Commentators have advocated the adoption of a similarly broad conception of "security of the person" in the interpretation of s. 7 of the *Charter.*

For purposes of the present appeal it is not necessary, in my opinion, to consider whether such an expansive approach to "security of the person" in s. 7 of the *Charter* should be taken. It seems to me that even if one adopts the narrow approach advocated by counsel for the Minister, "security of the person" must encompass freedom from threat of physical punishment or suffering as well as freedom from such punishment itself. I note particularly that a Convention refugee has the right under s. 55 of the Act not to "...be removed from Canada to a country where his life or freedom would be threatened...". In my view, the denial of such a right must amount to a deprivation of security of the person within the meaning of s. 7....

(2) Is Fundamental Justice Denied by the Procedures for the Determination of Convention Refugee Status Set out in the Act?

All counsel were agreed that at a minimum the concept of "fundamental justice" as it appears in s. 7 of the *Charter* includes the notion of procedural fairness articulated by Fauteux C.J.C. in *Duke v. The Queen* (1972):

Under s. 2(e) of the *Bill of Rights* no law of Canada shall be construed or applied so as to deprive him of "a fair hearing in accordance with the principles of fundamental justice". Without attempting to formulate any final definition of these words, I would take them to mean, generally, that the tribunal which adjudicates upon his rights must act fairly, in good faith, without bias and in a judicial temper, and must give to him the opportunity adequately to state his case.

Do the procedures set out in the Act for the adjudication of refugee status claims meet this test of procedural fairness? Do they provide an adequate opportunity for a refugee claimant to state his case and know the case he has to meet? This seems to be the question we have to answer and, in approaching it, I am prepared to accept [counsel for the Ministry] Mr. Bowie's submission that procedural fairness may demand different things in different contexts. Thus it is possible that an oral hearing before the decision-maker is not required in every case in which s. 7 of the *Charter is* called into play. However, I must confess to some difficulty in reconciling Mr. Bowie's argument that an oral hearing is not required in the context of this case with the interpretation he seeks to put on s. 7. If "the right to life, liberty and security of the person" is properly construed as relating only to matters such as death, physical liberty and physical punishment, it would seem on the surface at least that these are matters of such fundamental importance that procedural fairness would invariably require an oral hearing. I am prepared, nevertheless, to accept for present purposes that written submissions may be an adequate substitute for an oral hearing in appropriate circumstances .

I should note, however, that even if hearings based on written submissions are consistent with the principles of fundamental justice for some purposes, they will not be satisfactory for all purposes. In particular, I am of the view that where a serious issue of credibility is involved, fundamental justice requires that credibility be determined on the basis of an oral hearing. Appellate courts are well aware of the inherent weakness of written transcripts where questions of credibility are at stake and thus are extremely loath to review the findings of tribunals which have had the benefit of hearing the testimony of witnesses in person. I find it difficult to conceive of a situation in which compliance with fundamental justice could be achieved by a tribunal making significant findings of credibility solely on the basis of written submissions.

As I have suggested, the absence of an oral hearing need not be inconsistent with fundamental justice in every case. My greatest concern about the procedural scheme envisaged by ss. 45 to 58 and 70 and 71 of the *Immigration Act, 1976* is not, therefore, with the absence of an oral hearing in and of itself, but with the inadequacy of the opportunity the scheme provides for a refugee claimant to state his case and know the case he has to meet. Mr. Bowie argued that since the procedure under s. 45 was an administrative one, it was quite proper for the Minister and the Refugee Status Advisory Committee to take into account policy considerations and information about world affairs to which the refugee claimant had no opportunity to respond. However, in my view the proceedings before the Immigration Appeal Board were *quasi*-judicial and the board was not entitled to rely on material outside the record which the refugee claimant himself submitted on his application for redetermination. Mr. Bowie submitted that there was no case against the refugee claimant at that stage; it was merely his responsibility to make a written submission which demonstrated on the balance of probabilities that he would be able to establish his claim at a hearing. If the applicant failed to bring forward the requisite facts his claim would not be allowed to proceed, but there was nothing fundamentally unfair in this procedure.

It seems to me that the basic flaw in Mr. Bowie's characterization of the procedure under ss. 70 and 71 is his description of the procedure as non-adversarial. It is in fact highly adversarial but the adversary, the Minister, is waiting in the wings. What the Board has before it is a determination by the Minister based in part on information and policies to which the applicant has no means of access that the applicant for redetermination is not a Convention refugee. The applicant is entitled to submit whatever relevant material he wishes to the Board but he still faces the hurdle of having to establish to the Board that on the balance of probabilities the Minister was wrong. Moreover, he must do this without any knowledge of the Minister's case beyond the rudimentary reasons which the Minister has decided to give him in rejecting his claim. It is this aspect of the procedures set out in the Act which I find impossible to reconcile with the requirements of "fundamental justice" as set out in s. 7 of the *Charter*....

Under the Act as it presently stands, [moreover], a refugee claimant may never have the opportunity to make an effective challenge to the information or policies which underlie the Minister's decision to reject his claim. Because s. 71(1) requires the Immigration Appeal Board to reject an application for redetermination unless it is of the view that it is more likely than not that the applicant will usually be rejected before the refugee claimant has had an opportunity to discover the Minister's case against him in the context of a hearing. Indeed, given the fact that s. 71(1) resolves any doubt as to whether or not there should be a hearing against the refugee claimant, I find it difficult to see how a successful challenge to the accuracy of the undisclosed information upon which the Minister's decision is based could ever be launched.

I am accordingly of the view that the procedures for determination of refugee status claims as set out in the *Immigration Act, 1976* do not accord refugee claimants fundamental justice in the adjudication of those claims and are thus incompatible with s. 7 of the *Charter*....

CAROSELLA V. THE QUEEN

Supreme Court of Canada

[1997] 1 S.C.R. 80

In order to defence oneself against a criminal charge one needs relevant evidence. It has long been held that the crown cannot keep evidence that it has in its possession from the accused, especially if that evidence tends to exculpate. A failure of "disclosure" by the Crown could result in a stay of proceeding which, in practice, could mean that the accused is set free. Generally speaking, for centuries, courts have insisted that no obstacles should be placed before the accused that might hinder his or her right to "make full answer and defence". But does the duty to disclose potential evidence apply to someone other than the Crown?

In this case, the accused was charged with gross indecency. Shortly before laying the charge, the victim sought counseling from a social worker at a government-funded sexual assault crisis centre. When the defence made an application to have the notes of that interview released to them as evidence, it was found that the centre, in order to maintain the privacy of its clients and to ensure that women are not dissuaded from seeking their help, routinely shred notes of such interviews. The accused then brought this action claiming that his trial is procedurally unjust because, without those notes, he could not adequately defend himself.

* * * *

Mr. Justice Sopinka and Chief Justice Lamer and Justices Cory, Iacobucci and Major:

This appeal requires the court to determine the appropriate response of a trial court to the deliberate destruction of evidence which may be relevant to the defence of an accused person. The trial judge found that notes of interviews with the complainant conducted before she laid a charge of gross indecency were relevant material and that this destruction deprived the appellant of the right to make full answer and defence in breach of his constitutional rights. The trial judge ordered a stay of proceedings. The Court of Appeal reversed the trial judge and the appeal to this court is, therefore, as of right.

Was there a Breach of the Right to Full Answer and Defence?

The entitlement of an accused person to production [of documents] either from the Crown or third parties is a constitutional right. Breach of this right entitles the accused person to a remedy under s. 24(1) of the *Charter*. Remedies range from one or several adjournments to a stay of proceedings. To require the accused to show that the conduct of his or her defence was prejudiced would foredoom any application for even the most modest remedy where the material has not been produced. It would require the accused to show how the defence would be affected by the absence of material which the accused has not seen.

It is immaterial that the right to disclosure is not explicitly listed as one of the components of the principles of fundamental justice. That is true as well of the right to make full answer and defence and other rights. The components of the right cannot be separated from the right itself. An analogy can be made to the s. 10(b) right to counsel. Although s. 10(b) of the *Charter* makes no mention of the right to be informed of the availability of legal aid (or its equivalent), we have treated this requirement as a component of the s. 10(b) guarantee. As a result, an accused can satisfy the court that he or she was denied his or her s. 10(b) right to counsel as a result of the failure of the police to inform him or her as to the availability of legal aid. There is no further onus imposed on the accused to show that, in addition to the fact that his corollary right to be informed of the availability of legal aid was breached, this resulted in prejudice of such a magnitude that his right to counsel as a whole was also breached.

It follows from the foregoing that if the material which was destroyed meets the threshold test for disclosure or production, the appellant's *Charter* rights were breached without the requirement of showing additional prejudice. The Court of Appeal accepted the submission that the propriety of the order for production was not in issue by reason of the fact that both the Crown and the complainants consented to the application for production. As between the [Sexual Assault Crisis] centre and the complainant, it was the latter's consent that was required. The high-handed policy adopted by the centre appears to ignore the fact that the right to confidentiality resides in the complainant and that destruction of records without the consent of the complainant is a violation of that right. Some complainants may wish to waive any right to confidentiality for a variety of reasons including the fact that the records may tend to support the complainant's claim.

In my view, it is clear that the appellant could have made use of the information in the notes even though it is difficult to specify the precise manner in which the information could have been used without knowing the contents of the notes. The classic use of such evidence is, of course, to cross-examine the witness on inconsistent statements. Although in this case the complainant could not have been cross-examined on the notes themselves as the notes were not statements of the complainant, they could have afforded a foundation for cross-examination. If the notes indicated an inconsistency with evidence in the witness box, the witness could have been confronted with this inconsistency, and if denied, the statement could have been proved by calling the note-taker.

I conclude from the foregoing that there was abundant evidence before the trial judge to enable him to conclude that there was a reasonable possibility that the information contained in the notes that were destroyed was logically probative to an issue at the trial as to the credibility of the complainant. This information, therefore, would have satisfied the test for disclosure....The destruction of this material and its consequent non-disclosure resulted in a breach of the appellant's constitutional right to full answer and defence.

Madame Justice L'Heureux-Dubé, and Mr. Justices La Forest, Gonthier, and Madame Justice McLachlin (dissenting):

I disagree with the result reached by my colleague [Mr. Justice Sopinka] and would dismiss the appeal. I also take a very different approach to the issues raised. For this reason, it seems appropriate at this point to clarify a few matters, in light of the assertions about this case made by Sopinka J.

First, in my view, this case has absolutely nothing to do with disclosure. While Sopinka J. speaks at great length of the "right to disclosure" and the obligation which rests to disclose, I feel constrained to point out that disclosure is a concept which is binding *solely* upon the Crown, and not upon the public at large....Nor does [the duty to disclose] impose an obligation upon the Crown to comb the world for information which might be of possible relevance to the defence.

It is crucial to recall, therefore, that in the case at bar, the centre is a third party, a party which has no obligation to preserve evidence for prosecutions or otherwise. Its policy decisions are for itself to determine and not for the Crown, the accused or the courts to interfere with, so long as it acts within the confines of the law. In this case, when the notes were destroyed, the centre had not received any subpoena or court order to produce such notes. Whether its policy of destruction was appropriate is not for us to decide.

Does an accused automatically have the right to every piece of potentially relevant evidence in the world? My colleague suggests this is in fact the case...he suggests that there will be a breach of the right to full answer and defence and therefore an unfair trial anytime material is unavailable that would have been disclosed if in the hands of the Crown. Therefore, whenever information in the hands of a third party has the reasonable possibility of being of some use to the defence the fact that it is unavailable immediately causes a violation of the *Charter*. In my view, the adoption of this rationale could quite possibly lead one to the conclusion that there has never been a fair trial in this country. It goes against the grain of this court's *Charter* jurisprudence and is contrary to basic underlying notions of how the criminal justice system actually operates.

The *Charter* does not entitle an accused to a "perfect" trial, in which every piece of relevant information which might or might not affect the defence is diligently piled at the defence's door. An accused is entitled to a fair trial, where relevant, unprivileged material gathered by the Crown is disclosed, while evidence in the hands of third parties, after a balancing of considerations, is produced in appropriate cases. Where evidence is unavailable, the accused must demonstrate that a fair trial, and not a perfect one, cannot be had as a result of the loss.

In my view, for the appellant to suggest that he is unable to receive a fair trial because of the destroyed notes, he must be able to demonstrate that there was actually some harm to his position. It is not enough to speculate, as my colleague proposes, that there is the *potential* for harm, as the notes might somehow have proved useful....

In my view, the request [for the centre's notes] made here amounted to no more than what I stated should not be permitted: a fishing expedition in the hopes of uncovering a prior inconsistent statement. Despite the finding of the trial judge, there is absolutely nothing on the record to suggest that there was any discussion between the complainant and the counselor about the actual details of the events themselves....

In any event, I am not convinced that the crisis centre's conduct was "manifestly inappropriate" so as to meet the standard of an abuse of process....The crisis centre was not acting out of animus against this appellant; nor was it acting out of generalized *animus* against persons accused of sexual assault, or at the instigation of the Crown. Rather, the record indicates that the crisis centre was implementing a general policy designed to protect its clients' privacy and ensure that women would not be dissuaded from seeking assistance for fear that their private discussions will be communicated to the defence. The fact that this particular complainant had, to a certain extent, waived confidentiality does not affect the validity of the crisis centre's general policy. It is entirely legitimate and understandable for a centre to warn its clients that their files could be subpoenaed, and to obtain their consent to release the records in such an eventuality, while at the same time taking steps to defend the confidentiality of the records.

According to Sopinka J., the conduct of the crisis centre is an affront to the justice system and the crisis centre is flouting the authority of the courts. In my view, it is important to keep the actions of the centre in their proper perspective. First, this is not a case where a person shredded documents in respect of which a subpoena or court order had been issued. On the contrary, the crisis centre's policy on shredding states that "[W]e cannot shred a document if it has been subpoenaed or there is an application requesting a Court Order".

It is also highly significant that the centre was under no obligation whatsoever to create or maintain records. My colleague appears to suggests that an independent agency cannot destroy materials which *might* one day be required to be produced to the court. In my view, this type of obligation is completely inappropriate. The centre created notes for its own purposes. It was under no obligation to do so. Once it did, it had a legitimate property interest in them which it was able to do with as it saw fit. To suggest that the court should be able to enforce a maintenance obligation to property which *might one day be needed* by the courts is a hefty burden indeed.

Finally, I must comment upon the fact that these agencies have even felt it necessary to go to such lengths. From a quick perusal of lower court judgments, it would appear as if a request for therapeutic records in cases of sexual assault is becoming virtually automatic, with little regard to the actual relevancy of the documents. We have now come to a situation where people trying to help victims have resorted to forgoing the taking of notes or destroying them *en masse* in order to prevent what they see as a grave injustice. It is extremely likely that the therapeutical process for which these notes are actually created is being harmed in their absence....

R. V. HEYWOOD

Supreme Court of Canada

[1994] 174 N.R. 81

The language of legislation can itself violate the "principles of fundamental justice" referred to in section 7 of the *Charter*. If a crime is described in the *Criminal Code* using vague or ambiguous language, then not only will citizens be unsure as to what actions of theirs are criminal, but, if charged, they will not be able to defend themselves properly. Consider in this regard the problem of a criminal prohibition that suffers from "overbreadth". Overly broad language, though neither vague nor ambiguous, is unfair because it denotes a wider set of actions or behaviours than is necessary for public protection. The temptation to use such language is strong on the part of legislative drafters since the broader the term, the less likely an offender can argue that what he or she did was not quite the same as what was prohibited.

In this case, the issue is whether a prohibition against loitering was overly broad in light of the social goal of protecting children and others from convicted sex offenders who might prey on them in playgrounds or other public areas. By a narrow margin, the Supreme Court of Canada held that the provision was overly broad. The dissent, by contrast, argues that it is not by using the standard judicial technique of stipulating a narrower meaning for the term "loiter".

* * * *

Mr. Justice Cory, and Chief Justice Lamer and Justices Sopinka, Iacobucci and Major:

Section 179(1)(b) of the *Criminal Code* makes it a crime for persons convicted of specified offences to be "found loitering in or near a school ground, playground, public park or bathing area". It must be determined whether the section infringes s. 7 or 11(d) of the *Charter*.

The appellant submits that the word "loiter" in s. 179(1)(b) should be interpreted as requiring a malevolent intent while the respondent takes the position that "loiter" should be given its ordinary meaning.

When a statutory provision is to be interpreted the word or words in question should be considered in the context in which they are used, and read in a manner which is consistent with the purpose of the provision and the intention of the Legislature....If the ordinary meaning of the words is consistent with the context in which the words are used and with the object of the Act, then that is the interpretation which should govern....

There can be no question that s. 179(1)(b) restricts the liberty of those to whom it applies. Indeed, the appellant made no argument to the contrary. The section prohibits convicted sex offenders from attending (except perhaps to quickly walk through on their way to another location) at school grounds, playgrounds, public parks or bathing areas – places where the rest of the public is free to roam. The breach of this prohibition is punishable on summary conviction and, as this case demonstrates, imprisonment is the consequence.

The question this court must decide is whether this restriction on liberty is in accordance with the principles of fundamental justice. The respondent conceded in oral argument that a prohibition for the purpose of protecting the public does not *per se* infringe the principles of fundamental justice....The question, then, is whether some other aspect of the prohibition contained in s. 179(1)(b) violates the principles of fundamental justice. In my opinion it does. It applies without prior notice to the accused, to too many places, to too many people, for an indefinite period with no possibility of review. It restricts liberty far more than is necessary to accomplish its goal....

Overbreadth analysis looks at the means chosen by the state in relation to its purpose. In considering whether a legislative provision is overbroad, a court must ask the question: are those means necessary to achieve the state objective? If the state, in pursuing a legitimate objective, uses means which are broader than is necessary to accomplish that objective, the principles of fundamental justice will be violated because the individual's rights will have been limited for no reason. The effect of overbreadth is that in some applications the law is arbitrary or disproportionate.

Reviewing legislation for overbreadth as a principle of fundamental justice is simply an example of the balancing of the state interest against that of the individual....However, where an independent principle of fundamental justice is violated, such as the requirement of *mens rea* for penal liability, or of the right to natural justice, any balancing of the public interest must take place under s. 1 of the *Charter*.

In analyzing a statutory provision to determine if it is overbroad, a measure of deference must be paid to the means selected by the Legislature. While the courts have a constitutional duty to ensure that legislation conforms with the *Charter*, Legislatures must have the power to make policy choices. A court should not interfere with legislation merely because a judge might have chosen a different means of accomplishing the objective if he or she had been the legislator....

The purpose of 179(1)(b) is to protect children from becoming victims of sexual offences. This is apparent from the prohibition which applies to places where children are very likely to be found. In determining whether s. 179(1)(b) is overly broad and not in accordance with the principles of fundamental justice, it must be determined whether the means chosen to accomplish this objective are unreasonably tailored to effect this purpose. In those situations where legislation limits the liberty of an individual in order to protect the public, that limitation should not go beyond what is necessary to accomplish that goal....

In my opinion, s. 179(1)(b) suffers from overbreadth and thus the deprivation of liberty it entails is not in accordance with the principles of fundamental justice.

The section is overly broad in its geographical ambit. It applies not only to schoolgrounds and playgrounds, but also to all public parks and bathing areas. Its application to schools and playgrounds is appropriate, as these are the very places children are likely to congregate. But its application to all public parks and bathing areas is overly broad because not all such places are places where children are likely to be found....

Section 179(1)(b) is also overly broad in another aspect. It applies for life, with no possibility of review. The absence of review means that a person who has ceased to be a danger to children (or who indeed never was a danger to children), is subject to the prohibition in s. 179(1)(b)....

Section 179(1)(b) is overly broad in respect to the people to whom it applies. It applies to all persons convicted of the listed offences, without regard to whether they constitute a danger to children....It is difficult to accept that a person who had sexually assaulted an adult 15 years earlier with no subsequent offences should be assumed to still be a threat to children.

Mr. Justice Gonthier, and Mr. Justice La Forest and Madame Justices L'Heureux-Dubé, and McLachlin (dissenting):

I have read the opinion of Justice Cory and, with all due respect, find I am unable to agree. The central issue in this case concerns the interpretation of s. 179(1)(b) of the *Criminal Code*. By giving the word "loiter" its ordinary meaning, Cory J. would interpret the provision as prohibiting lingering, tarrying, standing idly around, sauntering, delaying, dawdling, etc., in the enumerated areas. This interpretation leads him to the conclude that the prohibition created by s. 179(1)(b) violates s. 7 of the *Charter* and is not saved by s. 1 because it is overbroad in terms of the persons, places and time period to which it applies and because notice to the accused is not required. In my view, however, s. 179(1)(b) should be interpreted as prohibiting the persons affected from being in one of the enumerated places for a malevolent or ulterior purpose related to the predicate offence. My reasons for favouring this interpretation are drawn from the purpose and legislative history of s. 179(1)(b) as well as precedent and statutory context.

...[T]he objectives embodied in the s. 179(1)(b) prohibition are relatively clear. The courts below have unanimously recognized that the section has at its foundation a concern for public safety and a desire to aid in the treatment and rehabilitation of offenders. I agree and would stress that the provision applies broadly to all persons convicted of the enumerated offences and therefore provides protection not only to children but also to others who could be victims of sexual assault in the listed areas. These areas, it should be remembered, are places where people will generally lower their guard.

The above, though, does not allow us to identify as easily the specific conduct prohibited. The identified objectives are clearly achieved, and perhaps most efficiently, by the broad interpretation of the prohibition adopted by Cory J. A less intrusive interpretation which prohibits the persons affected from being in one of the enumerated places for a malevolent or ulterior purpose related to the predicate offences, however, is also consistent with the objectives. The more narrow interpretation would go beyond a mere "attempts" offence. It would preserve the preventive aspect of the section by allowing the state to deal with activities that are part of the cycle of reoffending, such as taking photos, which can be proven to reflect a malevolent or ulterior purpose related to the predicate offences. At the same time, this interpretation would allow the affected persons to use the listed areas for the legitimate purposes for which they were intended.

Cory J. suggests that the prohibition created by s. 179(1)(b) is overbroad in terms of the persons, places and time period to which it applies. I express no opinion on the soundness of this analysis of liberty because it is not necessary in this case to decide the issue. The interpretation I advocate eliminates Cory J.'s concern that the prohibition is overbroad. A lifetime prohibition of activities with a malevolent or ulterior purpose related to reoffending is in no way objectionable or overbroad. Such a prohibition would impose a restriction on the liberty of the affected individuals to which ordinary citizens are not subject, but that restriction is directly related to preventing reoffending. The affected persons' history of offending, the uncertainties prevalent in treating offenders and a desire to disrupt the cycle of reoffending justify what is in effect a minor intrusion which does not breach the principles of fundamental justice.

That restraint of the affected person's liberty is minor and easily illustrated. As noted above, use of public parks for the legitimate purposes for which they are intended would not be caught. Furthermore, though trite, it must be remembered that the Crown will bear the burden of proving all elements of the offence between a reasonable doubt. This burden guarantees that only loitering which can be proven to be related to one of the predicate offences will be subject to the criminal prohibition. I recognize that this formulation of the offence will likely lead to certain evidentiary presumptions which, absent a satisfactory explanation, may cause a judge to draw an adverse inference. Take for example a person with a history of offences in relation to children who is observed hanging around a playground and offering children candy. Similarly, as discussed above, just lingering about a schoolyard with no apparent purpose, as distinct from a public park, would give rise to legitimate suspicions. Such presumptions, however, in no way reverse the burden of proof, nor do they violate the accused's right to silence.

One of the most obvious objections to the more narrow formulation is that it is potentially less efficient than the alternatives in terms of achieving the legislative objective. As I noted above, a broad prohibition preventing certain persons from even attending at areas where the risk of reoffending is high may be a superior way to achieve the objectives of public safety and offender treatment. As Cory J. convincingly demonstrates, however, for such a broad prohibition to be constitutional, it would probably have to be accompanied by [protections against overbreadth that s. 179(1)(b) lacks].

For the foregoing reasons, s. 179(1)(b) of the Code should be interpreted as prohibiting lingering or hanging about the enumerated areas for a malevolent or ulterior purpose related to any of the predicate offences. [So interpreted, the section would not violate s. 7 of the *Charter*.]

VI RESPONSIBILITY

The law not only protects our rights and respects our autonomy, it also holds us to our responsibilities. Cases involving public and private responsibilities constitutes by far the bulk of the common law. Of the various questions raised here, the philosophically most interesting concern the scope of our duties to others, the criteria for the judgment that we have failed in these duties, the circumstances when this failure is defensible or forgivable, and, finally, the limits to state sanctioning. More than any other area of law, the law of responsibility, defence and punishment seems the closest to the sphere of morality. Whether this is an intrinsic fact about the law, a coincidence or an illusion is itself a fundamental problem of jurisprudence.

Our law insists upon a distinction, however, that morality does not dwell on, namely the difference between crimes and private wrongs or delicts. In our law, this distinction is entrenched, both procedurally and substantively. With crime, the injury has been done to the state so it prosecutes; the victim fades into the background. With private wrongs, unless the victim brings a suit, the matter is not pursued by the state. Crimes are matters of serious concern that, at least potentially, threaten the very fabric of society. Private wrongs, on the other hand, involve disputes between individuals – nuisances, carelessly caused harms, unconscionable deals, and broken promises – that need to be peacefully, and finally, settled.

The first two sections of this Part explore various dimensions of the difference between public and private wrongs (using the tort of negligence as an example of the latter). The last section raises the issue of punishment, both what it is and the extent of the state's right to inflict it.

A: CRIMINAL RESPONSIBILITY AND DEFENCE

R. V. MACHEKEQUONABE

Ontario Court of Appeal

(1897) 28 O.R. 309

In this criminal case, an old one by Canadian standards, the problem of bridging a cultural gap was at issue, although it was clearly not taken very seriously by the court. A "pagan Indian" (his nation or tribe is never mentioned) was charged with manslaughter for killing what, from his cultural and religious perspective, was a dangerous evil spirit, a Wendigo. The question here is not whether Wendigos exist or not, but whether a person's sincere belief that they exist, are dangerous to the group and must be killed, should figure in some way into our assessment of the "guilty mind" or *mens rea*. (In the style of the day, the argument of the defence counsel is presented after the facts have been set out and before the court's actual judgment, which is starkly brief.)

* * * *

It appeared from the evidence that the prisoner was a member of a tribe of pagan Indians who believed in the existence of an evil spirit clothed in human flesh, or in human form called a Wendigo which would eat a human being.

That it was reported that a Wendigo had been seen and it was supposed was in the neighbourhood of their camp desiring to do them harm.

That among other precautions to protect themselves, guards and sentries, the prisoner being one, were placed out in pairs armed with firearms (the prisoner having a rifle); that the prisoner saw what appeared to be a tall human being running in the distance, which he supposed was the Wendigo; that he and another Indian gave chase, and after challenging three times and receiving no answer fired and shot the object, when it was discovered to be his own foster father, who died soon afterward.

The jury found affirmative answers to the following questions:

Are you satisfied the prisoner did kill the Indian?

Did the prisoner believe the object he shot at to be a Wendigo or spirit?

Did he believe the spirit to be embodied in human flesh?

Was it the prisoner's belief that the Wendigo could be killed by a bullet shot from a rifle?

Was the prisoner sane apart from the delusion or belief in the existence of a Wendigo?

The learned trial Judge then proceeded with his charge as follows: "Assuming these facts to be found by you, I think I must direct you as a matter of law that there is no justification in manslaughter so that unless you can suggest to yourselves something stated in the evidence, or drawn from the evidence to warrant a different conclusion, I think it will be your duty to return a verdict of manslaughter. You may confer among yourselves if you please, and if you take that view, I will reserve a case for consideration by the Court of Appeal as to whether he was properly convicted upon this evidence".

The jury found the prisoner guilty of manslaughter recommending him to mercy, and the learned Judge reserved a case for consideration whether upon the findings of the jury in answer to the questions he had submitted the prisoner was properly found guilty of manslaughter.

This case was argued on February 8th, 1897, before a Divisional Court composed of Armour, C.J., and Falconbridge, and Street, JJ. J.K. Kerr, Q.C., for the prisoner. The evidence shews the Indian tribe were pagans, and believed in an evil spirit clothed in human form which they called a Wendigo, and which attacked, killed and ate human beings. The man that was shot was thought to be a Wendigo, a spirit as distinguished from a human being. It is true there was a mistake, but there was no intention even to harm a human being much less to kill. The evidence shews the mistake was not unreasonable. At common law the following of a religious belief would be an excuse. The trial Judge wrongly directed the jury to find the prisoner guilty. There should be a new trial at least....

John Cartwright, Q.C., Deputy Attorney-General was not called on.

The judgment of the Court was delivered by *Armour, C.J.*:

Upon the case reserved if there was evidence upon which the jury could find the prisoner guilty of manslaughter it is not open to use to reverse that finding, and the question we have to decide is whether there was such evidence.

We think there was, and therefore do not see how we can say that the prisoner was not properly convicted of manslaughter.

R. V. CITY OF SAULT STE. MARIE

Supreme Court of Canada

[1978] 2 S.C.R. 1299

What makes a wrongdoing a *criminal* offence? For centuries, crimes have been distinguished from other wrongs, illegalities and delicts in terms of the quality of responsibility involved, and to a certain extent, the potential for the action to undermine the fabric of society. A determination of criminal responsibility requires more than proof that the accused performed some action or other; he or she must have possessed at the time a "guilty mind" or *mens rea*. To do an evil intentionally, or on purpose, or with "malice aforethought", is clearly to have a guilty mind. But over the years, courts have come to the conclusion that one's mind can be sufficiently guilty merely if one *knew* of the consequences of one's actions. Nonetheless, that the state is required to prove that the accused had a guilty mind before it convicts is one of the fundamental principles of justice. (See *Reference Re Section 94(2) of the Motor Vehicle Act* in Part V.)

Since it is a subjective state, it is not always easy to prove that someone had the required *mens rea*. Officials and legislators are therefore often tempted to fudge the question and create offences that either do not require the prosecutor to prove *mens rea*, or else allow the prosecutor to infer *mens rea* from objective behaviour. In the following case, the Supreme Court of Canada explored the problem raised by one very important class of such offences – the so-called "public welfare" offences that are concerned with pressing social problems (pollution, for example), but which do require the proving of *mens rea*.

* * * *

Mr. Justice Dickson:

In the present appeal the Court is concerned with offences variously referred to as "statutory", "public welfare", "regulatory", "absolute liability", or "strict responsibility", which are not criminal in any real sense, but are prohibited in the public interest. Although enforced as penal laws through the utilization of the machinery of the criminal law, the offences are in substance of a civil nature and might well be regarded as a branch of administrative law to which traditional principles of criminal law have but limited application. They relate to such everyday matters as traffic infractions, sales of impure food, violations of liquor laws, and the like. In this appeal we are concerned with pollution.

The doctrine of the guilty mind expressed in terms of intention or recklessness, but not negligence, is at the foundation of the law of crimes. In the case of true crimes there is a presumption that a person should not be held liable for the wrongfulness of his act if that act is without *mens rea*. Blackstone made the point over two hundred years ago in words still apt: "...to constitute a crime against human laws, there must be, first, a vicious will; and secondly, an unlawful act consequent upon such vicious will..." I would emphasize at the outset that nothing in the discussion which follows is intended to dilute or erode that basic principle....

To relate briefly the facts, the City on November 18, 1970, entered into an agreement with Cherokee Disposal and Construction Co. Ltd., for the disposal of all refuse originating in the City. Under the terms of the agreement, Cherokee became obligated to furnish a site and adequate labour, material and equipment. The site selected bordered Cannon Creek which, it would appear, runs into the Root River. The method of disposal adopted is known as the "area", or "continuous slope" method of sanitary land fill, whereby garbage is compacted in layers which are covered each day by natural sand or gravel.

Prior to 1970, the site had been covered with a number of freshwater springs that flowed into Cannon Creek. Cherokee dumped material to cover and submerge these springs and then placed garbage and wastes over such material. The garbage and wastes in due course formed a high mound sloping steeply toward, and within twenty feet of, the creek. Pollution resulted. Cherokee was convicted of a breach of s. 32(1) of the *Ontario Water Resources Act*, the section under which the City has been charged. The question now before the Court is whether the City is also guilty of an offence under that section.

In dismissing the charge at first instance, the Judge found that the City had had nothing to do with the actual disposal operations, that Cherokee was an independent contractor and its employees were not employees of the City. On the appeal *de novo* Judge Vannini found the offence to be one of strict liability and he convicted. The Divisional Court in setting aside the judgment found that the charge was duplicitous. As a secondary point, the Divisional Court also held that the charge required *mens rea* with respect to causing or permitting a discharge. When the case reached the Court of Appeal that Court held that the conviction could not be quashed on the ground of duplicity, because there had been no challenge to the information at trial. The Court of Appeal agreed, however, that the charge was one requiring proof of *mens rea*. A majority of the Court (Brooke and Howland JJ.A.) held there was not sufficient evidence to establish *mens rea* and ordered a new trial. In the view of Mr. Justice Lacourciere, dissenting, the inescapable inference to be drawn from the findings of fact of Judge Vannini was that the City had known of the potential impairment of waters of Cannon Creek and Root River and had failed to exercise its clear powers of control....

The Mens Rea *Point*

The distinction between the true criminal offence and the public welfare offence is one of prime importance. Where the offence is criminal, the Crown must establish a mental element, namely, that the accused who committed the prohibited act did so intentionally or recklessly, with knowledge of the facts constituting the offence, or with wilful blindness toward them. Mere negligence is excluded from the concept of the mental element required for conviction. Within the context of a criminal prosecution a person who fails to make such inquiries as a reasonable and prudent person would make, or who fails to know facts he should have known, is innocent in the eyes of the law.

In sharp contrast, "absolute liability" entails conviction on proof merely that the defendant committed the prohibited act constituting the *actus reus* of the offence. There is no relevant mental element. It is no defence that the accused was entirely without fault. He may be morally innocent in every sense, yet be branded as a malefactor and punished as such.

Public welfare offences obviously lie in a field of conflicting values. It is essential for society to maintain, through effective enforcement, high standards of public health and safety. Potential victims of those who carry on latently pernicious activities have a strong claim to consideration. On the other hand, there is a generally held revulsion against punishment of the morally innocent.

Public welfare offences evolved in mid-19th century Britain as a means of doing away with the requirement of *mens rea* for petty policy offences. The concept was a judicial creation, founded on expediency. That concept is now firmly embedded in the concrete of Anglo-American and Canadian jurisprudence, its importance heightened by the ever-increasing complexities of modern society.

Various arguments are advanced in justification of absolute liability in public welfare offences. Two predominate. Firstly, it is argued that the protection of social interests requires a high standard of care and attention on the part of those who follow certain pursuits and such persons are more likely to be stimulated to maintain those standards if they know that ignorance or mistake will not excuse them. The removal of any possible loophole acts, it is said, as an incentive to take precautionary measures beyond what would otherwise be taken, in order that mistakes and mishaps be avoided. The second main argument is one based on administrative efficiency. Having regard to both the difficulty of proving mental culpability and the number of petty cases which daily come before the Courts, proof of fault is just too great a burden in time and money to place upon the prosecution. To require proof of each person's individual intent would allow almost every violator to escape. This, together with the glut of work entailed in proving *mens rea* in every case would clutter the docket and impede adequate enforcement as virtually to nullify the regulatory statutes. In short, absolute liability, it is contended, is the most efficient and effective way of ensuring compliance with minor regulatory legislation and the social ends to be achieved are of such importance as to override the unfortunate byproduct of punishing those who may be free of moral turpitude. In further justification, it is urged that slight penalties are usually imposed and that conviction for breach of a public welfare offence does not carry the stigma associated with conviction for a criminal offence.

Arguments of greater force are advanced against absolute liability. The most telling is that it violates fundamental principles of penal liability. It also rests upon assumptions which have not been, and cannot be, empirically established. There is no evidence that a higher standard of care results from absolute liability. If a person is already taking every reasonable precautionary measure, is he likely to take additional measures, knowing that however much care he takes, it will not serve as a defence in the event of breach? If he has exercised care and skill, will conviction have a deterrent effect upon him or others? Will the injustice of conviction lead to cynicism and disrespect for the law, on his part and on the part of others? These are among the questions asked. The argument that no stigma attaches does not withstand analysis, for the accused will have suffered loss of time, legal costs, exposure to the processes of the criminal law at trial and, however one may downplay it, the opprobrium of conviction. It is not sufficient to say that the public interest is engaged and, therefore, liability may be imposed without fault. In serious crimes, the public interest is involved and *mens rea* must be proven. The administrative argument has little force. In sentencing, evidence of due diligence is admissible and therefore the evidence might just as well be heard when considering guilt....

Public welfare offences involve a shift of emphasis from the protection of individual interests to the protection of public and social interests. The unfortunate tendency in many past cases has been to see the choice as between two stark alternatives: (i) full *mens rea*; or (ii) absolute liability. In respect of public welfare offences (within which category pollution offences fall) where full *mens rea* is not required, absolute liability has often been imposed. English jurisprudence has consistently maintained this dichotomy. There has, however, been an attempt in Australia, in many Canadian Courts, and indeed in England, to seek a middle position, fulfilling the goals of public welfare offences while still not punishing the entirely blameless. There is an increasing and impressive stream of authority which holds that where an offence does not require full *mens rea*, it is nevertheless a good defence for the defendant to prove that he was not negligent....

We have the situation therefore in which many Courts of this country, at all levels, dealing with public welfare offences favour (i) *not* requiring the Crown to prove *mens rea*, (ii) rejecting the notion that liability inexorably follows upon mere proof of the *actus reus*, excluding any possible defence. The Courts are following the lead set in Australia many years ago and tentatively broached by several English courts in recent years.

It may be suggested that the introduction of a defence based on due diligence and the shifting of the burden of proof might better be implemented by legislative act. In answer, it should be recalled that the concept of absolute liability and the creation of a jural category of public welfare offences are both the product of the judiciary and not of the Legislature. The development to date of this defence in the numerous decisions I have referred to, of courts in this country as well as in Australia and New Zealand, has also been the work of judges. The present case offers the opportunity of consolidating and clarifying the doctrine.

The correct approach, in my opinion, is to relieve the Crown of the burden of proving *mens rea*, having regard to the virtual impossibility in most regulatory cases of proving wrongful intention. In a normal case, the accused alone will have knowledge of what he has done to avoid the breach and it is not improper to expect him to come forward with the evidence of due diligence. This is particularly so when it is alleged, for example, that pollution was caused by the activities of a large and complex corporation. Equally, there is nothing wrong with rejecting absolute liability and admitting the defence of reasonable care.

In this doctrine it is not up to the prosecution to prove negligence. Instead, it is open to the defendant to prove that all due care has been taken. This burden falls upon the defendant as he is the only one who will generally have the means of proof. This would not seem unfair as the alternative is absolute liability which denies an accused any defence whatsoever. While the prosecution must prove beyond a reasonable doubt that the defendant committed the prohibited act, the defendant must only establish on the balance of probabilities that he has a defence of reasonable care.

I conclude, for the reasons which I have sought to express, that there are compelling grounds for the recognition of three categories of offences rather than the traditional two:

1. Offences in which *mens rea*, consisting of some positive state of mind such as intent, knowledge, or recklessness, must be proved by the prosecution either as an inference from the nature of the act committed, or by additional evidence.

2. Offences in which there is no necessity for the prosecution to prove the existence of *mens rea;* the doing of the prohibited act *prima facie* imports the offence, leaving it open to the accused to avoid liability by proving that he took all reasonable care. This involves consideration of what a reasonable man would have done in the circumstances. The defence will be available if the accused reasonably believed in a mistaken set of facts which, if true, would render the act or omission innocent, or if he took all reasonable steps to avoid the particular event. These offences may properly be called offences of strict liability....

3. Offences of absolute liability where it is not open to the accused to exculpate himself by showing that he was free of fault.

Offences which are criminal in the true sense fall in the first category. Public welfare offences would, *prima facie*, be in the second category. They are not subject to the presumption of full *mens rea*. An offence of this type would fall in the first category only if such words as "wilfully", "with intent", "knowingly", or "intentionally" are contained in the statutory provision creating the offence. On the other hand, the principle that punishment should in general not be inflicted on those without fault applies. Offences of absolute liability would be those in respect of which the Legislature had made it clear that guilt would follow proof merely of the proscribed act. The over-all regulatory pattern adopted by the Legislature, the subject matter of the legislation, the importance of the penalty, and the precision of the language used will be primary considerations in determining whether the offence falls into the third category....

Turning to the subject-matter of s. 32(1) [of the *Ontario Water Resources Act*] – the prevention of pollution of lakes, rivers and streams – it is patent that this is of great public concern. Pollution has always been unlawful and, in itself, a nuisance. A riparian owner has an inherent right to have a stream of water "come to him in its nat-ural state, in flow, quantity and quality". Natural streams which for-merly afforded "pure and healthy" water for drinking or swimming purposes become little more than cesspools where riparian factory owners and municipal corporations discharge into them filth of all descriptions. Pollution offences are undoubtedly public welfare offences enacted in the interests of the public health. There is thus no presumption of a full *mens rea*....

Since s. 32(1) creates a public welfare offence, without clear indi-cation that liability is absolute, and without any words such as "know-ingly" or "wilfully" expressly to import *mens rea*, application of the cri-teria which I have outlined above undoubtedly places the offence in the category of strict liability.

Proof of the prohibited act *prima facie* imports the offence, but the accused may avoid liability by proving that he took reasonable care.

HUNDAL V. THE QUEEN

Supreme Court of Canada

[1993] 1 S.C.R. 867

The requirement of *mens rea* may be an essential feature of criminal offences, but what does the requirement mean? Does criminal guilt require an investigation into the actual thoughts and beliefs of the accused at the time of the offence? Or can we dispense with mind-reading, and infer from the harm that was done what the accused had in mind? Criminal lawyers call this the difference between a "subjective" and an "objective" approach to *mens rea,* and for centuries it was assumed that only the subjective approach, despite its problems, could satisfy the requirements of justice.

But increasingly, prosecutors and courts have expressed their frustration with the subjective approach: surely, since we can never know what really went on inside the accused's head, why should we dwell on this issue at all? Recently, the Supreme Court of Canada took a small, but important step in the direction of an "objective *mens rea"* in a case involving a fatal motor vehicle accident. One expert has said that this case represents the beginning of the "criminalization of civil negligence".

* * * *

Mr. Justice Cory and Justices L'Heureux-Dubé, Sopinka, Gonthier, and Iacobucci:

At issue on this appeal is whether there is a subjective element in the requisite *mens rea* which must be established by the Crown in order to prove the offence of dangerous driving described in s. 233 of the *Criminal Code.*

Factual Background

The accident occurred at about 3:40 in the afternoon in downtown Vancouver. The streets were wet at the time, a situation not uncommon to that city. The downtown traffic was heavy. The appellant was driving his dump truck eastbound on Nelson Street, a four lane road, approaching its intersection with Cambie Street. At the time, his truck was overloaded. It exceeded by 1160 kilograms the maximum gross weight permitted for the vehicle. He was travelling in the passing lane for eastbound traffic. The deceased was travelling southbound on Cambie Street. He had stopped for a red light at the intersection with Nelson Street. When the light turned green, the deceased proceeded into the intersection through a cross-walk, continued south across the two lanes for westbound traffic on Nelson Street and reached the passing lane for eastbound traffic. At that moment his car was struck on the right side by the dump truck killing him instantly.

The appellant stated that when he approached the intersection of Nelson and Cambie Streets he observed that the light had turned amber. He thought that he could not stop in time so he simply honked his horn and continued through the intersection when the impact occurred. Several witnesses observed the collision. They testified that the appellant's truck entered the intersection after the Nelson Street traffic light had turned red. It was estimated that at least one second had passed between the end of the amber light and the time when the dump truck first entered the intersection. A Vancouver police officer gave evidence that the red light for Nelson at this intersection is preceded by a three second amber light and there is a further one-half second delay before the Cambie light turned green. One witness observed that the deceased's vehicle had travelled almost the entire width of the intersection before it was struck by the truck. Another witness, Mr. Mumford, had been travelling close to the appellant's truck through some twelve intersections. He testified that on an earlier occasion, the appellant went through an intersection as the light turned red. He estimated the speed of the truck at the time of the collision was between 50 to 60 kilometres per hour....

Analysis

The relevant portions of s. 233 read as follows:

233. (1) Every one commits an offence who operates (a) a motor vehicle on a street, road, highway or other public p]ace in a manner that is dangerous to the public, having regard to all the circumstances, including the nature, condition and use of such place and the amount of traffic that at the time is or might reasonably be expected to be on such place;...

(4) Every one who commits an offence under subsection (1) and thereby causes the death of any other person is guilty of an

indictable offence and is liable to imprisonment for a term not exceeding fourteen years.

At the outset it must be admitted that the cases dealing with driving offences are not models of clarity. Professor Stuart in his book *Canadian Criminal Law* (2nd ed. 1987), at p. 202, states quite frankly that the law with regard to driving offences is a mess. He writes:

> As a matter of theory the law of driving offences has long been in a mess. The offence of careless driving may require simple or gross negligence; the more serious offence of dangerous driving involves simple negligence although sometimes the courts talk about an "advertence" requirement; and the most serious offence of negligent driving required on one view, advertent recklessness and on another gross inadvertent negligence. The law has been so confused that it has almost certainly been ignored. There is a fairyland quality to the esoteric analysis involved. Statistics indicate that most prosecutors have been content to rely on the provincial careless driving offence....

The Constitutional Requirement of Mens Rea

The appellant contends that the prison sentence which may be imposed for a breach of s. 233 makes it evident that an accused cannot be convicted without proof beyond a reasonable doubt of a subjective mental element of an intention to drive dangerously. Certainly every crime requires proof of an act or failure to act, coupled with an element of fault which is termed the *mens rea*. This Court has made it clear that s. 7 of the *Charter* prohibits the imposition of imprisonment in the absence of proof of that element of fault. See *Re B.C. Motor Vehicle Act* (1985).

Depending on the provisions of the particular section and the context in which it appears, the constitutional requirement of *mens rea* may be satisfied in different ways. The offence can require proof of a positive state of mind such as intent, recklessness or wilful blindness. Alternatively, the *mens rea* or element of fault can be satisfied by proof of negligence whereby the conduct of the accused is measured on the basis of an objective standard without establishing the subjective mental state of the particular accused. In the appropriate context, negligence can be an acceptable basis of liability which meets the fault requirement of s. 7 of the *Charter*. Thus, the intent required for a particular offence may be either subjective or objective.

A truly subjective test seeks to determine what was actually in the mind of the particular accused at the moment the offence is alleged to have been committed. In his very useful text, *Canadian Criminal Law* (2nd ed.) Professor Stuart puts it in this way at pp. 123-24 and at p. 125:

> What is vital is that *this accused* given his personality, situation and circumstances, actually intended, knew or foresaw the consequence and/or circumstance as the case may be. Whether he "could", "ought" or "should" have foreseen or whether a reasonable person would have foreseen is not the relevant criterion of liability....

> In trying to ascertain what was going on in the accused's mind, as the subjective approach demands, the trier of fact may draw reasonable inferences from the accused's actions or words at the time of his act or in the witness box. The accused may or may not be believed. To conclude that, considering all the evidence, the Crown has proved beyond a reasonable doubt that the accused "must" have thought in the penalized way is no departure from the subjective substantive standard. Resort to an objective substantive standard would only occur if the reasoning became that the accused "must have realized it if he had thought about it".

On the other hand, the test for negligence is an objective one requiring a marked departure from the standard of care of a reasonable person. There is no need to establish the intention of the particular accused. The question to be answered under the objective test concerns what the accused "should" have known. The potential harshness of the objective standard may be lessened by the consideration of certain personal factors as well as the consideration of a defence of mistake of fact. Nevertheless, there should be a clear distinction in the law between one who was aware (pure subjective intent) and one who should have taken care irrespective of awareness (pure objective intent).

What is the Mens Rea Required to Prove the Offence of Dangerous Driving?

The nature of driving offences suggests that an objective test, or more specially a modified objective test, is particularly appropriate to apply to dangerous driving. I say that for a number of reasons.

(a) The Licensing Requirement

First, driving can only be undertaken by those who have a licence.

The effect of the licensing requirement is to demonstrate that those who drive are mentally and physically capable of doing so. Moreover, it serves to confirm that those who drive are familiar with the standards of care which must be maintained by all drivers. There is a further aspect that must be taken into consideration in light of the licensing requirement for drivers. Licensed drivers choose to engage in the regulated activity of driving. They place themselves in a position of responsibility to other members of the public who use the roads.

As a result, it is unnecessary for a court to establish that the particular accused intended or was aware of the consequences of his or her driving. The minimum standard of physical and mental well-being coupled with the basic knowledge of the standard of care required of licensed drivers obviate that requirement. As a general rule, a consideration of the personal factors, so essential in determining subjective intent, is simply not necessary in light of the fixed standards that must be met by licensed drivers.

(b) The Automatic and Reflexive Nature of Driving

Second, the nature of driving itself is often so routine, so automatic that it is almost impossible to determine a particular state of mind of a driver at any given moment. Driving motor vehicles is something that is familiar to most adult Canadians. It cannot be denied that a great deal of driving is done with little conscious thought. It is an activity that is primarily reactive and not contemplative. It is every bit as routine and familiar as taking a shower or going to work. Often it is impossible for a driver to say what his or her specific intent was at any moment during a drive other than the desire to go from A to B.

It would be a denial of common sense for a driver, whose conduct was objectively dangerous, to be acquitted on the ground that he was not thinking of his manner of driving at the time of the accident.

(c) The Wording of Section 233

Third, the wording of the section itself which refers to the operation of a motor vehicle "in a manner that is dangerous to the public, having regard to all the circumstances" suggests that an objective standard is required. The "manner of driving" can only be compared to a standard of reasonable conduct. That standard can be readily judged and assessed by all who would be members of juries.

Thus, it is clear that the basis of liability for dangerous driving is negligence. The question to be asked is not what the accused subjectively intended but rather whether, viewed objectively, the accused exercised the appropriate standard of care. It is not overly difficult to determine when a driver has fallen markedly below the acceptable standard of care. There can be no doubt that the concept of negligence is well understood and readily recognized by most Canadians. Negligent driving can be thought of as a continuum that progresses, or regresses, from momentary lack of attention giving rise to civil responsibility through careless driving under a provincial Highway Traffic Act to dangerous driving under the *Criminal Code.*

(d) Statistics

Fourth, the statistics which demonstrate that all too many tragic deaths and disabling injuries flow from the operation of motor vehicles indicate the need to control the conduct of drivers. The need is obvious and urgent. Section 233 seeks to curb conduct which is exceedingly dangerous to the public. The statistics on car accidents in Canada indicate with chilling clarity the extent of the problem. The number of people killed and injured each year in traffic accidents is staggering. Data from Transport Canada shows that, in 1991, the number of deaths related to traffic accidents in Canada was 3,654. In 1990, there were 178,423 personal injury traffic accidents, 630,000 property damage accidents and 3,442 fatal accidents. These figures highlight the tragic social cost which can and does arise from the operation of motor vehicles. There is therefore a compelling need for effective legislation which strives to regulate the manner of driving vehicles and thereby lessen the carnage on our highways. It is not only appropriate but essential in the control of dangerous driving that an objective standard be applied.

In my view, to insist on a subjective mental element in connection with driving offences would be to deny reality. It cannot be forgotten that the operation of a motor vehicle is, as I have said so very often, automatic and with little conscious thought. It is simply inappropriate to apply a subjective test in determining whether an accused is guilty of dangerous driving.

(e) Modified Objective Test

Although an objective test must be applied to the offence of dangerous driving it will remain open to the accused to raise a reasonable doubt that a reasonable person would have been aware of the risks in the accused's conduct. The test must be applied with some measure of flexibility. That is to say the objective test should not be applied in a vacuum but rather in the context of the events surrounding the incident.

There will be occasions when the manner of driving viewed objectively will clearly be dangerous yet the accused should not be convicted. Take for example a driver who, without prior warning, suffers a totally unexpected heart attach, epileptic seizure or detached retina. As a result of the sudden onset of a disease or physical disability the manner of driving would be dangerous yet those circumstances could provide a complete defence despite the objective demonstration of dangerous driving. Similarly, a driver who, in the absence of any warning or knowledge of its possible effects, takes a prescribed medication which suddenly and unexpectedly affects the driver in such a way that the manner of driving was dangerous to the public, could still establish a good defence to the charge although it had been objectively established. These examples, and there may well be others, serve to illustrate the aim and purpose of the modified objective test. It is to enable a court to take into account the sudden and unexpected onset of disease and similar human frailties as well as the objective demonstration of dangerous driving....

In summary, the *mens rea* for the offence of dangerous driving should be assessed objectively but in the context of all the events surrounding the incident. That approach will satisfy the dictates both of common sense and fairness. As a general rule, personal factors need not be taken into account. This flows from the licensing requirement for driving which assures that all who drive have a reasonable standard of physical health and capability, mental health and a knowledge of the reasonable standard required of all licensed drivers.

In light of the licensing requirement and the nature of driving offences, a modified objective test satisfies the constitutional minimum fault requirement for s. 233 of the *Criminal Code* and is eminently well-suited to that offence.

It follows then that a trier of fact may convict if satisfied beyond a reasonable doubt that, viewed objectively, the accused was, in the words of the section, driving in a manner that was "dangerous to the public, having regard to all the circumstances, including the nature, condition and use of such place and the amount of traffic that at the time is or might reasonably be expected to be on such place". In making the assessment, the trier of fact should be satisfied that the conduct amounted to a marked departure from the standard of care that a reasonable person would observe in the accused's situation.

Next, if an explanation is offered by the accused, such as a sudden and unexpected onset of illness, then in order to convict, the trier of fact must be satisfied that a reasonable person in similar circumstances ought to have been aware of the risk and of the danger involved in the conduct manifested by the accused. If a jury is determining the fact, they may be instructed with regard to dangerous driving along the lines set out above. There is no necessity for a long or complex charge. Neither the section nor the offence requires it. Certainly the instructions should not be unnecessarily confused by any references to advertent or inadvertent negligence. The offence can be readily assessed by jurors who can arrive at a conclusion based on common sense and their own everyday experiences.

Application of These Principles to the Facts

Let us now consider whether the modified objective test was properly applied in this case. The trial judge carefully examined the circumstances of the accident. He took into account the busy downtown traffic, the weather conditions, and the mechanical conditions of the accused vehicle. He concluded, in my view very properly, that the appellant's manner of driving represented a gross departure from the standard of a reasonably prudent driver. No explanation was offered by the accused that could excuse his conduct. There is no reason for interfering with the trial judge's finding of fact and application of the law.

In the result the appeal must be dismissed.

R. V. JACOB

Ontario Court of Appeal

(1996) 31 O.R. (3d) 350

On an extremely hot and humid summer day in downtown Guelph, Ms Jacob went topless. When confronted by a police officer, she stated that since males were permitted to be in public with their chests uncovered, she had a constitutional right to do so to, and anyway, it was more comfortable in the heat. The constable decided not to charge Ms Jacob unless there was a complaint about her appearance. Soon enough, there were complaints and she was dutifully charged with a violation of section 173(1)(b) of the *Criminal Code*, which sets out the offence of wilfully committing an indecent act. The Ontario Court of Appeal asked itself why being topless should be an indecent act, indeed why should it be a crime? It answered that it should not (unless the context of the conduct was explicitly sexual, which in this case it clearly was not). Of special interest is Madam Justice Weiler's suggestion that the community's standard of tolerance – long used in the characterization of obscenity – is not a reliable guide to what conduct should be criminal.

* * * *

Madame Justice Weiler:

The appellant was charged with committing an indecent act by exposing her breasts in a public place contrary to s. 173(1)(a) of the *Criminal Code*. The provincial court judge found that the appellant's act was beyond the community standard of tolerance, convicted her of committing an indecent act and sentenced her to pay a fine of $75. She appealed her conviction to the Ontario Court (General Division). The appeal judge found that the trial judge's decision was not unreasonable, that it could be supported on the evidence, and that he had not erred in law. He dismissed the appeal. The appellant now seeks to appeal to this court. [Section 173(1) reads]:

173(1) Everyone who wilfully does an indecent act
(a) in a public place in the presence of one or more persons, or
(b) in any place, with intent thereby to insult or offend any person,
is guilty of an offence punishable on summary conviction.

Obscenity and indecency are part of the same continuum. There is, however, one important distinction. Whether or not a work is obscene is a function of the internal attributes of the work. A work does not become obscene by reason of the place or manner in which it is shown. Indecency, on the other hand, is contextual and depends on the circumstances.

In 1959, what is now s.163(8) of the *Criminal Code* was enacted, providing the first statutory definition of obscenity..."the undue exploitation of sex", or of sex and a series of enumerated subjects, namely, crime, horror, cruelty, and violence. The inherent characteristic of an obscene work is that sex is the dominant theme....[I]n order for there to be a conviction in respect of any charge of obscenity under the *Criminal Code* the Crown must prove two things: (1) the exploitation of sex as the dominant characteristic of the material or act, and (2) that this exploitation is "undue" in the sense that it is beyond the community standard of tolerance.

The community standard of tolerance test, used to measure whether the exploitation of sex was undue, was not restricted to obscenity. In *R. v. Popert* (1981), the court sought the advantage of a consistent test in relation to a charge of using the mails for "indecent, immoral or scurrilous matter" and adopted the community standard of tolerance test in relation to immorality and indecency....By linking indecency to the test used to determine whether an act is obscene, namely, the community standard of tolerance, the court imported the requirement of a sexual context. This conclusion is reinforced by the court's comment that the trial judge erred in purporting to apply the ordinary meaning of the term "indecent". In so doing, the court implicitly recognized that it is no longer appropriate to apply the ordinary or dictionary meaning of the word indecent.

Inasmuch as the term indecent is nowhere defined in the *Code*, and the dictionary definition has been rejected...it is within the role of the judiciary to attempt to interpret these terms. Determining the underlying values necessary for the coexistence of persons in places to which the public has access has never been an easy task. This is especially true now that conventional morality has been rejected as the basis for finding an act to be indecent. Instead, courts must seek to ground disapprobation of conduct by bearing in mind *Charter* rights and values. If the content of the conduct is ignored and regard is had only to community standards there is a danger of a majority deciding what values are important and coercing minorities to conform to those values on the basis of avoiding perceived harm to society from non-conformity. If resort is had only to the community standard of tolerance test without there being a context-based prerequisite, then it is possible that discrimination arising from social stereotyping will be legitimatized. In so far as community standards of tolerance are to be applied under s. 173(1)(a), therefore, an essential element is that the context of the conduct must first be sexual.

...[T]he question is, would a reasonable bystander, fully apprised of all the circumstances, have considered the appellant's act was sexual in the sense that she was exposing her breasts for the sexual gratification of herself or someone else. The exposure today of a woman's breasts in public does not automatically import a conclusion that this act is being done for the sexual gratification of the actor or the audience. For example, the exposure of a woman's breasts in public in order to breastfeed a child is not done for the sexual gratification of the woman or anyone else. It affords women, who choose to nourish a child by breastfeeding, mobility. This example illustrates the importance of the circumstances in determining whether an act is sexual....While the motive of the accused person is but one factor to consider, its importance will vary depending on the circumstances. Here, Ms. Jacob did not touch or stroke her breasts. With respect to words, I consider that underlying the remarks of the police officers and the mother who spoke to Ms. Jacob was a concern that Ms. Jacob was degrading the essential human dignity of herself and the members of her sex by exposing her breasts. The rude remarks made by some men upon seeing Ms. Jacob barebreasted would tend to support this view. But the reasonable bystander would not be fully informed without also considering Ms. Jacob's reply to the police officer protesting against what she viewed as discrimination, her conversation with the man working on his front lawn which was unremarkable, and her reply to the mother who spoke to her. Having regard to these conversations and weighing them in all the circumstances, the reasonable bystander would not, in my opinion, conclude beyond a reasonable doubt that the appellant was exposing her breasts for the sexual gratification of herself or someone else. As a result, the appellant's conduct lacks the sexual context for being an indecent act within the meaning of s. 173(1)(a).

Conclusion

In applying the community standard of tolerance test under s. 173(1)(a), one must bear in mind that this test is not an end in itself. If the term indecent were to mean whatever the community will not tolerate, there is a danger that discrimination by the community will be seen as harmful and legitimized. The community standard of tolerance is a measure of whether conduct is unduly sexual. In order for an act to be an indecent act under s. 173(1)(a), the act must be a sexual act in the sense that the act is done for the sexual gratification of the accused or others. In this case, a reasonable bystander, fully informed of all the circumstances, would not conclude that this was the case. Secondly, the trial judge erred in the manner in which he applied the community standard of tolerance test. For these reasons I would grant leave to appeal, allow the appeal and order that an acquittal be entered.

Mr Justices Osborne and Austin (concurring in the result):

I agree with Weiler J.A. that the appeal should be allowed. I do not, however, agree with her reasons for reaching that conclusion. In particular, I do not agree that to be an indecent act, as proscribed by s. 173(1)(a) of the *Criminal Code*, the act must have a sexual context.

In my opinion, the community standard of tolerance test must be used to answer the question whether the appellant's topless stroll in downtown Guelph constituted an indecent act. If the community standard of tolerance test is correctly applied (and I agree with Weiler J.A. that it was not) I do not think that the appellant committed the offence with which she was charged. I reach that conclusion in the light of the evidence which establishes the general context of the appellant's action, the trial judge's findings and significantly the absence of evidence that the appellant's choice of apparel caused any harm.

I agree with Weiler J.A. that if an act must have a sexual context to be an indecent act under s. 173(1)(a) and the act does not have a sexual context, there is no need to determine if the act exceed the community standard of tolerance. In my opinion, the context of the appellant's act (including any elements of moral turpitude) should be considered as part of the fabric of the community standard of tolerance, not as an element of the offence.

PERKA V. REGINA

Supreme Court of Canada

[1984] 2 S.C.R. 232

This Supreme Court of Canada case explores the philosophically rich part of the criminal law that deals with defences. Roughly, in defence, one can either argue that one has an excuse inasmuch as, at the time of the offence, one did not have the required *mens rea,* or one can argue that one's criminal conduct was justified under the circumstances. Here the accused tried to make a case for the defence of necessity, one of the most difficult and contentious defences recognized in our law. The Court took the opportunity to decide, once and for all, what the defence means and when it applies.

* * * *

Chief Justice Dickson and Justices Ritchie, Chouinard and Lamer:

The appellants are drug smugglers. At trial, they led evidence that in early 1979 three of the appellants were employed, with 16 crew members, to deliver, by ship (the "Samarkanda") a load of *cannabis* (marijuana) worth $6,000,000 or $7,000,000 from a point in international waters off the coast of Colombia, South America to a drop-point in international waters 200 miles off the coast of Alaska....

· ...*En route,* according to the defence evidence, the vessel began to encounter a series of problems; engine breakdowns, overheating generators and malfunctioning navigation devices, aggravated by deteriorating weather. In the meantime, the fourth appellant, Nelson, part-owner of the illicit cargo, and three other persons left Seattle in a small boat, the "Whitecap", intending to rendezvous with the "Samarkanda" at the drop-point in Alaska. The problems of the "Samarkanda" intensified as fuel was consumed. The vessel became lighter, the intakes in the hull for sea-water, used as a coolant, lost suction and took in air instead, causing the generators to overheat. At this point the vessel was 180 miles from the Canadian coastline. The weather worsened. There were eight-to-ten-foot swells and a rising wind. It was finally decided for the safety of ship and crew to seek refuge on the Canadian shoreline for the purpose of making temporary repairs. The "Whitecap" found a sheltered cove on the west coast of Vancouver Island, "No Name Bay". The "Samarkanda" followed the "Whitecap" into the bay but later grounded amidships on a rock because the depth sounder was not working. The tide ran out. The vessel listed severely to starboard, to the extent that the captain, fearing the vessel was going to capsize, ordered the men to off-load the cargo. That is a brief summary of the defence evidence.

Early on the morning of May 22, 1979, police officers entered No Name Bay in a marked police boat with siren sounding. The "Samarkanda" and the "Whitecap" were arrested, as were all the appellants except Perka and Nelson, the same morning. The vessels and 33.49 tons of *cannabis* marijuana were seized by the police officers.

Charged with importing *cannabis* into Canada and with possession for the purpose of trafficking, the appellants claimed they did not plan to import into Canada or to leave their cargo of *cannabis* in Canada. They had planned to make repairs and leave. Expert witnesses on marine matters called by the defence testified that the decision to come ashore was, in the opinion of one witness, expedient and prudent and in the opinion of another, essential. At trial, counsel for the Crown alleged that the evidence of the ship's distress was a recent fabrication. Crown counsel relied on the circumstances under which the appellants were arrested to belie the "necessity" defence; when the police arrived on the scene most of the marijuana was already onshore, along with plastic ground sheets, battery-operated lights, liquor, food, clothing, camp stoves and sleeping-bags. Nevertheless, the jury believed the appellants and acquitted them.

The acquittal was reversed on appeal....

[History of the Necessity Defence]

From earliest times it has been maintained that in some situations the force of circumstances makes it unrealistic and unjust to attach criminal liability to actions which, on their face, violate the law. Aristotle, in the *Nicomachean Ethics* discusses the jettisoning of cargo from a ship in distress and remarks that "any sensible man does so" to secure the safety of himself and his crew....In *Leviathan* Hobbes writes:

If a man by the terrour of present death, be compelled to doe a fact against the law, he is totally excused; because no law can oblige a man to abandon his own preservation. And supposing such a law were obligatory; yet a man would reason thus, if I doe it not, I die presently: if I doe it I die afterwards: therefore by doing it there is time of life gained: nature therefore compels him to the fact.

To much the same purpose Kant, in *The Metaphysical Elements of Justice,* discussing the actions of a person who, to save his own life sacrifices that of another, says:

> A penal law applying to such a situation could never have the effect intended, for the threat of an evil that is still uncertain (being condemned to death by a judge) cannot outweigh the fear of an evil that is certain (being drowned). Hence, we must judge that, although an act of self-preservation through violence is not inculpable, it still is unpunishable.

In those jurisdictions in which such a general principle has been recognized or codified it is most often referred to by the term "necessity". Classic and harrowing instances which have been cited to illustrate the arguments both for and against the principle include the mother who steals food for her starving child, the shipwrecked mariners who resort to cannibalism (*R. v. Dudley and Stephens* (1884)), or throw passengers overboard to lighten a sinking lifeboat (*United States v. Holmes* (1842)), and the more mundane case of the motorist who exceeds the speed-limit taking an injured person to the hospital....

In England, opinion as to the existence of a general defence of necessity has varied. Blackstone, in his *Commentaries on the Laws of England,* mentioned two principles capable of being read as underlying such a defence: "As punishments are only inflicted for the abuse of that free will, which God has given to man, it is just that a man should be excused for those acts, which are done through unavoidable force and compulsion". Then under the rubric "Choice Between Two Evils" he writes:

> *Choice Between Two Evils.* This species of necessity is the result of reason and reflection and obliges a man to do an act, which, without such obligation, would be criminal. This occurs, when a man has his choice of two evils set before him, and chooses the less pernicious one. He rejects the greater evil and chooses the less. As where a man is bound to arrest another for a capital offence, and being resisted, kills the offender, rather than permit him to escape....

In Canada the existence and the extent of a general defence of necessity was discussed by this Court in *Morgentaler v. The Queen* (1975). As to whether or not the defence exists at all I had occasion to say:

> On the authorities it is manifestly difficult to be categorical and state that there is a law of necessity, paramount over other laws, relieving obedience from the letter of the law. If it does exist it can go no further than to justify non-compliance in urgent situations of clear and imminent peril when compliance with the law is demonstrably impossible....

[Conceptual Foundations of Necessity]

...[T]he "defence" of necessity in fact is capable of embracing two different and distinct notions. As Mr. Justice Macdonald observed succinctly but accurately: "Generally speaking, the defence of necessity covers all cases where noncompliance with law is excused by an emergency or justified by the pursuit of some greater good...".

Criminal theory recognizes a distinction between "justifications" and "excuses". A "justification" challenges the wrongfulness of an action which technically constitutes a crime. The police officer who shoots the hostage-taker, the innocent object of an assault who uses force to defend himself against his assailant, the good Samaritan who commandeers a car and breaks the speed laws to rush an accident victim to the hospital, these are all actors whose actions we consider *rightful*, not wrongful. For such actions people are often praised, as motivated by some great or noble object. The concept of punishment often seems incompatible with the social approval bestowed on the doer.

In contrast, an "excuse" concedes the wrongfulness of the action but asserts that the circumstances under which it was done are such that it ought not to be attributed to the actor. The perpetrator who is incapable, owing to a disease of the mind, of appreciating the nature and consequences of his acts, the sleepwalker; these are all actors of whose "criminal" actions we disapprove intensely, but whom, in appropriate circumstances, our law will not punish....

...I retain the scepticism I expressed in *Morgentaler*. It is still my opinion that "[n]o system of positive law can recognize any principle which would entitle a person to violate the law because on his view the law conflicted with some higher social value". The *Criminal Code* has specified a number of identifiable situations in which an actor is justified in committing what would otherwise be a criminal offence. To go beyond that and hold that ostensibly illegal acts can be validated on the basis of their expediency, would import an undue subjectivity into the criminal law. It would invite the courts to second-guess the Legislature and to assess the relative merits of social policies underlying criminal prohibitions. Neither is a role which fits well with the judicial function. Such a doctrine could well become the last resort of scoundrels and...it could "very easily become simply a mask for anarchy".

Conceptualized as an "excuse", however, the residual defence of necessity is, in my view, much less open to criticism. It rests on a realistic assessment of human weakness, recognizing that a liberal and humane criminal law cannot hold people to the strict obedience of laws in emergency situations where normal human instincts, whether of self-preservation or of altruism, overwhelmingly impel disobedience. The objectivity of the criminal law is preserved; such acts are still wrongful, but in the circumstances they are excusable. Praise is indeed not bestowed, but pardon is, when one does a wrongful act under pressure which, in the words of Aristotle "overstrains human nature and which no one could withstand".

George Fletcher, *Rethinking Criminal Law*, describes this view of necessity as "compulsion of circumstance" which description points to the conceptual link between necessity as an excuse and the familiar criminal law requirement that in order to engage criminal liability, the actions constituting the *actus reus* of an offence must be voluntary. Literally, this voluntariness requirement simply refers to the need that the prohibited physical acts must have been under the conscious control of the actor. Without such control, there is, for purposes of the criminal law, no act. The excuse of necessity does not go to voluntariness in this sense. The lost Alpinist who, on the point of freezing to death, breaks open an isolated mountain cabin is not literally behaving in an involuntary fashion. He has control over his actions to the extent of being physically capable of abstaining from the act. Realistically, however, his act is not a "voluntary" one. His "choice" to break the law is no true choice at all; it is remorselessly compelled by normal human instincts. This sort of involuntariness is often described as "moral or normative involuntariness"....

...At the heart of this defence is the perceived injustice of punishing violations of the law in circumstances in which the person had no other viable or reasonable choice available; the act was wrong but it is excused because it was realistically unavoidable....

Relating necessity to the principle that the law ought not to punish involuntary acts leads to a conceptualization of the defence that integrates it into the normal rules for criminal liability rather than constituting it as a *sui generis* exception and threatening to engulf large portions of the criminal law. Such a conceptualization accords with our traditional legal, moral and philosophic views as to what sorts of acts and what sorts of actors ought to be punished. In this formulation it is a defence which I do not hesitate to acknowledge and would not hesitate to apply to relevant facts capable of satisfying its necessary prerequisites.

[Limitations on the Defence]

If the defence of necessity is to form a valid and consistent part of our criminal law it must, as has been universally recognized, be strictly controlled and scrupulously limited to situations that correspond to its underlying *rationale*. That *rationale* as I have indicated, is the recognition that it is inappropriate to punish actions which are normatively "involuntary". The appropriate controls and limitations on the defence of necessity are, therefore, addressed to ensuring that the acts for which the benefit of the excuse of necessity is sought are truly "involuntary" in the requisite sense.

In *Morgentaler v. The Queen (1975)* I was of the view that any defence of necessity was restricted to instances of non-compliance "in urgent situations of clear and imminent peril when compliance with the law is demonstrably impossible". In my opinion, this restriction focuses directly on the "involuntariness" of the purportedly necessitous behaviour by providing a number of tests for determining whether the wrongful act was truly the only realistic reaction open to the actor or whether he was in fact making what in fairness could be called a choice. If he was making a choice, then the wrongful act cannot have been involuntary in the relevant sense....At a minimum the situation must be so emergent and the peril must be so pressing that normal human instincts cry out for action and make a counsel of patience unreasonable.

The requirement that compliance with the law be "demonstrably impossible" takes this assessment one step further. Given that the accused had to act, could he nevertheless realistically have acted to avoid the peril or prevent the harm, without breaking the law? *Was there a legal way out?*...The question to be asked is whether the agent had any real choice: could he have done otherwise? If there is a reasonably legal alternative to disobeying the law, then the decision to disobey becomes a voluntary one, impelled by some consideration beyond the dictates of "necessity" and human instincts.

The importance of this requirement that there be no reasonable legal alternative cannot be overstressed.

Even if the requirements for urgency and "no legal way out" are met, there is clearly a further consideration. There must be some way of assuring proportionality. No rational criminal justice system, no matter how humane or liberal, could excuse the infliction of a greater harm to allow the actor to avert a lesser evil. In such circumstances we expect the individual to bear the harm and refrain from acting illegally. If he cannot control himself we will not excuse him....

I would therefore add to the preceding requirements a stipulation of proportionality expressible by the proviso that the harm inflicted must be less than the harm sought to be avoided.

The Crown submits that there is an additional limitation on the availability of the defence of necessity....[I]t argues that because the appellants were committing a crime when their necessitous circumstances arose, they should be denied the defence of necessity as a matter of law....

...I have considerable doubt as to the cogency of such a limitation. If the conduct in which an accused was engaging at the time the peril arose was illegal, then it should clearly be punished, but I fail to see the relevance of its illegal character to the question of whether the accused's subsequent conduct in dealing with this emergent peril ought to be excused on the basis of necessity. At most the illegality...of the preceding conduct will colour the subsequent conduct in response to the emergency as also wrongful. But that wrongfulness is never in any doubt. Necessity goes to *excuse* conduct, not to *justify* it. Where it is found to apply it carries with it no implicit vindication of the deed to which it attaches. That cannot be over-emphasized. Were the defence of necessity to succeed in the present case, it would not in any way amount to a vindication of importing controlled substances nor to a critique of the law prohibiting such importation. It would also have nothing to say about the comparative social utility of breaking the law against importing as compared to obeying the law. The question, as I have said, is never whether what the accused has done is wrongful. The question is whether what he has done is voluntary. Except in the limited sense I intend to discuss below, I do not see the relevance of the legality or even the morality of what the accused was doing at the time the emergency arose to this question of the voluntariness of the subsequent conduct....

In my view the accused's fault in bringing about the situation later invoked to excuse his conduct *can* be relevant to the availability of the defence of necessity....Insofar as the accused's "fault" reflects on the moral quality of the action taken to meet the emergency, it is irrelevant to the issue of the availability of the defence on the same basis as the illegality or immorality of the actions preceding the emergency are irrelevant. If this fault is capable of attracting criminal or civil liability in its own right, the culprit should be appropriately sanctioned. I see no basis, however, for "transferring" such liability to the actions taken in response to the emergency, especially where to do so would result in attaching criminal consequences on the basis of negligence to actions which would otherwise be excused.

In my view, the better approach to the relationship of fault to the availability of necessity as a defence is based once again on the question of whether the actions sought to be excused were truly "involuntary". If the necessitous situation was clearly foreseeable to a reasonable observer, if the actor contemplated or ought to have contemplated that his actions would likely give rise to an emergency requiring the breaking of the law, then I doubt whether what confronted the accused was in the relevant sense an emergency. His response was in that sense not "involuntary"....

...If the accused's "fault" consists of actions whose clear consequences were in the situation that actually ensued, then he was not "really" confronted with an emergency which compelled him to commit the unlawful act he now seeks to have excused. In such situations the defence is unavailable. Mere negligence, however, or the simple fact that he was engaged in illegal or immoral conduct when the emergency arose will not disentitle an individual to rely on the defence of necessity.

Although necessity is spoken of as a defence, in the sense that it is raised by the accused, the Crown always bears the burden of proving a voluntary act. The prosecution must prove every element of the crime charged. One such element is the voluntariness of the act. Normally, voluntariness can be presumed, but if the accused places before the court, through his own witnesses or through cross-examination of Crown witnesses, evidence sufficient to raise an issue that the situation created by external forces was so emergent that failure to act could endanger life or health and upon any reasonable view of the facts, compliance with the law was impossible, then the Crown must be prepared to meet that issue. There is no onus of proof on the accused....

It is now possible to summarize a number of conclusions as to the defence of necessity in terms of its nature, basis and limitations: (1) the defence of necessity could be conceptualized as either a justification or an excuse; (2) it should be recognized in Canada as an excuse, operating by virtue of s. 7(3) of the *Criminal Code;* (3) necessity as an excuse implies no vindication of the deeds of the actor; (4) the criterion is the moral involuntariness of the wrongful action; (5) this involuntariness is measured on the basis of society's expectation of appropriate and normal resistance to pressure; (6) negligence or involvement in criminal or immoral activity does not disentitle the actor to the excuse of necessity; (7) actions or circumstances which indicate that the wrongful deed was not truly involuntary do disentitle; (8) the existence of a reasonable legal alternative similarly disentitles; to be involuntary the act must be inevitable, unavoidable and afford no reasonable opportunity for an alternative course of action that does not involve a breach of the law; (9) the defence only applies in circumstances of imminent risk where the action was taken to avoid a direct and immediate peril; (10) where the accused places before the court sufficient evidence to raise the issue, the onus is on the Crown to meet it beyond a reasonable doubt.

[Application to the Facts]

In his charge [to the jury], the trial judge did not...tell the jury that they must find facts capable of showing that "compliance with the law was demonstrably impossible..." but on his recharge he put before the jury a significantly different test. The test, he said, is:

> ...can you find facts from this evidence, and that means all the evidence, of course, that the situation of the Samarkanda at sea was so appallingly dire and dangerous to life that a reasonable doubt arises as to whether or not their decision was justified?...

[This passage implies] that the crucial consideration was whether the accused acted reasonably in coming into shore with their load of *cannabis* rather than facing death at sea. That is not sufficient as a test. Even if it does deal with the reality of the peril, its imminence and the proportionality of putting into shore, it does not deal at all with the question of whether there existed any other reasonable responses to the peril that were not illegal. Indeed...the trial judge did not advert to this consideration at all, nor did he direct the jury's attention to the relevance of evidence indicating the possibility of such alternative courses of action. In these respects I believe he erred in law. He did not properly put the question of a "legal way out" before the jury.

In my view, this was a serious error and omission going to the heart of the defence of necessity. The error justifies a new trial.

R. V. LAVALLEE

Supreme Court of Canada

[1990] 1 S.C.R. 852

Lyn Lavallee was acquitted of murdering her common law spouse by a jury who had heard expert evidence from a psychiatrist who described Lavallee's actions in terms of the "battered wife syndrome". Lavallee had convinced the jury that she fatally shot Kevin Rust out of self-defence. The Manitoba Court of Appeal overturned the acquittal on the grounds that the psychiatric evidence should not have been admitted, since it was based on unsworn and hearsay evidence, and without the expert evidence the jury would not have accepted the plea of self-defence.

In rejecting this argument, and reinstating the acquittal, the Supreme Court of Canada found it necessary to look carefully at the requirements for self-defence as well as the conditions that can be imposed on exculpatory expert evidence. Along the way, Madam Justice Bertha Wilson also considered the role of juries in cases, such as this, in which it can not be presumed that ordinary, reasonable people can fully appreciate or understand the circumstances some accused people were in at the time of the offence.

* * * *

Madam Justice Wilson, Chief Justice Dickson and Justices Lamer, L'Heureux-Dubé, Gonthier and Cory:

The expert evidence which forms the subject matter of the appeal came from Dr. Fred Shane, a psychiatrist with extensive professional experience in the treatment of battered wives. At the request of defence counsel Dr. Shane prepared a psychiatric assessment of the appellant. The substance of Dr. Shane's opinion was that the appellant had been terrorized by Rust to the point of feeling trapped, vulnerable, worthless and unable to escape the relationship despite the violence. At the same time, the continuing pattern of abuse put her life in danger. In Dr. Shane's opinion the appellant's shooting of the deceased was a final desperate act by a woman who sincerely believed that she would be killed that night....

Relevant Legislation: Criminal Code

34. (2) Every one who is unlawfully assaulted and who causes death or grievous bodily harm in repelling the assault is justified if

(a) he causes it under reasonable apprehension of death or grievous bodily harm from the violence with which the assault was originally made or with which the assailant pursues his purposes, and

(b) he believes on reasonable and probable grounds, that he cannot otherwise preserve himself from death or grievous bodily harm....

Analysis

(i) Admissibility of Expert Evidence

The bare facts of this case, which I think are amply supported by the evidence, are that the appellant was repeatedly abused by the deceased but did not leave him (although she twice pointed a gun at him), and ultimately shot him in the back of the head as he was leaving her room. The Crown submits that these facts disclose all the information a jury needs in order to decide whether or not the appellant acted in self-defence. I have no hesitation in rejecting the Crown's submission.

Expert evidence on the psychological effect of battering on wives and common law partners must, it seems to me, be both relevant and necessary in the context of the present case. How can the mental state of the appellant be appreciated without it? The average member of the public (or of the jury) can be forgiven for asking: Why would a woman put up with this kind of treatment? Why should she continue to live with such a man? How could she love a partner who beat her to the point of requiring hospitalization? We would expect the woman to pack her bags and go. Where is her self-respect? Why does she not cut loose and make a new life for herself? Such is the reaction of the average person confronted with the so-called "battered wife syndrome". We need help to understand it and help is available from trained professionals.

The gravity, indeed, the tragedy of domestic violence can hardly be overstated. Greater media attention to this phenomenon in recent years has revealed both its prevalence and its horrific impact on women from all walks of life. Far from protecting women from it the law historically sanctioned the abuse of women within marriage as an aspect of the husband's ownership of his wife and his "right" to chastise her. One need only recall the centuries old law that a man is entitled to beat his wife with a stick "no thicker than his thumb".

Laws do not spring out of a social vacuum. The notion that a man has a right to "discipline" his wife is deeply rooted in the history of our society. The woman's duty was to serve her husband and to stay in the marriage at all costs "till death do us part" and to accept as her due any "punishment" that was meted out for failing to please her husband. One consequence of this attitude was that "wife battering" was rarely spoken of, rarely reported, rarely prosecuted, and even more rarely punished. Long after society abandoned its formal approval of spousal abuse tolerance of it continued and continues in some circles to this day.

Fortunately, there has been a growing awareness in recent years that no man has a right to abuse any woman under any circumstances. Legislative initiatives designed to educate police, judicial officers and the public, as well as more aggressive investigation and charging policies all signal a concerted effort by the criminal justice system to take spousal abuse seriously. However, a woman who comes before a judge or jury with the claim that she has been battered and suggests that this may be a relevant factor in evaluating her subsequent actions still faces the prospect of being condemned by popular mythology about domestic violence. Either she was not as badly beaten as she claims or she would have left the man long ago. Or, if she was battered that severely, she must have stayed out of some masochistic enjoyment of it.

Expert testimony on the psychological effects of battering have been admitted in American courts in recent years. In *State v. Kelly (1984)* the New Jersey Supreme Court commended the value of expert testimony in these terms:

> It is aimed at an area where the purported common knowledge of the jury may be very much mistaken, an area where jurors' logic, drawn from their own experience, may lead to a wholly incorrect conclusion, an area where expert knowledge would enable the jurors to disregard their prior conclusions as being common myths rather than common knowledge.

The Court concludes that the battering relationship is "subject to a large group of myths and stereotypes". As such, it is "beyond the ken of the average juror and thus is suitable for the explanation through expert testimony". I share that view.

(ii) The relevance of Expert Testimony to the Elements of Self-Defence

In my view, there are two elements of the defence under s. 34(2) of the *Code* which merit scrutiny for present purposes. The first is the temporal connection in s. 34(2)(a) between the apprehension of death or grievous bodily harm and the act allegedly taken in self-defence. Was the appellant "under reasonable apprehension of death or grievous bodily harm" from Rust as he was walking out of the room? The second is the assessment in s. 34(2)(b) of the magnitude of the force used by the accused. Was the accused's belief that she could not "otherwise preserve herself from death or grievous bodily harm" except by shooting the deceased based on "reasonable grounds"?

The feature common to both s. 34(2)(a) and (b) is the imposition of an objective standard of reasonableness on the apprehension of death and the need to repel the assault with deadly force. In *Reilly v. The Queen* (1984), this Court considered the interaction of the objective and subjective components of s. 34(2), at p. 404:

> Subsection (2) of s. 34 places in issue the accused's state of mind at the time he caused death. The subsection can only afford protection to the accused if he apprehended death or grievous bodily harm from the assault he was repelling and if he believed he could not preserve himself from death or grievous bodily harm otherwise than by the force he used. Nonetheless, his apprehension must be a *reasonable* one and his belief must *be based upon reasonable and probable grounds*. The subsection requires that the jury consider, and be guided by, what they decide on the evidence was the accused's appreciation of the situation and his belief as to the reaction it required, so long as there exists an objectively verifiable basis for his perception.

> Since s. 34(2) places in issue the accused's perception of the attack upon and the response required to meet it, the accused may still be found to have acted in self-defence even if he was mistaken in his perception. Reasonable and probable grounds must still exist for this mistaken perception in the sense that the mistake must have been one which an ordinary man using ordinary care could have made in the same circumstances.

If it strains credulity to imagine what the "ordinary man" would do in the position of a battered spouse, it is probably because men do not typically find themselves in that situation. Some women do, however. The definition of what is reasonable must be adapted to circumstances which are, by and large, foreign to the world inhabited by the hypothetical "reasonable man"....

A. *Reasonable Apprehension of Death*

In the present case, the assault precipitating the appellant's alleged defensive act was Rust's threat to kill her when everyone else was gone.

It will be observed that s. 34(2)(a) does not actually stipulate that the accused apprehend *imminent* danger when he or she acts. Case law has, however, read that requirement into the defence. The sense in which "imminent" is used conjures up the image of "an uplifted knife" or a pointed gun. The rationale for the imminence rule seems obvious. The law of self-defence is designed to ensure that the use of defensive force is really necessary. It justifies the act because the defender reasonably believed that he or she had no alternative but to take the attacker's life. If there is a significant time interval between the original unlawful assault and the accused's response, one tends to suspect that the accused was motivated by revenge rather than self-defence. In the paradigmatic case of a one-time barroom brawl between two men of equal size and strength, this inference makes sense. How can one feel endangered to the point of firing a gun at an unarmed man who utters a death threat, then turns his back and walks out of the room? One cannot be certain of the gravity of the threat or his capacity to carry it out. Besides, one can always take the opportunity to flee or to call the police. If he comes back and raises his fist, one can respond in kind if need be. These are the tacit assumptions that underlie the imminence rule....

...[T]he appellant...was routinely beaten over the course of her relationship with the man she ultimately killed. According to the testimony of Dr. Shane these assaults were not entirely random in their occurrence....

Dr. [Lenore] Walker defines a battered woman as a woman who has gone through the battering cycle at least twice. As she explains in the introduction to *The Battered Woman (1979)*, at p. xv, "Any woman may find herself in an abusive relationship with a man once. If it occurs a second time, and she remains in the situation, she is defined as a battered woman".

Given the relational context in which the violence occurs, the mental state of an accused at the critical moment she pulls the trigger cannot be understood except in terms of the cumulative effect of months or years of brutality. As Dr. Shane explained in his testimony, the deterioration of the relationship between the appellant and Rust in the period immediately preceding the killing led to feelings of escalating terror on the part of the appellant....

Another aspect of the cyclical nature of the abuse is that it begets a degree of predictability to the violence that is absent in an isolated violent encounter between two strangers. This also means that it may in fact be possible for a battered spouse to accurately predict the onset of violence before the first blow is struck, even if an outsider to the relationship cannot. Indeed it has been suggested that a battered woman's knowledge of her partner's violence is so heightened that she is able to anticipate the nature and extent (though not the onset) of the violence by his conduct beforehand....

Where evidence exists that an accused is in a battering relationship, expert testimony can assist the jury in determining whether the accused had a "reasonable" apprehension of death when she acted by explaining the heightened sensitivity of a battered woman to her partner's acts. Without such testimony I am skeptical that the average fact-finder would be capable of appreciating why her subjective fear may have been reasonable in the context of the relationship. After all, the hypothetical "reasonable man" observing only the final incident may have been unlikely to recognize the batterer's threat as potentially lethal. Using the case at bar as an example the "reasonable man" might have thought, as the majority of the Court of Appeal seemed to, that it was unlikely that Rust would make good on his threat to kill the appellant that night because they had guests staying overnight.

The issue is not, however, what an outsider would have reasonably perceived but what the accused reasonably perceived, given her situation and her experience.

Even accepting that a battered woman may be uniquely sensitized to danger from her batterer, it may yet be contended that the law ought to require her to wait until the knife is uplifted, the gun pointed or the fist clenched before her apprehension is deemed reasonable. This would allegedly reduce the risk that the woman is mistaken in her fear, although the law does not require her fear to be correct, only reasonable. In response to this contention, I need only point to the observation made by Huband J.A. that the evidence showed that when the appellant and Rust physically fought the appellant "invariably got the worst of it". I do not think it is an unwarranted generalization to say that due to their size, strength, socialization and lack of training, women are typically no match for men in hand-to-hand combat. The requirement...that a battered woman wait until the physical assault is "underway" before her apprehensions can be validated in law would, in the words of an American court, be tantamount to sentencing her to 'murder by installment'. I share the view expressed by Willoughby in "Rendering Each Woman Her Due: Can a Battered Woman Claim Self-Defense When She Kills Her Sleeping Batterer" (1989), that "society gains nothing, except perhaps the additional risk that the battered woman will herself be killed, because she must wait until her abusive husband instigates another battering episode before she can justifiably act".

B. Lack of Alternatives to Self-Help

Section 34(2) requires an accused who pleads self-defence to believe "on reasonable grounds" that it is not possible to otherwise preserve him or herself from death or grievous bodily harm. The obvious question is if the violence was so intolerable, why did the appellant not leave her abuser long ago? This question does not really go to whether she had an alternative to killing the deceased at the critical moment. Rather, it plays on the popular myth already referred to that a woman who says she was battered yet stayed with her batterer was either not as badly beaten as she claimed or else she liked it. Nevertheless, to the extent that her failure to leave the abusive relationship earlier may be used in support of the proposition that she was free to leave at the final moment, expert testimony can provide useful insights....

I emphasize at this juncture that it is not for the jury to pass judgment on the fact that an accused battered woman stayed in the relationship. Still less is it entitled to conclude that she forfeited her right to self-defence for having done so. I would also point out that traditional self-defence doctrine does not require a person to retreat from her home instead of defending it. A man's home may be his castle but it is also the woman's home even if it seems to her more like a prison in the circumstances.

If, after hearing the evidence (including the expert testimony), the jury is satisfied that the accused had a reasonable apprehension of death or grievous bodily harm and felt incapable of escape, it must ask itself what the "reasonable person" would do in such a situation. The situation of the battered woman as described by Dr. Shane strikes me as somewhat analogous to that of a hostage. If the captor tells her that he will kill her in three days time, is it potentially reasonable for her to seize an opportunity presented on the first day to kill the captor or must she wait until he makes the attempt on the third day? I think the question the jury must ask itself is whether, given the history, circumstances and perceptions of the appellant, her belief that she could not preserve herself from being killed by Rust that night except by killing him first was reasonable. To the extent that expert evidence can assist the jury in making that determination, I would find such testimony to be both relevant and necessary....

I would accordingly allow the appeal, set aside the order of the Court of Appeal, and restore the acquittal.

•

B: LIABILITY IN PRIVATE LAW

COOK V. LEWIS

Supreme Court of Canada

[1952] S.C.R. 830

In order to prove liability for the tort of negligence the plaintiff must prove that the defendant acted carelessly in circumstances in which there was a duty to be more careful and that this conduct caused the plaintiff to be harmed in some way. On the face of it one might suspect that the element of causation would be the least difficult to prove, and this is usually true. The general rule for causation in torts (or "cause-in-fact") is the so-called "but for" test: the plaintiff must show that, but for the defendant's negligent conduct, the plaintiff would not have suffered harm. What could be more straightforward? *Cook v. Lewis* shows cause-in-fact to be anything but straightforward.

Stripped to its essentials, the situation was this: plaintiff Lewis was struck by birdshot in the face immediately after defendants Cook and Akenhead, who were hunting in the vicinity, had discharged their guns at the same moment. One of these shots hit Lewis, but it was not possible to tell which one. The jury found that since Lewis could not prove which of Cook and Akenhead caused his injury, neither was liable. The Court of Appeal said this was perverse and the case made its way up to the Supreme Court of Canada. That Court offered two different solutions to the causal conundrum.

* * * *

Mr. Justice Cartwright:

...I am of opinion...that if under the circumstances of the case at bar the jury, having decided that the plaintiff was shot by either Cook or Akenhead, found themselves unable to decide which of the two shot him because in their opinion both shot negligently in his direction, both defendants should have been found liable....

Mr. Justice Rand:

I agree with the Court of Appeal that the finding of the jury exculpating both defendants from negligence was perverse and it is unnecessary to examine the facts on which that conclusion is based.

There remains the answer that, although shots from one of the two guns struck the respondent [Lewis], the jury could not determine from which they came. This is open to at least four interpretations: first, believing that only one discharge could have inflicted the injuries, they found it difficult to decide which testimony, whether that of Cook or Akenhead, was to be accepted, the evidence of each, taken at its face, excluding guilt; or that the shots from both guns having been fired so nearly at the same time and to have been aimed so nearly at the same target, it was impossible for them to say which struck the eye; or that they were unable to say whether the situation was either of those two alternatives; or finally, that they were not unanimous on any one or more of these views.

It will be seen that there is one feature common to the first three: having found that either A or B had been the cause of injury to C, the jury declare that C has not satisfied them which of the two it was. It is then a problem in proof and must be considered from that standpoint.

A cause may be said to be an operating element which in *de facto* co-operation with what may be called environment is considered the factor of culpability in determining legal responsibility for damage or loss done to person or property. But in that determination the practical difficulty turns on the allocation of elements to the one or other of these two divisions of data. In considering the second and third possibilities in this case, the essential obstacle to proof is the fact of multiple discharges so related as to confuse their individual effects: it is the fact that bars final proof. But if the victim, having brought guilt down to one or both of the two persons before the Court, can bring home to either of them a further wrong done him in relation to his remedial right of making that proof, then I should say that on accepted principles, the barrier to it can and should be removed.

The Court of Appeal of England has laid down this principle: that if A is guilty of a negligent act toward B, the total direct consequences of that act are chargeable against A notwithstanding that they arise from reactions unforeseeable by the ordinary person acting reasonably: *Re Polemis & Furness, Withy* (1921)....

Similarly would that result follow where, instead of an unforeseen potentiality, an element is introduced into the scene at the critical moment of which or its probability the negligent actor knows or ought to have known. That element becomes, then, one of the circumstances in reaction with which the consequences of his act manifest themselves, among which, here, is the confusion of consequences. If the new element is innocent, no liability results to the person who introduces it; if culpable, its effect in law remains to be ascertained.

What, then, the culpable actor has done by his initial negligent act is, first, to have set in motion a dangerous force which embraces the injured person within the scope of its probable mischief; and next, in conjunction with circumstances which he must be held to contemplate, to have made more difficult if not impossible the means of proving the possible damaging results of his own act or the similar results of the act of another. He has violated not only the victim's substantive right to security, but he has also culpably impaired the latter's remedial right of establishing liability. By confusing his act with environmental conditions, he has, in effect, destroyed the victim's power of proof.

The legal consequences of that is, I should say, that the onus is then shifted to the wrongdoer to exculpate himself; it becomes in fact a question of proof between him and the other and innocent member of the alternatives, the burden of which he must bear. The onus attaches to culpability, and if both acts bear that taint, the onus or *prima facie* transmission of responsibility attaches to both, and the question of the sole responsibility of one is a matter between them.

On the first interpretation, the answer of the jury was insufficient as a return. Their duty was to determine the facts from the evidence laid before them as best they could on the balance of probabilities, and it could not be evaded in the face of such divergent testimony either because of a tender regard for distasteful implications or for any other reason. The jury might have reached a deadlock from which there was no escape: but with the proper direction as to onus, that would have been obviated. The result is that there has been no verdict on an essential question, and the judgment based upon the answer cannot stand....

If, next, the answer means, as it may, that lack of unanimity was the frustrating factor, there is again a fatal incompleteness of findings, because of which, likewise, the judgment cannot stand.

The remaining interpretations fall within the considerations already expressed. The dominating fact is a confusion of causal factors and consequences resulting in what was, in substance, a small shower of flying shot. In dealing with such a situation, we must keep in mind that the task of the Court is to determine responsibility, not cause, but obviously for that purpose cause as ordinarily conceived is a controlling factor. Ultimately, it is cause in a juridical sense that we are to find. In the judicial process also, auxiliary mechanisms have been adopted which experience has vindicated, such as, for example, onus, estoppel, presumption. Although the facts here, in their precise form, have not, then, previously been presented to the courts of either this country or England, they are such as to which onus is properly invoked.

The risks arising from these sporting activities by increased numbers of participants and diminishing opportunity for their safe exercise, as the facts here indicate, require appropriate refinements in foresight. Against the private and public interests at stake, is the privilege of the individual to engage in a sport not inherently objectionable. As yet, certainly, the community is not ready to assume the burden of such a mishap. The question is whether a victim is to be told that such a risk, not only in substantive right but in remedy, is one he must assume. When we have reached the point where, as here, shots are considered spent at a distance of between 150 feet and 200 feet and the woods are "full" of hunters, a somewhat stringent regard to conduct seems to me to be obvious. It would be a strange commentary on its concern toward personal safety, that the law, although forbidding the victim any other mode of redress, was powerless to accord him any in its own form of relief. I am unable to assent to the view that there is any such helplessness.

Liability would, *a fortiori*, be the legal result if the acts of several were intended to be co-operative for a common object or if the act of one was so aided or abetted or induced by the act or conduct of another that it could be said to have had the will and the influence of that other behind it; and in determining that fact, the usual understandings between hunters in relation to the existence of conditions that would make shooting in particular situation dangerous, are relevant.

Assuming, then, that the jury have found one or both of the defendants here negligent, as on the evidence I think they must have, and at the same time have found that the consequences of the two shots, whether from a confusion in time or in area, cannot be segregated, the onus on the guilty person arises. This is a case where each hunter would know of or expect the shooting by the other and the negligent actor has culpably participated in the proof-destroying fact, the multiple shooting and its consequences. No liability will, in any event, attach to an innocent act of shooting, but the culpable actor, as against innocence, must bear the burden of exculpation.

These views of the law were not as adequately presented to the jury as I think they should have been.

I would, therefore, dismiss the appeal with costs.

MARCONATO AND MARCONATO V. FRANKLIN

British Columbia Supreme Court

[1974] 6 W.W.R. 676

Should people who negligently harm others be responsible for *all* the damage that actually results, even if it is unforeseeable? Suppose you have a very rare condition – a thin skull – and I, negligently, hit your head causing you far greater injury than a similar blow would have caused anyone else. Should I be liable for all of this harm or only part of it? In this case the law's answer – tortfeasors must take their victims as they find them – is applied to a different kind of "thin skull".

* * * *

Mr. Justice Aikins:

The plaintiffs are husband and wife. On 1st February 1971 Mrs. Marconato was driving her car in Vancouver; a car driven by the defendant collided with the left side of her car. Mrs. Marconato was injured. The left side of her head and body was thrown against some part of her car. Mrs. Marconato sues for damages for personal injury and her husband sues for damages for loss of consortium and servitium. Liability is admitted. The parties have agreed on special damages.

I shall first consider the amount of general damages that should be awarded to Mrs. Marconato. Her physical injuries were fortunately not of major severity. However, assessment of damages presents some difficulty because it is asserted that because of the collision, caused by the admitted negligence of the defendant, Mrs. Marconato suffered psychiatric injury referred to in the statement of claim as "traumatic neurosis" and "conversion hysteria"....

I propose to review Mrs. Marconato's evidence and the evidence of the two doctors...at length because much of the difficulty in the case stems from somewhat bizarre symptoms of which Mrs. Marconato complained from time to time after she was hurt and to which she testified. Many of her complaints cannot be explained by straightforward physical causation. That is to say, clinical examination does not reveal any physiological line of causation running from the force to which she was subjected in the collision to many of the aches, pains and disabilities of which she has complained over the following years. Mrs. Marconato's doctors cannot clinically find any physiological reasons for many of Mrs. Marconato's complaints. In the face of this, it might be thought that Mrs. Marconato was malingering. I think it convenient at this point to state plainly that I thought Mrs. Marconato to be an honest witness. I do not think that she lied to her doctors and I do not think she lied to me. I found some support for Mrs. Marconato's evidence in the evidence given by her husband and I add that I thought him to be an honest witness....

I find that Mrs. Marconato had a paranoid type personality. She was not, however, mentally ill before she was hurt. I accept Dr. Whitman's diagnosis: a neurotic or psychoneurotic reaction with mixed anxiety and depression. Indeed I am satisfied that Mrs. Marconato has suffered great anxiety and great depression. She has had to cope with a great deal of pain. I find that the main cause of her continued pain and disability has been anxiety and tension but that, as well, conversion hysteria has played some part. She has developed unfounded mistrust of her medical advisers. She has shown some characteristics of paranoia. She has undergone what can best be described, I suppose, as a personality change; she was a happy and contented woman in her role in life and she has become a very unhappy woman. She has given up hobbies and activities which gave her pleasure.

I turn to the question of causation. One would not ordinarily anticipate, using reasonable foresight, that a moderate cervical strain with soft tissue damage would give rise to the consequences which followed for Mrs. Marconato. These arose, however, because of her pre-existing personality traits. She had a peculiar susceptibility or vulnerability to suffer much greater consequences from a moderate physical injury than the average person. The consequences for Mrs. Marconato could no more be foreseen than it could be foreseen by a tortfeasor that his victim was thin-skulled and that a minor blow to the head would cause very serious injury. It is plain enough that the defendant could foresee the probability of physical injury. It is implicit, however, in the principle that a wrongdoer takes his victim as he finds him, that he takes his victim with all the victim's peculiar susceptibilities and vulnerabilities. The consequences of Mrs. Marconato's injuries were unusual but arose involuntarily. Granted her type of personality they arose as night follows day because of the injury and the circumstances in which she found herself because of the injury.

As to the argument that the damage suffered is too remote because not reasonably foreseeable, I refer first to an English case *Smith v. Leech Brain & Co. Ltd. (1962)*. In this case the plaintiff widow claimed damages for the death of her husband under the Fatal Accidents Acts. The defendant was the deceased's employer. The deceased suffered a burn on his lip; as a result cancer developed at that site, from which the injured man died some three years later. Remoteness on the ground of lack of foreseeability was argued. I cite two passages from the judgment of Lord Parker C.J.:

> ...It has always been the law of this country that a tortfeasor takes his victim as he finds him. It is unnecessary to do more than refer to the short passage in the decision of Kennedy J. in *Dulieu v. White & Sons*, (1901) where he said: 'If a man is negligently run over or otherwise negligently injured in his body, it is no answer to the sufferer's claim for damages that he would have suffered less injury, or no injury at all, if he had not had an unusually thin skull or an unusually weak heart."

The second passage is:

> The test is not whether these employers could reasonably have foreseen that a burn would cause cancer and that he would die. The question is whether these employers could reasonably foresee the type of injury he suffered, namely, the burn. What, in the particular case, is the amount of damage which he suffers as a result of that burn, depends upon the characteristics and constitution of the victim....

What I have cited might well be transposed in the present case to go as follows: Mrs. Marconato was predisposed by her personality to suffer the consequences which she did suffer as a result of the modest physical injury caused by the accident and it was that predisposition which brought on the unusual consequences of the injury. The defendant must pay damages for all the consequences of his negligence.

NORBERG V. WYNRIB

Supreme Court of Canada

[1992] 2 S.C.R. 226

Laura Norberg became addicted to pain killers and maintained her supply by "double doctoring" – obtaining narcotic prescriptions from doctors without telling them that she already had other prescriptions. She eventually went to Dr. Morris Wynrib who confronted her about her addiction. But instead of recommending treatment, Dr. Wynrib made it clear that he would provide her with the drug in exchange for sexual intercourse. She gave in to his demands, and soon Dr. Wynrib was directly giving her the narcotic after each sexual encounter. Not long after, Norberg was charged criminally for double doctoring and went to a rehabilitation centre on her own initiative. Then she sued Dr. Wynrib.

The Supreme Court of Canada split three ways, not on the question of *whether* Dr. Wynrib had done something wrong and so was liable to Laura Norberg for damages, but on the issue of *what* duty he owed her and which he failed to live up to. Two of the justices sought to capture this duty in a highly innovative way, one which may signal a change in our understanding of the patient-physician and other professional relationships.

* * * *

Madam Justices McLachlin and L'Heureux-Dubé:

The relationship of physician and patient can be conceptualized in a variety of ways. It can be viewed as a creature of contract, with the physician's failure to fulfil his or her obligations giving rise to an action for breach of contract. It undoubtedly gives rise to a duty of care, the breach of which constitutes the tort of negligence. In common with all members of society, the doctor owes the patient a duty not to touch him or her without his or her consent; if the doctor breaches this duty he or she will have committed the tort of battery. But perhaps the most fundamental characteristic of the doctor-patient relationship is *its fiduciary* nature. All the authorities agree that the relationship of physician to patient also falls into that special category of relationships which the law calls fiduciary....

...I think it is readily apparent that the doctor-patient relationship shares the peculiar hallmark of the fiduciary relationship – trust, the trust of a person with inferior power that another person who has assumed superior power and responsibility will exercise that power for his or her good and only for his or her good and in his or her best interests. Recognizing the fiduciary nature of the doctor-patient relationship provides the law with an analytic model by which physicians can be held to the high standards of dealing with their patient which the trust accorded them requires.

The foundation and ambit of the fiduciary obligation are conceptually distinct from the foundation and ambit of contract and tort. Sometimes the doctrines may overlap in their application, but that does not destroy their conceptual and functional uniqueness. In negligence and contract the parties are taken to be independent and equal actors, concerned primarily with their own self-interest. Consequently, the law seeks a balance between enforcing obligations by awarding compensation when those obligations are breached, and preserving optimum freedom for those involved in the relationship in question. The essence of a fiduciary relationship, by contrast, is that one party exercises power on behalf of another and pledges himself or herself to act in the best interests of the other....

The fiduciary relationship has trust, not self-interest, at its core, and when breach occurs, the balance favours the person wronged. The freedom of the fiduciary is limited by the obligation he or she has undertaken – an obligation which "betokens loyalty, good faith and avoidance of a conflict of duty and self-interest": *Canadian Aero Service Ltd. v. O'Malley* (1973). To cast a fiduciary relationship in terms of contract or tort (whether negligence or battery) is to diminish this obligation. If a fiduciary relationship is shown to exist, then the proper legal analysis is one based squarely on the full and fair consequences of a breach of that relationship.

As La Forest J. went on to note in *McInerney v. MacDonald* (1992), characterizing the doctor-patient relationship as fiduciary is not the end of the analysis: "not all fiduciary relationships and not all fiduciary obligations are the same; these are shaped by the demands of the situation. A relationship may properly be described as "fiduciary" for some purposes, but not for others". So the question must be asked, did a fiduciary relationship exist between Dr. Wynrib and Ms. Norberg? And assuming that such relationship did exist, is it properly described as fiduciary for the purposes relevant to this appeal?

[Several previous Supreme Court of Canada decisions have] attributed the following characteristics to a fiduciary relationship: "(1) the fiduciary has scope for the exercise of some discretion or power; (2) the fiduciary can unilaterally exercise that power or discretion so as to affect the beneficiary's legal or practical interests; (3) the beneficiary is peculiarly vulnerable or at the mercy of the fiduciary holding the discretion or power."

Dr. Wynrib was in a position of power vis-à-vis the plaintiff; he had scope for the exercise of power and discretion with respect to her. He had the power to advise her, to treat her, to give her the drug or to refuse her the drug. He could unilaterally exercise that power or discretion in a way that affected her interests. And her status as a patient rendered her vulnerable and at his mercy, particularly in light of her addiction....All of the classic characteristics of a fiduciary relationship were present. Dr. Wynrib and Ms. Norberg were on an unequal footing. He pledged himself – by the act of hanging out his shingle as a medical doctor and accepting her as his patient – to act in her best interests and not permit any conflict between his duty to act only in her best interests and his own interests – including his interest in sexual gratification – to arise. As a physician, he owed her the classic duties associated with a fiduciary relationship – the duties of "loyalty, good faith, and avoidance of a conflict of duty and self-interest".

Closer examination of the principles enunciated by Wilson, J. in *Frame v. Smith (1987)* confirms the applicability of the fiduciary analysis in this case. The possession of power or discretion needs little elaboration. That one party in a fiduciary relationship holds such power over the other is not in and of itself wrong; on the contrary, "the fiduciary must be entrusted with power in order to perform his function". What will be a wrong is if the risk inherent in entrusting the fiduciary with such power is realized and the fiduciary abuses the power which has been entrusted to him or her. As Wilson J. noted in *Frame,* in the absence of such a discretion or power and the possibility of abuse of power which it entails, "there is no need for a super-added obligation to restrict the damaging use of the discretion or power."

As to the second characteristic, it is, as Wilson J. put it, "the fact that the power or discretion may be used to affect the beneficiary in a damaging way that makes the imposition of a fiduciary duty necessary". Wilson J. went on to state that fiduciary duties are not confined to the exercise of power which can affect the legal interests of the beneficiary, but extend to the beneficiary's "vital non-legal or `practical' interests". This negates the suggestion inherent in some of the other judgments which this case has engendered that the fiduciary obligation should be confined to legal rights such as confidentiality and conflict of interest and undue influence in the business sphere....

The case at bar is not concerned with the protection of what has traditionally been regarded as a legal interest. It is, however, concerned with the protection of interests, both societal and personal, of the highest importance. Society has an abiding interest in ensuring that the power entrusted to physicians by us, both collectively and individually, not be used in corrupt ways. On the other side of the coin, the plaintiff, as indeed does every one of us when we put ourselves in the hands of a physician, has a striking personal interest in obtaining professional medical care free of exploitation for the physician's private purposes. These are not collateral duties and rights created at the whim of an aggrieved patient. They are duties universally recognized as essential to the physician-patient relationship. The Hippocratic Oath reflects this universal concern that physicians not exploit their patients for their own ends, and in particular, not for their own sexual ends....

To the extent that the law requires that physicians who breach them be disciplined, these duties have legal force. The interests which the enforcement of these duties protect are, to be sure, different from the legal and economic interests which the law of fiduciary relationships has traditionally been used to safeguard. But as Wilson J. said in *Frame* "[t]o deny relief because of the nature of the interest involved, to afford protection to material interests but not to human or personal interests would, it seems to me, be arbitrary in the extreme". At the very least, the societal and personal interests at issue here constitute "a vital and substantial `practical' interest" within the meaning of the second characteristic of a fiduciary duty set out in *Frame v. Smith.*

The third requirement is that of vulnerability. This is the other side of the differential power equation which is fundamental to all fiduciary relationships. In order to be the beneficiary of a fiduciary relationship a person need not be *per se* vulnerable....It is only where there is a material discrepancy, in the circumstances of the relationship in question, between the power of one person and the vulnerability of the other that the fiduciary relationship is recognized by the law. Where the parties are on a relatively equal footing, contract and tort provide the appropriate analysis....

At the case at bar, this requirement too is fulfilled. A physician holds great power over the patient. The recent decision of the Ontario Court (General Division) in *College of Physicians & Surgeons of Ontario v. Gillen* (1990), contains a reminder that a patient's vulnerability may be as much physical as emotional, given the fact that a doctor "has the right to examine the patient in any state of dress or undress and to administer drugs to render the patient unconscious". Visits to doctors occur in private; the door is closed; there is rarely a third party present; everything possible is done to encourage the patient to feel that the patient's privacy will be respected. This is essential to the meeting of the patient's medical and emotional needs; the unfortunate concomitant is that it also creates the conditions under which the patient may be abused without fear of outside intervention. Whether physically vulnerable or not, however, the patient, by reason of lesser expertise, the "submission" which is essential to the relationship, and sometimes, as in this case, by reason of the nature of the illness itself, is typically in a position of comparative powerlessness. The fact that society encourages us to trust our doctors, to believe that they will be persons worthy of our trust, cannot be ignored as a factor inducing a heightened degree of vulnerability....

Women, who can so easily be exploited by physicians for sexual purposes, may find themselves particularly vulnerable. That female patients are disproportionately the targets of sexual exploitation by physicians is borne out by the [College of Physicians and Surgeons of Ontario, *Final Report of the Task Force on Sexual Abuse of Patients*]. Of the 303 reports they received of sexual exploitation at the hands of those in a position of trust (the vast majority of whom were physicians), 287 were by female patients, 16 by males....

The principles outlined by Wilson J. in *Frame v. Smith* may apply with varying force depending on the nature of the particular doctor-patient relationship. For example, the uniquely intimate nature of the psychotherapist-patient relationship, the potential for transference, and the emotional fragility of many psychotherapy patients make the argument for a fiduciary obligation resting on psychotherapists, and in particular an obligation to refrain from any sexualizing of the relationship, especially strong in that context. American courts have, as a result, imposed higher duties on psychiatrists than they have on other physicians. The Task Force of the Ontario College of Physicians and Surgeons has in its report also recognized the greater danger of breach of trust inherent in psychotherapeutic relationships, and has as a consequence recommended even more stringent guidelines for appropriate psychotherapist behaviour than it has for physicians practising in other areas. While the medical relationship between Dr. Wynrib and Ms. Norberg was not psychotherapeutic in orientation, the treatment of a patient dependent on drugs would seem to me to share many of the same characteristics, thereby rendering the addicted patient even more vulnerable and in need of the protection which the law of fiduciary obligations can afford than other patients might be....

But, it is said, there are a number of reasons why the doctrine of breach of fiduciary relationship cannot apply in this case. I turn then to these alleged conditions of defeasibility.

The first factor which is said to prevent application of the doctrine of breach of fiduciary duty is Ms. Norberg's conduct. Two terms have been used to raise this consideration to the status of a legal or equitable bar – the equitable maxim that he who comes into equity must come with clean hands and the tort doctrine of ex *turpi causa non orbitur actio*. For our purposes, one may think of the two respectively as the equitable and legal formulations of the same type of bar to recovery. The trial judge found that although Dr. Wynrib was under a trust obligation to Ms. Norberg, she was barred from claiming damages against him because of her "immoral" and "illegal" conduct. While he referred to the doctrine of ex *turpi*, there seems to be little doubt that in equity the appropriate term is "clean hands" and consequently that is the expression I will use.

The short answer to the arguments based on wrongful conduct of the plaintiff is that she did nothing wrong in the context of this relationship. She was not a sinner, but a sick person, suffering from an addiction which proved to be uncontrollable in the absence of a professional drug rehabilitation program. She went to Dr. Wynrib for relief from that condition. She hoped he would give her relief by giving her the drug; "hustling" doctors for drugs is a recognized symptom of her illness. Such behaviour is commonly seen by family physicians. Patients may, as did Ms Norberg, feign physical problems which, if bona fide, would require analgesic relief. They may, as Ms. Norberg also did, specify the drug they wish to receive. Once a physician has diagnosed a patient as an addict who is "hustling" him for drugs, the recommended response is to "(1) maintain control of the doctor-patient relationship, (2) remain professional in the face of ploys for sympathy or guilt and (3) regard the drug seeker as a patient with a serious illness"....

The law might accuse Ms. Norberg of "double doctoring" and moralists might accuse her of licentiousness; but she did no wrong because not she but the doctor was responsible for this conduct. He had the power to cure her of her addiction, as her successful treatment after leaving his "care" demonstrated; instead he chose to use his power to keep her in her addicted state and to use her for his own sexual purposes.

It is difficult not to see the attempt to bar Ms. Norberg from obtaining redress for the wrong she has suffered through the application of the clean hands maxim as anything other than "blaming the victim"....

A[nother] objection raised to viewing the relationship between

Dr. Wynrib and Ms. Norberg as fiduciary is that it will open the flood-gates to unfounded claims based on the abuse of real or perceived inequality of power. The spectre is conjured up of a host of actions based on exploitation – children suing parents, wives suing husbands, mistresses suing lovers, all for abuse of superior power. The answer to this objection lies in defining the ambit of the fiduciary obligation in a way that encompasses meritorious claims while excluding those without merit. The prospect of the law's recognizing meritorious claims by the powerless and exploited against the powerful and exploitive should not alone serve as a reason for denying just claims. This Court has an honourable tradition of recognizing new claims of the disempowered against the exploitive.

The criteria for the imposition of a fiduciary duty already enunciated by this court...provide a good starting point for the task of defining the general principles which determine whether such a relationship exists. As we have seen, an imbalance of power is not enough to establish a fiduciary relationship. It is a necessary but not sufficient condition. There must also be the potential for interference with a legal interest or a non-legal interest of "vital and substantial 'practical' interest". And I would add this. Inherent in the notion of fiduciary duty...is the requirement that the fiduciary have assumed or undertaken to "look after" the interest of the beneficiary....It is not easy to bring relationships within this rubric. Generally people are deemed by the law to be motivated in their relationships by mutual self-interest. The duties of trust are special, confined to the exceptional case where one person assumes the power which would normally reside with the other and undertakes to exercise that power solely for the other's benefit. It is as though the fiduciary has taken the power which rightfully belongs to the beneficiary on the condition that the fiduciary exercise the power entrusted exclusively for the good of the beneficiary. Thus, the trustee of an estate takes the financial power that would normally reside with the beneficiaries and must exercise those powers in their stead and for their exclusive benefit. Similarly, a physician takes the power which a patient normally has over her body, and which she cedes to him for the purposes of treatment. The physician is pledged by the nature of his calling to use the power the patient cedes to him exclusively for her benefit. If he breaks that pledge, he is liable.

In summary, the constraints inherent in the principles governing fiduciary relationships belie the contention that the recognition of a fiduciary obligation in this case will open the floodgates to unmeritorious claims. Taking the case at its narrowest, it is concerned with a relationship which has long been recognized as fiduciary – the physician-patient relationship; it represents no extension of the law. Taking the case more broadly, with reference to the general principles governing fiduciary obligations, it is seen to fall within principles previously recognized by this court, and again represents no innovation. In so far as application of those principles in this case might be argued to give encouragement to new categories of claims, the governing principles offer assurance against unlimited liability while at the same time promising a great measure of justice for the exploited.

C. PUNISHMENT

R. V. SMITH

Supreme Court of Canada

[1987] 1 S.C.R. 1047

Two sections of the *Charter of Rights and Freedoms* deal with punishment. Section 9 states that "Everyone has the right not to be arbitrarily detained or imprisoned", while section 12 guarantees that "Everyone has the right not to be subjected to any cruel and unusual treatment or punishment". *R. v. Smith* gave the Supreme Court of Canada its first opportunity to discuss these two provisions, and constitutional limits to punishment in Canada. At issue was the much-criticized section 5(2) of the federal *Narcotic Control Act* which set out a mandatory *minimum* sentence of seven years upon a conviction for importing a narcotic substance. Although a clear majority declared the section constitutionally invalid, there was disagreement over how the two sections of the *Charter* interact.

* * * *

Mr. Justice Lamer and Chief Justice Dickson:

It is generally accepted in a society such as ours that the state has the power to impose a "treatment or punishment" on an individual where it is necessary to do so to attain some legitimate end and where the requisite procedure has been followed....

The limitation at issue here is s. 12 of the *Charter*. In my view, the protection afforded by s. 12 governs the quality of the punishment and is concerned with the effect that the punishment may have on the person on whom it is imposed. I would agree with Laskin C.J.C. in *Miller and Cockriell* (1977), where he defined the phrase "cruel and unusual" as a "compendious expression of a norm". The criterion which must be applied in order to determine whether a punishment is cruel and unusual within the meaning of s. 12 of the *Charter* is, to use the words of Laskin C.J.C., "whether the punishment prescribed is so excessive as to outrage standards of decency". In other words, though the state may impose punishment, the effect of that punishment must not be grossly disproportionate to what would have been appropriate.

In imposing a sentence of imprisonment, the judge will
circumstances of the case in order to arrive at an approp
tence. The test for review under s. 12 of the *Charter is* one of
proportionality, because it is aimed at punishments that are more
than merely excessive. We should be careful not to stigmatize every
disproportionate or excessive sentence as being a constitutional violation, and should leave to the usual sentencing appeal process the
task of reviewing the fitness of a sentence. Section 12 will only be
infringed where the sentence is so unfit having regard to the offence
and the offender as to be grossly disproportionate.

In assessing whether a sentence is grossly disproportionate, the
court must first consider the gravity of the offence, the personal characteristics of the offender and the particular circumstances of the
case in order to determine what range of sentences would have been
appropriate to punish, rehabilitate or deter this particular offender
or to protect the public from this particular offender. The other purposes which may be pursued by the imposition of punishment, in
particular the deterrence of other potential offenders, are thus not
relevant at this stage of the inquiry. This does not mean that the
judge or the legislator can no longer consider general deterrence or
other pennological purposes that go beyond the particular offender
in determining a sentence, but only that the resulting sentence must
not be grossly disproportionate to what the offender deserves. If a
grossly disproportionate sentence is "prescribed by law", then the
purpose which it seeks to attain will fall to be assessed under s. 1. Section 12 ensures that individual offenders receive punishments that
are appropriate, or at least not grossly disproportionate, to their particular circumstances, while s. 1 permits this right to be overridden to
achieve some important societal objective.

One must also measure the effect of the sentence actually
imposed. If it is grossly disproportionate to what would have been
appropriate, then it infringes s. 12. The effect of the sentence is often
a composite of many factors and is not limited to the quantum or
duration of the sentence but includes its nature and the conditions
under which it is applied. Sometimes by its length alone or by its very
nature will the sentence be grossly disproportionate to the purpose
sought. Sometimes it will be the result of the combination of factors
which, when considered in isolation, would not in and of themselves
amount to gross disproportionality. For example, 20 years for a first
offence against property would be grossly disproportionate, but so
would three months of imprisonment if the prison authorities decide
it should be served in solitary confinement. Finally, I should add that
some punishments or treatments will always be grossly dispropor-

tionate and will always outrage our standards of decency: for example, the infliction of corporal punishment, such as the lash, irrespective of the number of lashes imposed, or, to give examples of treatment, the lobotomisation of certain dangerous offenders or the castration of sexual offenders.

...[T]o refer to tests listed by Professor Tarnopolsky, the determination of whether the punishment is necessary to achieve a valid penal purpose, whether it is founded on recognized sentencing principles, and whether there exist valid alternatives to the punishment imposed, are all guidelines which, without being determinative in themselves, help to assess whether the punishment is grossly disproportionate.

There is a further aspect of proportionality which has been considered on occasion by the American courts: a comparison with punishments imposed for other crimes in the same jurisdiction. Of course, the simple fact that penalties for similar offences are divergent does not necessarily mean that the greater penalty is grossly disproportionate and thus cruel and unusual. At most, the divergence in penalties is an indication that the greater penalty may be excessive, but it will remain necessary to assess the penalty in accordance with the facts discussed above. The notion that there must be a gradation of punishments according to the malignity of offences may be considered to be a principle of fundamental justice under s. 7, but, given my decision under s. 12, I do not find it necessary to deal with that issue here.

On more than one occasion the courts in Canada have alluded to a further factor, namely, whether the punishment was arbitrarily imposed. As regards this factor, some comments should be made, because arbitrariness of detention and imprisonment is addressed by s. 9, and, to the extent that the arbitrariness, given the proper context, could be in breach of a principle of fundamental justice, it could trigger a *prima facie* violation under s. 7. As indicated above, s. 12 is concerned with the *effect* of a punishment, and, as such, the process by which the punishment is imposed is not, in my respectful view, of any great relevance to a determination under s. 12. For example, s. 12 would not be infringed if a judge, after having refused to hear any submissions on sentencing, indicated that he would not take into consideration any relevant factors, but then went on to impose arbitrarily a preconceived but appropriate sentence. In my view, because this result would be appropriate, the sentence cannot be characterized as grossly disproportionate and violative of s. 12....

At issue in this appeal is the minimum term of imprisonment

provided for by s. 5(2) of the *Narcotic Control Act*. The minimum seven-year imprisonment fails the proportionality test enunciated above and therefore *prima facie* infringes the guarantees established by s. 12 of the *Charter*. The simple fact that s. 5(2) provides for a mandatory term of imprisonment is obviously not in and of itself cruel and unusual. The legislature may, in my view, provide for a compulsory term of imprisonment upon conviction for certain offences without infringing the rights protected by s. 12 of the *Charter*. For example, a long term of penal servitude for he or she who has imported large amounts of heroin for the purpose of trafficking would certainly not contravene s. 12 of the *Charter*, quite the contrary. However, the seven-year minimum prison term of s. 5(2) is grossly disproportionate when examined in light of the wide net cast by s. 5(1).

As indicated above, the offence of importing enacted by s. 5(1) of the *Narcotic Control Act* covers numerous substances of varying degrees of dangerousness and totally disregards the quantity of the drug imported. The purpose of a given importation, such as whether it is for personal consumption or for trafficking, and the existence of nonexistence of previous convictions for offences of a similar nature or gravity are disregarded as irrelevant. Thus, the law is that it is inevitable that, in some cases, a verdict of guilt will lead to the imposition of a term of imprisonment which will be grossly disproportionate.

This is what offends s. 12, the certainty, not just the potential. Absent the minimum, the section still has the potential of operating so as to impose cruel and unusual punishment. But that would only occur if and when a judge chose to impose, let us say, seven years or more on the "small offender". Remedy will then flow from s. 24. It is the judge's sentence, but not the sentence, that is in violation of the *Charter*. However, the effect of the minimum is to insert the certainty that, in some cases, as of conviction the violation will occur. It is this aspect of certainty that makes the section itself a *prima facie* violation of s. 12, and the minimum must, subject to s. 1, be declared of no force or effect.

[Mr. Justice Lamer then went on to argue that s. 5(1) can not be saved by section 1 of the Charter.]

Madame Justice Wilson (concurring):

Section 12 on its face appears to me to be concerned primarily with the nature or type of a treatment or punishment. Indeed, its historical origins would appear to support this view. The rack and the thumbscrew, the stocks, torture of any kind, unsanitary prison conditions, prolonged periods of solitary confinement were progressively recognized as inhuman and degrading and completely inimical to the rehabilitation of the prisoner who sooner or later was going to have to be released back into the community. I agree, however, with my colleague that s. 12 is not confined to punishments which are in their nature cruel. It also extends to punishments which are, to use his words, "grossly disproportionate". And by that I mean that they are cruel and unusual in their disproportionality in that no one, not the offender and not the public, could possibly have thought that that particular accused's offence would attract such a penalty. It was unexpected and unanticipated in its severity either by him or by them. It shocked the communal conscience. It was "unusual" because of its extreme nature. Adopting Laskin C.J.C.'s concept of "interacting expressions colouring each other", it was so unusual as to be cruel and so cruel as to be unusual....

I disagree, however, with Lamer J. that the arbitrary nature of the minimum sentence under s. 5(2) of the Act is irrelevant to its designation as "cruel and unusual" under s. 12. On the contrary, I believe it is quite fundamental. A seven-year sentence for drug importation is not *per se* cruel and unusual. It may be very well deserved and completely appropriate. It is the fact that the seven-year sentence must be imposed regardless of the circumstances of the offence or the circumstances of the offender that results in its being grossly disproportionate in some cases and therefore cruel and unusual in those particular cases. The concept of "the fit sentence" to which I made reference in my concurring reasons in *Re B.C. Motor Vehicle Act* (1985) as basic to modern day theories of punishment is effectively precluded by the mandatory minimum in s. 5(2). Judicial discretion to impose a shorter sentence if circumstances warrant is foreclosed and the inevitable result is a legislatively ordained grossly disproportionate sentence in some cases.

Punishments may undoubtedly be cruel and unusual within the meaning of s. 12 without being arbitrarily imposed. Punishments may be arbitrary within the meaning of s. 9 without also being cruel and unusual. But I do not share my colleague's anxiety to keep the two sections mutually exclusive. I believe this is a case where the arbitrary nature of the legislatively prescribed minimum sentence must inevitably in some cases result in the imposition of a cruel and unusual punishment. This might not be so if the legislatively prescribed minimum was, for example, six months or a year because, although this might be arbitrary, it arguably would not be "so excessive as to outrage standards of decency". Seven years, on the other hand, is that excessive and this, in my view, is why it cannot survive the constitutional challenge under s. 12.

Mr. Justice McIntyre (dissenting):

I would...say, in short, that to be "cruel and unusual treatment or punishment" which would infringe s. 12 of the *Charter,* the punishment or treatment must be "so excessive as to outrage standards of decency". While not a precise formula for cruel and unusual treatment or punishment, this definition does capture the purpose and intent of s. 12 of the *Charter* and is consistent with the views expressed in Canadian jurisprudence on this subject. To place stress on the words "to outrage standards of decency" is not, in my view, to erect too high a threshold for infringement of s. 12.

As noted above, while the prohibition against cruel and unusual treatment or punishment was originally aimed at punishments which by their nature and character were inherently cruel, it has since been extended to punishments which, though not inherently cruel, are so disproportionate to the offence committed that they become cruel and unusual. However, when considerations of proportionality arise in an inquiry under s. 12 of the *Charter,* great care must be exercised in applying the standard of cruel and unusual treatment or punishment. Punishment not *per se* cruel and unusual, may become cruel and unusual due to excess or lack of proportionality only where it is so excessive that it is an outrage to standards of decency. Not every departure by a court or legislature from what might be called the truly appropriate degree of punishment will constitute cruel and unusual punishment. Sentencing, at the best of times, is an imprecise and imperfect procedure and there will always be a substantial range of appropriate sentences. Further, there will be a range of sentences which may be·considered excessive, but not so excessive or so disproportionate as to "outrage standards of decency" and thereby justify judicial interference under s. 12 of the *Charter.* In other words, there is a vast gray area between the truly appropriate sentence and a cruel and unusual sentence under the *Charter.* Entry into that gray area will not alone justify the application of the absolute constitutional prohibition voiced in s. 12 of the *Charter....*

A punishment will be cruel and unusual and violate s. 12 of the *charter* if it has any one or more of the following characteristics:

(1) The punishment is of such character or duration as to outrage the public conscience or be degrading to human dignity;

(2) The punishment goes beyond what is necessary for the achievement of a valid social aim, having regard to the legitimate purposes of punishment and the adequacy of possible alternatives; or

(3) The punishment is arbitrarily imposed in the sense that it is not applied on a rational basis in accordance with ascertained or ascertainable standards.

[Mr. Justice McIntyre then went on to argue that s. 5(2) does not have any of these characteristics.]

By way of summary, I express the view that s. 12 of the *Charter* is a special constitutional provision which is not concerned with general principles of sentencing nor with related social problems. Its function is to provide the constitutional outer limit beyond which Parliament, or those acting under parliamentary authority, may not go in imposing punishment or treatment respecting crime or penal detention. Parliament retains, while acting within the limits so prescribed, a full discretion to enact laws and regulations concerning sentencing and penal detention. The courts, on the other hand, in the actual sentencing process have a duty to prevent an incursion into the field of cruel and unusual treatment or punishment and, where there has been no such incursion, to impose appropriate sentences within the permissible limits established by Parliament. In so doing, the courts will apply the general principles of sentencing accepted in the courts in an effort to make the punishment fit the crime and the individual criminal.

The *Charter* provision in s. 12 is the device by which the parliamentary discretion as to punishment was to be constitutionally limited. It cannot be said that the *Charter* sought to effect that purpose by giving an absolute discretion in the matter to the courts. If s. 12 were to be construed to permit a trial judge to ameliorate a sentence mandated by Parliament simply because he considered it to be too severe, then the whole parliamentary role with regard to punishment for criminal conduct would become subject to discretionary judicial review. The role of Parliament in the determination and definition of this aspect of public policy would be eliminated. The concept of cruel and unusual treatment or punishment would be deprived of its special character and would become, in effect, a mere caution against severe punishment. It must be remembered that s. 12 voices an absolute prohibition. If that prohibition is not confined within definite limits, if it may be invoked by the courts on an individual case-by-case basis according to judicial discretion, then what is cruel and unusual in respect of "A", on one occasion, may become acceptable in respect of "B" on another occasion. Such a result reduces the significance of the absolute prohibition in s. 12 of the *Charter* and does not afford, in my view, an acceptable approach to a constitutional question.

KINDLER V. CANADA (MINISTER OF JUSTICE)

Supreme Court of Canada

[1991] 2 S.C.R. 779

Is capital punishment "cruel and unusual"? Although there has not been an execution in Canada since 1962 and Parliament voted against reinstating capital punishment in 1987, *Kindler v. Minister of Justice of Canada* shows that the legal question is still debatable. The circumstances under which the issue came through the federal court system and eventually to the Supreme Court of Canada were unique. Kindler, the appellant, had been convicted of murder in Pennsylvania and sentenced to death. He escaped to Canada and the United States sought his extradition. Under the terms of a bi-national extradition treaty, Canada had the option of refusing to extradite unless it got assurances that the death penalty would not be carried out. To bolster his argument that that option should be exercised in his case, Kindler argued that capital punishment violated both sections 7 and 12 of the *Charter*. Although a majority of the Court rejected Kindler's argument, the Court was still dramatically divided on the question of capital punishment.

* * * *

Madam Justice McLachlin and Justices L'Heureux-Dubé, and Gonthier:

This appeal, and the companion case, *Reference Re Ng Extradition (Canada)*, raise the issue of whether the Minister of Justice can order the extradition of fugitives to the United States without obtaining an assurance from that country's authorities that the death penalty will not be imposed. Canadian law does not impose the death penalty, except for certain military offences. The question is whether our government is obliged, in all cases, to obtain assurances from the state requesting extradition that the death penalty will not be carried out by them....

The minister's orders of extradition are attacked on two grounds: (1) that section [25] of the *Extradition Act* under which they are made is unconstitutional; and (2) that the minister's exercise of his discretion under the order was unconstitutional.

For the reasons that follow, I conclude that it is not contrary to the *Canadian Charter of Rights and Freedoms* to give the minister discretion on the question of whether to seek assurances from the requesting state that the death penalty will not be carried out. I further conclude that the minister did not err in the way he exercised his discretion in the cases of Ng and Kindler....

Section 25 of the *Extradition Act is* attacked because it permits the Minister to order the extradition of a fugitive to a state where he or she may, if convicted, face capital punishment. To allow this, it is said, is to offend the principles of fundamental justice.

I do not agree. The question...is not whether the death penalty is constitutional, or even desirable in this country, but whether returning a fugitive to face it in another jurisdiction offends the Canadian sense of what is fair and right. The answer to this question turns on attitudes in this country toward the death penalty, and toward extradition, considered along with other factors such as the need to preserve an effective extradition policy and to deter American criminals fleeing to Canada as a "safe haven".

The practice of extradition...has deep roots in this country, and the practice *per se* has never been controversial. This reflects a strong belief that crime must not go unpunished. Fairness requires that alleged criminals be brought to justice and extradition is the normal means by which this is achieved when the offence was committed in a foreign jurisdiction.

When an accused person is to be tried in Canada there will be no conflict between our desire to see an accused face justice, and our desire that the justice he or she faces conforms to the most exacting standards which have emerged from our judicial system. However, when a fugitive must face trial in a foreign jurisdiction if he or she is to face trial at all, the two desires may come into conflict. In some cases the social consensus may clearly favour one of these values above the other, and the resolution of the conflict will be straightforward. This would be the case if, for instance, the fugitive faced torture on return to his or her country. In many cases, though, neither value will be able to claim absolute priority; rather, one will serve to temper the other. There may be less unfairness in requiring an accused to face a judicial process which may be less than perfect according to our standards, than in having him or her escape the judicial process entirely.

For this reason, in considering the attitude of Canadians toward the death penalty we must consider not only whether Canadians consider it unacceptable, but whether they consider it to be so absolutely unacceptable that it is better that a fugitive not face justice at all rather than face the death penalty.

With this in mind I turn to consider Canadian attitudes to the death penalty. Much has been said and written in this country on the death penalty. While it is difficult to generalize about a subject so controversial, this much can be ventured. There is no clear consensus in this country that capital punishment is morally abhorrent and absolutely unacceptable.

Capital punishment was a component of Canadian criminal law from this country's colonial beginnings until it was abolished by Parliament in 1976. For most of that period the penalty was accepted with little question, although executions became increasingly rare in the latter years of its existence in Canada. The last execution in Canada was in 1962. Yet, while the death penalty has been formally abolished in this country, its possible return continues to be debated. In 1987, in response to persistent calls to bring back the death penalty, Members of Parliament conducted a free vote on a resolution to reinstate capital punishment. The result was a defeat of the motion, but the vote – 148 to 127 – fell far short of reflecting a broad consensus even among Parliamentarians .

To this day, capital punishment continues to apply to certain military offences. At the same time, public opinion polls continue to show considerable support among Canadians for the return of the death penalty for certain offences. Can it be said, in light of such indications as these, that the possibility that a fugitive might face the death penalty in California or Pennsylvania "shocks" the Canadian conscience or leads Canadians to conclude that the situation the fugitive faces is "simply unacceptable"? The case is far from plain.

When other considerations are brought into the picture, the matter becomes even less clear. In some cases, the unconditional surrender of a fugitive to face the death penalty may "sufficiently shock" the national conscience as to render it mandatory that the minister seek an assurance that the penalty will not be imposed. But in other cases, this may not be so. These instances provide an example. Both fugitives are sought for crimes involving brutal, and in the case of Ng, multiple, murders. In both Pennsylvania and California the legal system is the product of democratic government, and includes the substantial protections of a constitutional rights document which dates back over two centuries. The variance between cases supports legislation which accords to the Minister a measure of discretion on the question of whether an assurance that the death penalty will not be imposed should be demanded....

Another relevant consideration in determining whether surrender without assurances regarding the death penalty would be a breach of fundamental justice is the danger that if such assurances were mandatory, Canada might become a safe haven for criminals in the United States seeking to avoid the death penalty. This is not a new concern. The facility with which American offenders can flee to Canada has been recognized since the nineteenth century....

The fugitives, in suggesting that s. 25 should be struck down, in effect urge that the only constitutional law is one which absolutely forbids extradition in the absence of assurances that the death penalty will not be imposed. The foregoing discussion suggests that such a law might well prove too inflexible to permit the government of Canada to deal with particular situations in a way which maintains the required comity with other nations, while at the same time going beyond what is required to conform to our fundamental sense of fairness. What is required is a law which permits the minister, in the particular case before her, to act in a way which preserves the effectiveness of the extradition process, while conforming to the Canadian sense of what is fundamentally just. Section 25 does this; the less flexible alternative proposed by the fugitives would not.

I conclude that the fugitives have not established that the law which permits their extradition without assurances that the death penalty will not be applied in the requesting states offends the fundamental principles of justice enshrined in s. 7 of the *Charter.*

Mr. Justices Cory and Lamer (dissenting):

At the very heart of this appeal is a conflict between two concepts. On one side is the concept of human dignity and the belief that this concept is of paramount importance in a democratic society. On the other side is the concept of retributive justice and the belief that capital punishment is necessary to deter murderers. An historical review reveals an increasing tendency to resolve this tension in favour of human dignity....

...[F]rom the 12th century forward there was a reluctance on the part of jurors to impose the death sentence. The jurors, the very people who might have been expected to be most interested in enforcing the criminal law particularly with regard to property offences, were loath to condemn the accused to death. Their verdicts gave early recognition to the fundamental importance of human dignity and of the need to accord that dignity to all. As well, reformers for over 300 years advocated not only the reduction but the total abolition of the death penalty....[O]pposition to the imposition of the death penalty has a long and honoured history....

The international community has affirmed its commitment to the principle of human dignity through various international instruments....Except for the United States, the western world has reinforced this commitment to human dignity, both internationally and nationally, through the express abolition of the death penalty. Canada's action in the international forum affirms its own commitment to the preservation and enhancement of human dignity and to the abolition of the death penalty....

What then is the constitutional status of the death penalty under s. 12 of the *Charter?*

The American experience provides no guidance. Cases dealing with the constitutional validity of the death penalty were decided on very narrow bases unique to the wording of the American *Constitution* and rooted in early holdings of the United States Supreme Court. Canadian courts should articulate a distinct Canadian approach with respect to cruel and unusual punishment based on Canadian traditions and values.

The approach to be taken by this Court in determining whether capital punishment contravenes s. 12 of the *Charter* should, in my view, be guided by two central considerations. First is the principle of human dignity which lies at the heart of s. 12. It is the dignity and importance of the individual which is the essence and the cornerstone of democratic government. Second is the decision of this court in *R. v. Smith (1987)*....

A consideration of the effect of the imposition of the death penalty on human dignity is enlightening. Descriptions of executions demonstrate that it is state-imposed death which is so repugnant to any belief in the importance of human dignity. The methods utilized to carry out the execution serve only to compound the indignities inflicted upon the individual....

The death penalty not only deprives the prisoner of all vestiges of human dignity, it is the ultimate desecration of the individual as a human being. It is the annihilation of the very essence of human dignity.

Let us now consider the principles set out in *R. v. Smith* to determine whether the death penalty is of the same nature as corporal punishment, lobotomy or castration which were designated as cruel and unusual punishment.

What is acceptable as punishment to a society will vary with the nature of that society, its degree of stability and its level of maturity. The punishments of lashing with the cat-o-nine tails and keel-hauling were accepted forms of punishment in the 19th century in the British navy. Both of those punishments could, and not infrequently, did result in death to the recipient. By the end of the 19th century, however, it was unthinkable that such penalties would be inflicted. A more sensitive society had made such penalties abhorrent.

Similarly, corporal punishment is now considered cruel and unusual yet it was an accepted form of punishment in Canada until it was abolished in 1973. The explanation, it seems to me, is that a maturing society has recognized that the imposition of the lash would now be a cruel and intolerable punishment.

If corporal punishment, lobotomy and castration are no longer acceptable and contravene s. 12, then the death penalty cannot be considered to be anything other than cruel and unusual punishment. It is the supreme indignity to the individual, the ultimate corporal punishment, the final and complete lobotomy and the absolute and irrevocable castration.

As the ultimate desecration of human dignity, the imposition of the death penalty in Canada is a clear violation of the protection afforded by s. 12 of the *Charter*. Capital punishment is *per se* cruel and unusual.

If Kindler had committed the murder in Canada, then not simply the abolition of the death penalty in this country but more important, the provisions of s. 12 of the *Charter* would prevent his execution....

[Moreover], the respondent's contention that the *Charter* would not apply to cruel and unusual punishments inflicted by the requesting state must be rejected. In my view, since the death penalty is a cruel punishment, that argument is an indefensible abdication of moral responsibility. Historically such a position has always been condemned. The ceremonial washing of his hands by Pontius Pilate did not relieve him of responsibility for the death sentence imposed by others and has found little favour over the succeeding centuries.

Notwithstanding the fact that it is the United States and not Canada which would impose the death penalty, Canada has the obligation not to extradite a person to face a cruel and unusual treatment or punishment. To surrender a fugitive who may be subject to the death penalty violates s. 12 of the *Charter* just as surely as would the execution of the fugitive in Canada. Therefore, the Minister's decision to extradite Kindler without obtaining Article 6 assurances violates Kindler's s. 12 rights....

It was also argued that, in order to comply with its international commitments arising out of the Treaty, Canada should not uniformly seek Article 6 assurances. In essence the respondent argues that Kindler is an evil man. Regardless of the fact that he is subject to the death penalty, it is said, he should be extradited to the United States in order to fulfil Canada's obligations under the Treaty.

However, it must be remembered that, no matter how vile the killing, Kindler would not be executed in Canada had he committed the murder in this country. Further, Canada has committed itself in the international community to the recognition and support of human dignity and to the abolition of the death penalty. These commitments were not lightly made. They reflect Canadian values and principles. Canada cannot, on the one hand, give an international commitment to support the abolition of the death penalty and at the same time extradite a fugitive without seeking the very assurances contemplated by the Treaty. To do so would mean that Canada either was not honouring its international commitments or was applying one standard to the United States and another to other nations. Neither alternative is acceptable, Both would contravene Canadian values and commitments.

R. V. BELCZOWSKI

Federal Court of Appeal

[1992] 2 F.C. 440

The two standard philosophical accounts of punishment are retributivism and consequentialism. The first seeks to justify punishment by exploring the concepts of *responsibility, blame* and *desert*, the second looks to the socially beneficial consequences of deterrence and crime prevention. Both accounts lead us to conclusions about what forms of state sanction are justifiable as punishment. In this case, the Federal Court of Appeal is asked to assess the constitutionality of a long-standing disqualification of prisoners from the right to vote. Is this punishment, and if so, is it justified? But if it is not punishment, then what is it? Mr. Justice Hugessen argues that the professed rationale for the disqualification is "symbolic and abstract" and declares it an unjustifiable violation of the democratic right to vote, found in section 3 of the *Charter*.

* * * *

Mr. Justice Hugessen:

This is an appeal from the judgment of Strayer J. in the Trial Division, wherein he granted declaratory relief and held that the provisions of the *Canada Elections Act* disqualifying prison inmates from voting were contrary to the *Canadian Charter of Rights and Freedoms*.

While it is true that the disqualification of prisoners from the right to vote is not strictly speaking a part of the criminal law, it is, in my view, far more analogous to legislation for dealing with and punishing criminals....In disputes centred around compulsory retirement, or the rights of non-citizens to practise law, or even the control of advertising directed to children, it is relatively simple to identify competing groups each of which constitutes only a part of the body politic. To say, however, as the appellant does...that the legislation, here under review, balances the claims of the respondent to those of "society at large", is surely to say no more than that the state, which represents the latter, has interests directly opposed to those targeted by the impugned legislation. This is surely most nearly comparable to the case where the state, representing society at

large, decrees that certain types of conduct are forbidden and prosecutes with a view to punishing those who breach the proscrip-
tion.

What is more, the right to vote in s. 3 of the *Charter* (and the kin-
dred rights set out in ss. 4 and 5) are cast in straightforward and
unambiguous terms singularly amenable to judicial interpretation.
Indeed, it might be more accurate to state that they require no interpretation at all. The courts should have no difficulty in measuring
legislation against them with a high degree of certainty and it is very
difficult to see how such legislation could raise any question of rec-
onciliation of competing claims or the distribution of limited
resources....

What then is the objective or legislative purpose of s. 51 (e) [*Canada Elections Act*]? Certainly it is not immediately apparent and does
not leap from the page on a reading of the section as a matter of first
impression. Indeed, s. 51, when read as a whole, seems to have a variety of disparate purposes:

51. The following persons are not qualified to vote at an election
and shall not vote at an election:

(a) the Chief Electoral Officer;
(b) the Assistant Chief electoral Officer;
(c) the returning officer for each electoral district...;
(d) every judge appointed by the Governor in Council...;
(e) *every person undergoing punishment as an inmate in any penal insti-
     tution for the commission of any offence;*
(f) every person who is restrained of his liberty of movement or
     deprived of the management of his property by reason of men-
     tal disease; and
(g) every person who is disqualified from voting under any law
     relating to the disqualification of electors for corrupt or ille-
     gal practices.

The objective of the exclusions mentioned in paras. (a), (b) and
(c) seems obviously to be to guarantee the fairness of the electoral
process. To adopt a sporting analogy, the referee, umpire and lines-
men are not to take part in the game.

The objective of the exclusion in para. (d) is quite different. It is
aimed not at the fairness of elections but at the appearance of impartiality and freedom from partisanship of those who are called upon
to decide disputes between the state and its citizens.

Paragraph (f), by contrast, seems to have for its purpose a guarantee of an absolute minimum of intellectual capacity in those who exercise the franchise.

Finally, para. (g) is manifestly a punitive provision attaching to past conduct related to the electoral process itself.

What are we to make of para. (e) which is located in the middle of this list? It seems to bear no logical relationship to the objectives underlying paras. (a), (b) and (c) nor to that underlying para. (d). It equally cannot today share a common purpose with para. (f), although it may well be the case that historically, and before the advent of proxy and mail votes, it was thought to be simply impossible that anyone deprived of his liberty of movement, for whatever reason, would be physically able to cast a vote. Finally, there may be a superficial resemblance between the objectives of paras. (e) and (g) although it should be noted that the latter exclusion is expressly framed in terms of fitting the punishment to the crime in a way that is wholly absent from the former.

In my view, and based solely upon a textual analysis of the section, one cannot, with confidence, assign any legislative purpose to para. 51(e). The appellant, however, asserts, based on the opinion evidence given at trial by a professor of political science, that the paragraph has three objectives as follows:

(a) to affirm and maintain the sanctity of the franchise in our democracy;

(b) to preserve the integrity of the voting process; and

(c) to sanction offenders.

The appellant adopts these objectives and expands on them in the following manner.

The objective of maintaining the sanctity of the franchise is based on the need for a liberal democracy to have a "decent and responsible citizenry" which will voluntarily abide by the laws, or at any rate most of them....

The objective of preserving the integrity of the voting process has nothing to do with the practicalities of permitting prisoners to vote: the appellant concedes that administrative and security problems cannot be invoked to justify s. 51 (e)....

In any event the Crown's present position is that one of the purposes of disqualifying prisoners is to ensure that only those who can truly participate in the democratic process should be allowed to cast ballots. Prisoners being isolated from society at large, and being temporarily removed from the local communities and constituencies of which other voters form part, cannot participate fully in the debate, discussion and interchange which are essential to the democratic process.

Finally, the objective of sanctioning offenders is said to arise from the state's legitimate interests in punishing those who disobey the law and in expressing collective disapproval of deliberate actions in breach of the social contract.

Viewed together and collectively, the most striking point about the alleged objectives of s. 51 (e) is that they are all symbolic and abstract. The appellant admits as much, but maintains that this fact does not prevent them from being legitimate objectives for legislation. With respect, it seems to me that this misses the mark. It is, of course, true that legislation may legitimately have a purely symbolic objective. The question on the first branch of the *Oakes* test, however, is not the *legitimacy* of the legislative purpose but rather its *importance*, that is to say whether it is "pressing and substantial". For my part, I must say that I have very serious doubts whether a wholly symbolic objective can ever be sufficiently important to justify the taking away of rights which are themselves so important and fundamental as to have been enshrined in our Constitution....

Assuming, however, for the sake of argument, that a purely symbolic objective may be sufficiently serious in some circumstances, it is my view that it cannot be so in this case. Depriving prisoners of the vote is not a ringing and unambiguous public declaration of principle. On the contrary it is an almost invisible infringement of the rights of a group of persons who, as long as they remain inside the walls are, to our national disgrace, almost universally unseen and unthought of. If, as I think, therefore, the alleged symbolic objective is one whose symbolism is lost on the great majority of citizens, it is impossible to characterize that objective as pressing or substantial....

Given the foregoing comments, I am not prepared to accept the objectives advanced by the Crown in support of s. 51 (e). Indeed, it seems to me far more likely...that the legislation represents nothing more than a historic holdover from the time when it was thought, for practical, security and administrative reasons, that it was quite simply impossible that prisoners should vote. As I have indicated that ground has now been abandoned by the Crown and would in any event be unsustainable in modern conditions....

Alternatively, and far less commendably, it would appear to me that the true objective of s. 51 (e) may be to satisfy a widely held stereotype of the prisoner as a no-good almost subhuman form of life to which all rights should be indiscriminately denied. That, it need hardly be said, is not an objective which would satisfy s. 1 of the *Charter*....

To summarize, it is my view that s. 51 (e) does not have the objectives which are claimed for it. While I do not deny that at least some of those objectives, notably that of punishing offenders, may be legitimate, neither the text nor the operation of the legislation supports the view that this is in fact what Parliament was aiming at. Even assuming the validity and legitimacy of the ends, the means are irrational, arbitrary and disproportionate. I conclude...that s. 51 (e) impairs the rights granted by s. 3 of the *Charter* and that it is not a reasonable limit thereon such as can be demonstrably justified in a free and democratic society.

I would dismiss the appeal with costs.

[This decision was upheld, without comment, by the Supreme Court of Canada]

CANADIAN CHARTER OF RIGHTS AND FREEDOMS

Constitution Act, 1982

Part I

Preamble

Whereas Canada is founded upon principles that recognize the supremacy of God and the rule of law;

Guarantee of Rights and Freedoms

1. The *Canadian Charter of Rights and Freedoms* guarantees the rights and freedoms set out in it subject only to such reasonable limits prescribed by law as can be demonstrably justified in a free and democratic society.

Fundamental Freedoms

2. Everyone has the following fundamental freedoms:

   (a) freedom of conscience and religion;

   (b) freedom of thought, belief, opinion and expression, including freedom of the press and other media of communication;

   (c) freedom of peaceful assembly; and

   (d) freedom of association.

Democratic Rights

3. Every citizen of Canada has the right to vote in an election of members of the House of Commons or of a legislative assembly and to be qualified for membership therein.

4. (1) No House of Commons and no legislative assembly shall continue for longer than five years from the date fixed for the return of the writs at a general election of its members.

   (2) In time of real or apprehended war, invasion or insurrection, a House of Commons may be continued by Parliament and a legislative assembly may be continued by the legislature beyond five years if such continuation is not opposed by the votes of more than one-third of the members of the House of Commons or the legislative assembly, as the case may be.

5. There shall be a sitting of Parliament and of each legislature at least once every twelve months.

Mobility Rights

6. (1) Every citizen of Canada has the right to enter, remain in and leave Canada.

(2) Every citizen of Canada and every person who has the status of a permanent resident of Canada has the right

(a) to move to and take up residence in any province; and

(b) to pursue the gaining of a livelihood in any province.

(3) The rights specified in subsection (2) are subject to

(a) any laws or practices of general application in force in a province other than those that discriminate among persons primarily on the basis of province of present or previous residence; and

(b) any laws providing for reasonable residency requirements as a qualification for the receipt of publicly provided social services.

(4) Subsections (2) and (3) do not preclude any law, program or activity that has as its object the amelioration in a province of conditions of individuals in that province who are socially or economically disadvantages if the rate of employment in that province is below the rate of employment in Canada.

Legal Rights

7. Everyone has the right to life, liberty and security of the person and the right not to be deprived thereof except in accordance with the principles of fundamental justice.

8. Everyone has the right to be secure against unreasonable search or seizure.

9. Everyone has the right not to be arbitrarily detained or imprisoned.

10. Everyone has the right on arrest or detention

(a) to be informed promptly of the reasons therefor;

(b) to retain and instruct counsel without delay and to be informed of that right; and

(c) to have the validity of the detention determined by way of habeas corpus and to be released if the detention is not lawful.

11. Any person charged with an offence has the right

(a) to be informed without unreasonable delay of the specific offence;

(b) to be tried within a reasonable time;

(c) not to be compelled to be a witness in proceedings against that person in respect of the offence;

(d) to be presumed innocent until proven guilty according to law in a fair and public hearing by an independent and impartial tribunal;

(e) not to be denied reasonable bail without just cause;

(f) except in the case of an offence under military law tried before a military tribunal, to the benefit of trial by jury where the maximum punishment for the offence is imprisonment for five years or a more severe punishment;

(g) not to be found guilty on account of any act of omission unless, at the time of the act or omission, it constituted an offence under Canadian or international law or was criminal according to general principles of law recognized by the community of nations;

(h) if finally acquitted of the offence, not to be tried for it again and, if finally found guilty and punishment for the offence, not to be tried or punished for it again; and

(i) if found guilty of the offence and if the punishment for the offence has been varied between the time of the commission and the time of the sentencing, to the benefit of the lesser punishment.

12. Everyone has the right not to be subjected to any cruel and unusual treatment or punishment.

13. A witness who testifies in any proceedings has the right not to have any incriminating evidence so given used to incriminate that witness in any other proceedings, except in a prosecution for perjury or for the giving of contradictory evidence

14. A party or witness in any proceedings who does not understand or speak the language in which the proceedings are conducted or who is deaf has the right to the assistance of an interpreter.

Equality Rights

15. (1) Every individual is equal before and under the law and has the right to the equal protection and equal benefit of the law without discrimination and, in particular, without discrimination based on race, national or ethnic origin, colour, religion, sex, age or mental or physical disability.

(2) Subsection (1) does not preclude any law, program or activity that has as its object the amelioration of conditions of disadvantaged individuals or groups including those that are disadvantaged because of race, national or ethnic origin, colour, religion, sex, age or mental or physical disability.

Official Languages of Canada

16. (1) English and French are the official languages of Canada and have equality of status and equal rights and privileges as to their use in all institutions of the Parliament and government of Canada.

(2) English and French are the official languages of New Brunswick and have equality of status and equal rights and privileges as to their use in all institutions of the Parliament and government of New Brunswick.

(3) Nothing in this Charter limits the authority of Parliament or

a legislature to advance the equality of status or use of English and French.

17. (1) Everyone has the right to use English or French in any debates and other proceedings of Parliament.

(2) Everyone has the right to use English or French in any debates and other proceedings of the legislature of New Brunswick.

18. (1) The statutes, records and journals of Parliament shall be printed and published in English and French and both language versions are equally authoritative.

(2) The statutes, records and journals of the legislature of New Brunswick shall be printed and published in English and French and both language versions are equally authoritative.

19. (1) Either English or French may be used by any person in, or in any pleading in or process issuing from, any court established by Parliament.

(2) Either English or French may be used by any person in, or in any pleading in or process issuing from, any court in New Brunswick.

20. (1) Any member of the public in Canada has the right to communicate with, and to receive available services from, any head or central office of an institution of Parliament or government of Canada in English or French, and has the same right with respect to any other office of any such institution where

(a) there is a significant demand for communications with and services from that office in such language; or

(b) due to the nature of the office, it is reasonable that communications with and services from that office be available in both English and French.

(2) Any member of the public in New Brunswick has the right to communicate with, and to receive available services from, any office of an institution of the legislature or government of New Brunswick in english or French.

21. Nothing in sections 16 to 20 abrogates or derogates from any right, privilege or obligation with respect to the English and French languages, or either of them, that exists or is continued by virtue of any other provision of the Constitution of Canada.

22. Nothing in sections 16 to 20 abrogates or derogates from any legal or customary right or privilege acquired or enjoyed either before or after the coming into force of this Charter with respect to any language that is not English or French.

Minority Language Educational Rights

23. (1) Citizens of Canada

(a) whose first language learned and still understood is that of the English or French linguistic minority population of the province in which they reside, or

(b) who have received their primary school instruction in Canada in the English or French and reside in a province where the language in which they received that instruction is the language of the English or French linguistic minority population of the province, have the right to have their children receive primary and secondary school education in that language in that province.

(2) Citizens of Canada of whom any child has received or is receiving primary or secondary school instruction in English or French in Canada, have the right to have all their children receive primary and secondary school instruction in the same language .

(3) The right of citizens of Canada under subsection (1) and

(2) to have their children receive primary and secondary school instruction in the language of the English or French linguistic minority population of a province

(a) applies wherever in the province the number of children of citizens who have such a right is sufficient to warrant the provision to them out of public funds of minority language instruction; and

(b) includes, where the number of those children so warrants, the right to have them receive that instruction in minority language educational facilities provided out of public funds.

Enforcement

24. (1) Anyone whose rights or freedoms, as guaranteed by this Charter, have been infringed or denied may apply to a court of competent jurisdiction to obtain such remedy as the court considers appropriate and just in the circumstances.

(2) Where, in proceedings under the subsection (1), a court concludes that evidence was obtained in a manner that infringed or denied any rights or freedoms guaranteed by this Charter, the evidence shall be excluded if it is established that, having regard to all the circumstances, the admission of it in the proceedings would bring the administration of justice into disrepute.

General

25. The guarantee in this Charter of certain rights and freedoms shall not be construed so as to abrogate or derogate from any aboriginal, treaty or other rights or freedoms that pertain to the aboriginal peoples of Canada including

(a) any rights or freedoms that have been recognized by the Royal Proclamation of October 7, 1763; and

(b) any rights or freedoms that now exist by way of land claims agreements or may be so acquired.

26. The guarantee in this Charter of certain rights and freedoms shall not be construed as denying the existence of any other rights or freedoms that exist in Canada.

27. This Charter shall be interpreted in a manner consistent with the preservation and enhancement of the multicultural heritage of Canadians.

28. Notwithstanding anything in this Charter, the rights and freedoms referred to in it are guaranteed equally to male and female persons.

29. Nothing in this Charter abrogates or derogates from any rights or privileges guaranteed by or under the Constitution of Canada in respect of denominational, separate or dissentient schools.

30. A reference in this Charter to a province or to the legislative assembly or legislature of a province shall be deemed to include a reference to the Yukon Territory and the Northwest Territories, or to the appropriate legislative authority thereof, as the case may be.

31. Nothing in this Charter extends the legislative powers of any body or authority.

Application of Charter

32. (1) This Charter applies

    (a) to the Parliament and government of Canada in respect of all matters within the authority of Parliament including all matters relating to the Yukon Territory and Northwest Territories; and

    (b) to the legislature and governments of each province in respect of all matters within the authority of the legislature of each province.

(2) Notwithstanding subsection (1), section 15 shall not have effect until three years after this section comes into force.

33. (1) Parliament or the legislature of a province may expressly declare in an Act of Parliament or of the legislature, as the case may be, that the Act or a provision thereof shall operate notwithstanding a provision included in section 20 or sections 7 to 15 of this Charter.

(2) An Act or a provision of an Act in respect of which a declaration made under this section is in effect shall have such operation as it would have but for the provision of this Charter referred to in the declaration.

(3) A declaration made under subsection (1) shall cease to have effect five years after it comes into force or on such earlier date as may be specified in the declaration.

(4) Parliament or the legislature of a province may re-enact a declaration made under subsection (1).

(5) Subsection (3) applies in respect of a re-enactment made under subsection (4).

* * *

Part VII

52. (1) The Constitution of Canada is the supreme law of Canada, and any law that is inconsistent with the provisions of the Constitution is, to the extent of the inconsistency, of no force or effect.

(2) The Constitution of Canada includes

    (a) the *Canada Act 1982*, including this Act;

    (b) the Acts and orders referred to in the schedules; and

    (c) any amendment to any Act or order referred to in paragraph (a) or (b).

(3) Amendments to the Constitution of Canada shall be made only in accordance with the authority contained in the Constitution of Canada.